BIOFIELD ALCHEMY

NAMITA AGGARWAL

BLUEROSE PUBLISHERS
India | U.K.

Copyright © Namita Aggarwal 2024

All rights reserved by author. No part of this publication may be reproduced, stored in a retrieval system or transmitted in any form or by any means, electronic, mechanical, photocopying, recording or otherwise, without the prior permission of the author. Although every precaution has been taken to verify the accuracy of the information contained herein, the publisher assume no responsibility for any errors or omissions. No liability is assumed for damages that may result from the use of information contained within.

BlueRose Publishers takes no responsibility for any damages, losses, or liabilities that may arise from the use or misuse of the information, products, or services provided in this publication.

For permissions requests or inquiries regarding this publication, please contact:

BLUEROSE PUBLISHERS
www.BlueRoseONE.com
info@bluerosepublishers.com
+91 8882 898 898
+4407342408967

ISBN: 978-93-6452-711-8

First Edition: December 2024

ACKNOWLEDGEMENT

The journey of bringing 'Biofield Alchemy' to life has been an immensely transformative and rewarding experience. The path to understanding the intricacies of 'Biofield Alchemy' is neither solitary nor straightforward; it is paved with the wisdom, support, and contributions of many remarkable individuals and sources. I would like to extend my deepest gratitude to everyone who has played a vital part in this journey, as their influence has been integral to the creation of this book.

First and foremost, I want to express my soulful gratitude to my Divine Mother Goddess, 'Maa Kamakhya Devi', and 'Lord Shiva', along with all the positive and supporting energies associated with them. With a heart overflowing with profound devotion, I humbly bow before my Maa Kamakhya Devi and Lord Shiva

Their sacred presence, along with the compassionate and uplifting energies that surround them, has been the guiding force in my life. Maa Kamakhya is not just a deity to me; She is the infinite wellspring of energy, the boundless reservoir of power, and the eternal font of wisdom. She is the Great Goddess of wish fulfillment, the compassionate force that shapes the very fabric of my existence. Every day, in every moment, I feel 'Her' loving presence and 'Her' blessings pouring into my being. This 'feeling of bliss', is the very foundation of 'Biofield Alchemy.'

Secondly, I express my heartfelt gratitude to Swami Awdheshanand Giri Ji Maharaj for nurturing my mind from childhood. As my family's Gurudev, his influence began when I was just a small child, and his teachings became a way of life for me. Waking up before sunrise, maintaining dietary discipline, embracing the power of chanting mantras and performing regular rituals are among the many practices he instilled in me. The power of the mind training, the power of patience and silence, the power of conscious and mindful thinking and speaking, the power of sharing knowledge, and the power of following the path of dharma and truthfulness (even in the toughest situations in life) - were the potent seeds planted by him in my mind.

Through his example, I learned that wisdom is gained not just by reading books but by observing and spending quality time with those role models who embody wisdom in their daily lives.

With all my heart and soul, I want to express my deepest gratitude to my beloved parents, Shri. Ashok Aggarwal and Shrimati Shanti Devi. They are not just the givers of my life - they are the very essence of my being, the core of everything I am. Words fail to capture the immense love and appreciation I have for them. Bruce Lipton beautifully said that parents are the ultimate genetic engineers, shaping us in ways we cannot even fathom. And so, with every fiber of my existence, I can proudly declare: "I am what I am because of them."

Thirdly, with a heart overflowing with soulful gratitude, I dedicate this to my one and the only angel - my son, Abhay. He is the pure essence of my being, the true light that showed me the real meaning of 'unconditional love.' Through him, I have come to understand the depths of love and life that transcend this world, awakening and illuminating my soul in ways I never thought possible.

Without Abhay, my journey into true alchemy would have remained a distant dream. Thank you, Abhay, for being the 'Alchemist' of my Soul!

My soulful and heartfelt gratitude for my dearest soul friend and unwavering business partner, Shri Bhuvneshwar. For over 25 years, he has been the 'Philosopher's Stone,' painstakingly refining me into the gold I am today. Without his steadfast support, I would never have reached this transformative moment in my life. Shri Bhuvneshwar is a living proof that, even in today's world, there are still those rare, extraordinary souls with hearts of pure gold.

My deepest and most heartfelt gratitude goes out to Shri. Devrathjee, whose unwavering belief in me has been a spark of a miracle. To be chosen by him as his business partner is an honor beyond words, and I am profoundly grateful for the privilege of earning his trust. Thank you, Devrathjee, for giving me so many treasured years and a promise of working together for many more years ahead.

I would also like to express my soulful gratitude for my incredible brother and business partner, Mr. Rene Stevens, who has been nothing short of a magician in my life. He took me from being 'Miss Shy' to 'Miss Photogenic' with such grace and patience. Rene, your unwavering support and endless hours spent behind the camera, capturing thousands of pictures and videos have been the key to unlocking my confidence. You stood by me, helping me conquer my deepest fears and guiding me through every step. A million thanks could never be enough for your dedication, and for teaching me invaluable business lessons along the way. I am beyond blessed to have you by my side.

With all the love in my heart, I extend my deepest, most soulful gratitude to the most extraordinary couple - Mr. Pierre Stevens and Miep Stevens-Hansen for embracing me as their own daughter, offering me a sanctuary of unconditional love with a strong 'family feel' - gifting me a 'real home' away from home. The purity of their love, the way they enveloped me into their family, is a miraculous blessing beyond words. They have shown me that true love transcends all languages, borders, and religions. It is a love that is boundless and eternal - a love that I will treasure forever.

I also take this opportunity to express my soulful gratitude to my entire family and all friends, who have been my pillars of strength and encouragement. A million thanks to their patience, understanding, and love. Their support has allowed me the freedom to explore the depths of 'Biofield Alchemy' and for that I am eternally thankful

I am also deeply indebted to all my Masters and Mentors who have provided guidance, feedback, and encouragement throughout my life process and also the writing process. Their critical insights, constructive critiques, and unwavering support have been instrumental in shaping the content and direction of this book. Their belief in the importance of this work has kept me motivated and focused, even during the most challenging phases of the writing process.

I am extremely grateful to the pioneers and scholars in the field of biofield science whose tireless research and discoveries have laid the groundwork for our understanding of the biofield and its profound implications. Their commitment to exploring the unseen dimensions of human physiology and consciousness has been a source of inspiration and a cornerstone for the discussions in this book. Their work has provided a foundation upon which I have built my exploration of 'Biofield Alchemy', and I am honored to contribute to the ongoing conversation in this dynamic field.

I would like to express my sincere appreciation to the practitioners and teachers of ancient healing traditions, whose knowledge and practices have enriched the scope of this book. Their insights into the energy systems of the body and their techniques for protecting, balancing and enhancing these systems have been invaluable. The integration of their wisdom with modern scientific perspectives has allowed for a holistic approach to 'Biofield Alchemy', bridging the gap between ancient and contemporary understandings of human potential.

My Special thanks also go to the researchers and scientists who have dedicated their careers to studying the subtle energies that influence our health and well-being. Their rigorous methodologies and innovative approaches have brought credibility and clarity to a field that was once considered purely esoteric. By shining a light on the measurable effects of biofield therapies, they have opened new avenues for exploration and validation, which are thoroughly discussed in this book.

In addition, I am thankful for the feedback and experiences shared by readers, followers and participants of 'Biofield Alchemy' workshops and seminars. Their stories of transformation and healing have not only validated the principles of 'Biofield Alchemy' but have also provided rich, real-world examples that illustrate the concepts discussed in this book. Their openness and willingness to share their journeys have been a source of inspiration and have added a personal touch to the theoretical and practical aspects of this work.

I would also like to acknowledge the contributions of my editors and publishers, whose expertise and professionalism have been vital in bringing this book to fruition. Their meticulous attention to detail and commitment to excellence have ensured that the message of 'Biofield Alchemy' is communicated clearly and effectively to a wide audience. Their partnership has been a crucial element in the successful realization of this project.

Finally, with all the passion in my heart, I extend infinite gratitude - millions upon trillions of 'Thank Yous' - to every opponent who stood in my path. You were not just competitors; you were the relentless forces that pushed me beyond my limits, the fierce challenges that demanded my evolution at every turn. It is you who have been my greatest source of encouragement and inspiration. Without your unyielding pressure, I would never have blossomed into the person I am today. You are the reason for my growth, and for that, I am eternally, immeasurably grateful.

'Biofield Alchemy' is the result of a collective effort, a tapestry woven from the threads of many minds and hearts. To all who have contributed to this tapestry, directly or indirectly, I extend my deepest thanks. This book is a testament to the power of collaboration and the limitless potential of human exploration.

ABOUT THE AUTHOR
DR. NAMITA AGGARWAL
'BIOFIELD ALCHEMIST'™

INDIA'S FIRST 'BIOFIELD ALCHEMIST'™

Dr. Namita Aggarwal is a luminary in the world of Alternative Healing Sciences, celebrated as India's first 'Biofield Alchemist'. Over the past 25 years, she has dedicated herself to exploring the depths of 'Biofield Alchemy', an ancient and mysterious practice that she has meticulously developed through her extensive education, research, and real-world application. Her pioneering work in the field has redefined the way we understand and interact with the human biofield, a complex and dynamic energy system that influences every aspect of our existence. With over 25 years of relentless dedication to the exploration and practice of 'Biofield Alchemy', Dr. Namita has emerged as a visionary leader who bridges the gap between ancient wisdom and modern science.

Her profound contributions to the field are not just rooted in her extensive qualifications but are also a reflection of her deep spiritual insight and unwavering commitment to healing and bettering humanity.

EARLY LIFE & EDUCATION

From her earliest years, Dr. Namita Aggarwal was driven by a profound curiosity about the unseen forces that shape our lives. Raised in an environment that encouraged both intellectual exploration and spiritual growth, she developed a unique perspective that combined the best of both worlds.

Her formal education began in conventional subjects, where she excelled and quickly demonstrated a talent for understanding complex systems. However, her journey took a transformative turn when she discovered alternative healing methods, leading her to delve into disciplines that, at that time, were considered unconventional yet held profound potential for healing and personal growth.

Her educational journey is as diverse as it is distinguished. Dr. Namita holds an array of degrees, each representing a different facet of her expansive knowledge. Her background in economics, where she earned a distinguished degree, provided her with a deep understanding of the global financial systems and the intricate forces that govern them. This unique perspective allowed her to approach 'Biofield Alchemy' not just as a healing science but as a system that interacts with the broader economic and social structures of society.

Beyond her grounding in conventional economics, Dr. Namita pursued advanced degrees in alternative medicine, earning a Doctor of Medicine (M.D.), a Doctor of Naturopathy (N.D.), a Ph.D., a Doctor of Science (D.Sc.), and a Doctor of Literature (D.Litt.), all in the field of Alternative Medicine. Her academic achievements are further enriched by Master's degrees in Psychotherapy and Counseling (M.P.C.) and another Master's degree in Cosmetology (M.I.C.), disciplines that contribute to her holistic approach to healing, which addresses not just the physical body but also the mind and spirit.

In addition to her formal education, Dr. Namita Aggarwal trained as a Life Design Program Coach and a Silva Method Trainer, further enhancing her skills in personal development and mind-body healing. She is also an International Reiki Master and a Mind Power Coach, credentials that highlight her expertise in energy healing and mental empowerment. These roles have allowed her to integrate a wide range of healing modalities into her practice, creating a comprehensive approach to 'Biofield Alchemy' that is both deeply intuitive and scientifically grounded.

PROFESSIONAL EXPERIENCE

Dr. Namita's professional journey is equally impressive. She has held key leadership positions, including serving as the Director of Atelier V Real Estate B.V. in The Netherlands, where she combined her knowledge of energy fields with architectural design to create spaces that promote well-being. She was also the Co-founder and Director of the International Institute of Metaphysical Research & Sciences B.V. (IIMRS) in the Netherlands, a pioneering institution dedicated to the study and application of metaphysical sciences. Additionally, she Co-founded and Chaired the Dutch N.G.O., I-People Metaphysical Foundation (IPMF), where she worked tirelessly to bring the benefits of metaphysical research to the broader public.

Throughout her career, Dr. Namita Aggarwal has remained committed to the advancement of alternative healing sciences. Her work has been characterized by a unique blend of scientific rigor and intuitive understanding, a combination that has allowed her to bridge the gap between ancient wisdom and modern science. She has not only mastered over 100 alternative healing modalities but has also synthesized these into practical, actionable formulas that can be used to address a wide range of human challenges, from physical ailments to emotional and spiritual crises. Her work is characterized by a deep respect for the traditions she draws from, combined with a forward-thinking approach that seeks to innovate and expand the boundaries of what is possible in the field of healing.

THE BIRTH OF 'BIOFIELD ALCHEMY'

The concept of 'Biofield Alchemy', as developed by Dr. Namita, is the culmination of decades of research, practice, and experimentation. The biofield, an intricate and dynamic energy field that surrounds and permeates the human body, has long been a subject of fascination and study in various traditional energy healing systems. However, Dr. Namita's approach to the biofield is unique in its synthesis of these ancient traditions with cutting-edge scientific research.

For Dr. Namita, 'Biofield Alchemy' is more than just a method of healing; it is an art, a way of understanding the interconnectedness of all life.

She describes 'Biofield Energy' as the 'Real Currency' of human life, a powerful and versatile resource that can be harnessed to achieve both material and spiritual goals.

'ART OF BIOFIELD ALCHEMY'™ PROGRAM

'Art of 'Biofield Alchemy' Program is one of Dr. Namita's most significant contributions to the field of 'Biofield Alchemy'

'Art of Biofield Alchemy' Program is the result of Dr. Namita's rigorous exploration of over 100 alternative healing sciences, her study of more than 10,000 books, and her execution of thousands of experiments. Through this exhaustive process, she has identified more than 1,000 formulas that do not work and more than 100 formulas that will always work. These formulas are designed to act as a guide, leading individuals from problem to solution in a way that is both scientifically sound and deeply transformative.

As the founder of 'Art of Biofield Alchemy' Program, Dr. Namita dreams of sharing this mysterious alchemical program with a billion people to help them achieve their own superpowers through the power of Alternative Sciences (A.S) and Emotional Intelligence (EI)

Just as a mother's milk provides complete nourishment for an infant, 'biofield energy' serves as a complete and ultimate solution to all human challenges, offering a path to healing that is both profound and practical. This 'biofield energy' is the true power for manifesting both material and spiritual aspirations.

'Art of Biofield Alchemy' Program is not just about healing; it's about transformation at every level of existence. Participants learn to identify and remove energy blockages, align their biofield with their highest intentions, and manifest their desires with greater ease and clarity. The program's success lies in its simplicity and accessibility, allowing anyone, regardless of their prior experience or knowledge, to tap into the immense power of their biofield.

'BIOFIELD CURRENCY' ™ &
'BIOFIELD CURRENCY GENERATOR FORMULA'™

Another groundbreaking innovation by Dr. Namita Aggarwal is the 'Biofield Currency Generator Formula.' This program teaches individuals how to generate and utilize the most potent currencies of the universe - The

"Biofield Currency." Dr. Namita's discovery of this ancient and dynamic 'Biofield Currency' has revolutionized the way we understand energy.

Dr. Namita, having rediscovered the most ancient and dynamic 'Currency' of the universe, and having decoded and re-created a specific formula to generate these most potent currencies of the universe - inspires and encourages her followers to invest in the most potent 'currency' of the universe!

This powerful formula is designed to empower individuals by teaching them how to generate and utilize their own 'biofield energy' to create the highest possible change in their lives. The program is built on the foundation of the 'Art of Biofield Alchemy', a set of principles and practices that Dr. Namita has distilled from her extensive research and experience.

INSPIRATION & IMPACT

Dr. Namita Aggarwal's work has inspired countless individuals around the world to explore the depths of their own potential. Her teachings resonate with those who seek more than just tangible effects; they are drawn to her holistic approach that addresses the totality of the human experience. Through her innovative programs and dedicated mentorship, Dr. Namita has transformed the lives of many, helping them to achieve greater health, wealth, power, happiness, bliss and overall fulfillment.

Her influence extends beyond the individual level; her vision is to catalyze a global movement toward higher consciousness and collective well-being. By empowering people with the knowledge and tools to harness their 'biofield energy', Dr. Namita is contributing to a larger shift in how humanity understands and interacts with the fundamental energies of life.

A VISION FOR THE FUTURE

Dr. Namita's vision extends far beyond the immediate benefits of 'Biofield Alchemy'. She envisions a billion people to unlock their superpowers through the power of alternative sciences and emotional intelligence. This ambitious goal reflects her belief that everyone has the potential to achieve greatness and that by harnessing the power of the biofield, individuals can overcome any obstacle and realize their highest aspirations.

To achieve this vision, Dr. Namita is committed to sharing her knowledge and experience with as many people as possible. She plans to do this through her books, workshops, seminars and retreat programs, where she will teach the principles of 'Biofield Alchemy' and provide practical tools for applying these principles in everyday life. Her approach is one of inclusivity and accessibility, ensuring that anyone, regardless of their background or experience, can benefit from the wisdom she has gathered over her long and distinguished career.

THE LEGACY OF 'ART OF 'BIOFIELD ALCHEMY' ™ & 'BIOFIELD CURRENCY'™

The 'Art of Biofield Alchemy', is more than a set of techniques; it is a comprehensive system designed to bring about transformation at every level of existence. Dr. Namita's innovative approach integrates physical, mental, emotional, and spiritual dimensions, creating a holistic pathway to well-being. The program's success lies in its simplicity and accessibility, allowing anyone, regardless of their prior experience or knowledge, to tap into the immense power of their biofield.

Participants of 'Art of Biofield Alchemy' Program often describe their experiences as life-changing. By following the program's structured guidelines, they learn to identify and remove energy blockages, align their biofield with their highest intentions, and manifest their desires with greater ease and clarity. Testimonials from those who have completed the program highlight profound improvements in health, relationships, career, and personal growth.

The program is not just about healing; it's about unlocking the full spectrum of human potential. Participants often report a deep sense of empowerment as they learn to consciously direct their energy to create the life they desire. The 'Art Of Biofield Alchemy' Program provides a clear roadmap for this journey, offering both the wisdom of ancient traditions and the cutting-edge insights of modern science.

THE FUTURE OF 'BIOFIELD ALCHEMY'

Looking to the future, Dr. Namita is focused on expanding the reach of 'Biofield Alchemy' even further. She is currently working on a series of new books and programs that will delve deeper into the advanced concepts and practices of 'biofield energy'. These upcoming works will build on the foundation laid in her earlier teachings, offering readers and practitioners the opportunity to explore the more intricate and powerful aspects of 'Biofield Alchemy'.

Dr. Namita is also committed to furthering research in the field of biofield science. She is actively collaborating with scientists and researchers to explore the mechanisms behind 'biofield energy' and its effects on the human body and mind. Her goal is to contribute to the growing body of scientific evidence that supports the efficacy of alternative healing methods, ultimately leading to greater acceptance and integration of these practices within mainstream healthcare.

MASTERING THE 'ART OF BIOFIELD ALCHEMY'™

Over the years, Dr. Namita has mastered more than 100 alternative healing modalities, each of which contributes to her unique approach to 'Biofield Alchemy'. These modalities include:

1) Psychic Surgery, 2) Biofield Tuning, 3) Metaphysical Healing, 4) Genetic Pattern Healing, 5) Psychosomatic Healing, 6) Holographic Healing, 7) Hypnotherapy, 8) Emotional Intelligence (EI), 9) NeuroLinguistics Programming (NLP), 10) Mind power Techniques, 11) Mentalism, 12) Silva Method, 13) Theta Healing, 14) Heart Math Methods, 15) Emotional Freedom Technique (EFT), 16) Tension Release Exercises (TRE), 17) White Magic, 18) Psychotherapy, 19) Living On Light, 20) Twin Soul Healing, 21) Energy Medicine, 22) Energy Shields, 23) Divine DNA Activation, 24) Shamanism, 25) Vedic Astrology, 26) Vaastu Shastra, 27) Palmistry, 28) Feng-Shui, 29) Naturopathy, 30) Ashtanga Yoga, 31) Usui Reiki, 32) Rainbow Reiki, 33) Melchizedek Method, 34) Past Life Regression Therapy, 35) Cosmetology, 36) Divine Blueprint Healing, 37) Ayurveda, 38) Homeopathy, 39) Pranic Healing, 40) Vipassana, 41) Divination Method, 42)

Tarot cards, 43) I-Ching, 44) Runes Divination, 45) Body Language, 46) Face Reading, 47) Acupressure, 48) Relationship Healing, 49) Vedic Rituals, 50) Mandala Therapy, 51) Holistic Diet & Nutrition Therapy, 52) Color Therapy, 53) Mantra Science, 54) Magnified healing, 55) Five Element Healing, 56) Mental Health Therapy, 57) Sound Healing, 58) Sacred Geometry, 59) Lama Fera, 60) Rebirthing, 61) Mindfulness Meditations, 62) Bach Flower Remedies, 52) Aromatherapy, 63) Reflexology, 64) Kinesiology, 65) Magnet Therapy, 66) White Light Healing, 67) Martial Arts, 68) Tai Chi, 69) Art Therapy, 70) Music Therapy, 71) Dance Therapy, 72) Drama Therapy, 73) Play Therapy, 74) Mudra Science, 75) Higher Self Connection, 76) Inner Child Healing, 77) Pendulum Dowsing, 78) Fertility Therapy, 79) Gaia Earth Healing, 80) Merkaba Activation, 81) Panchakarma, 82) Chakra Healing, 83) Kriya Yoga, 84) Pyramid Science, 85) Crystal Healing, 86) Ancestral Healing, 87) Akashic Record Reading, 88) Transcendental Meditation, 89) Zen Meditation, 90) Soul Retrieval Therapy, 91) Light Therapy, 92) Core Healing, 93) Kundalini Activation, 94) Pregnancy Healing, 95) Womb Healing, 96) Home Energizing, 97) Time Line Therapy, 98) Metal Magic, 99) Gem Elixirs, 100) Light Body Activation, 101) Psychic Protection,

CONTRIBUTIONS TO ALTERNATIVE HEALING SCIENCES

Dr. Namita's contributions to the field of alternative healing sciences extend far beyond her work in 'Biofield Alchemy'. At the core of Dr. Namita Aggarwal's work, is a profound love for humanity and a deep desire to help others realize their full potential. Her journey as a 'Biofield Alchemist' is a testament to the power of dedication, knowledge, and compassion. Her life is a testament to the power of living in alignment with one's highest values. Whether through her charitable work, her teaching, or her personal practice, she continues to embody the ideals she embraces, leading by example and inspiring others to do the same.

A LIFE DEDICATED TO HEALING & EMPOWERMENT

In a world increasingly dominated by materialism and external validation, Dr. Namita's message is a refreshing reminder of the importance of inner work and spiritual growth. She encourages her students and followers to cultivate a deep connection with their own 'biofield energy', using it not only to achieve personal goals but also to contribute to the greater good. Through her teachings, writings, and personal interactions, she has created a legacy that will continue to inspire and uplift people for generations to come.

Dr. Namita's life is a shining example of what can be achieved when one follows their passion with unwavering determination. Her work has not only transformed the lives of individuals but has also contributed to a broader understanding of the human biofield and its role in health and well-being. As she continues her mission to empower a billion people, Dr. Namita remains a guiding force in the world of alternative healing, a true pioneer whose impact will be felt for years to come.

LOOKING AHEAD: DR. NAMITA'S CONTINUING JOURNEY...

As Dr. Namita Aggarwal looks to the future, she remains focused on her mission to spread the principles of 'Biofield Alchemy' to as many people as possible. Her plans include expanding her educational programs, publishing more books, and continuing to offer workshops and retreats that bring her teachings to a global audience.

Her legacy will undoubtedly be one of profound impact - both on the individuals she directly teaches, and on the broader field of alternative medicine. Through her work, Dr. Namita is not only transforming lives but also contributing to a deeper understanding of the human biofield and its potential to bring about lasting change.

CONCLUSION

Dr. Namita Aggarwal's journey as a 'Biofield Alchemist' is a testament to the power of dedication, curiosity, and an unwavering belief in the potential of human beings to transcend their limitations. Her work is a harmonious blend of ancient wisdom and modern science, offering a path to healing that is as accessible as it is profound. Through her books, programs, and teachings, Dr. Namita has created a legacy that will inspire generations to come. Her commitment to sharing her knowledge is evident in every aspect of her work, from her detailed research to her compassionate approach to healing. For Dr. Namita's 'Art of Biofield Alchemy' is not just a concept; it is a sacred mission to empower individuals to live their best lives by harnessing the untapped potential within them.

In conclusion, Dr. Namita Aggarwal's work embodies a unique blend of scientific inquiry, spiritual wisdom, and compassionate service, making her a true luminary in her field. As she continues to share her knowledge and expand her influence, Dr. Namita is helping to shape a future where holistic, energy-based healing is recognized as a vital component of human health and well-being.

As she continues to explore and share the mysteries of the biofield, she offers all of us the opportunity to tap into our own innate power and create a life of health, wealth, happiness, harmony and bliss.

PREFACE

In an age where science and spirituality often seem to walk divergent paths, 'Biofield Alchemy' emerges as a bridge between these two seemingly disparate worlds. This book is not merely a collection of ideas, practices, and research; it is a journey into the very essence of what it means to be human, exploring the subtle energies that animate our physical, mental, emotional, and spiritual existence. The biofield - a term that may be unfamiliar to some - represents an ancient concept reimagined for the modern age, an intricate web of energy that surrounds and penetrates every living being. It is the very fabric that connects us to the universe, to each other, and to ourselves.

The idea for 'Biofield Alchemy' was born out of a deep curiosity about the unseen forces that govern our lives. Over the years, as I delved deeper into various disciplines - from quantum physics to ancient mysticism - I realized that there is a profound interconnectedness between these fields. The biofield is not a new concept; it has been known by many names across different cultures. In Vedic traditions, it is referred to as 'prana', in Chinese medicine as 'qi', and in various indigenous cultures as 'life force'. Yet, despite its ancient roots, the biofield has often been relegated to the fringes of scientific inquiry, dismissed as pseudoscience or superstition.

However, recent advancements in science, particularly in the fields of quantum biology and energy medicine, have begun to shed light on the biofield, offering a more comprehensive understanding of its role in human health and well-being. Researchers like Dr. Beverly Rubik and Dr. Konstantin Korotkov have made significant strides in measuring and visualizing the biofield, lending credibility to what was once considered esoteric knowledge. Their work, along with that of many others, has laid the groundwork for a new paradigm, one where the biofield is recognized as a vital component of human physiology and consciousness.

'Biofield Alchemy' seeks to explore this paradigm in depth. The word 'alchemy' is often associated with the transmutation of base metals into gold, but in the context of this book, it represents the transformation of human consciousness through the understanding and manipulation of the biofield. Just as the ancient alchemists sought to refine and purify matter, we can refine and purify our own energy fields, leading to profound shifts in our physical, mental, emotional, and spiritual states.

The purpose of this book is threefold. First, it aims to provide a comprehensive overview of the biofield, drawing from both scientific research and ancient wisdom. Second, it seeks to offer practical tools and techniques for harnessing the power of the biofield in everyday life. These practices - ranging from meditation and breathwork to the use of crystals and sound - are not merely theoretical; they are grounded in centuries of experiential knowledge and backed by contemporary scientific studies. Finally, this book aspires to inspire a deeper understanding of the interconnectedness of all life, encouraging readers to view themselves as integral parts of a vast, energetic tapestry.

Writing 'Biofield Alchemy' has been both a labor of love and a process of discovery. As I embarked on this journey, I found myself continually amazed by the depth and breadth of knowledge available on this subject. From the ancient texts of the Vedas and to the latest research in quantum physics and epigenetics, there is a wealth of information that supports the existence and significance of the biofield. But more than just gathering data, this journey has been deeply personal, challenging me to integrate these teachings into my own life. The practices and concepts discussed in this book are not abstract ideas; they are living, breathing realities that have had a transformative impact on my own well-being.

One of the key themes of 'Biofield Alchemy' is the concept of self-empowerment. In a world where we are often taught to look outside ourselves for answers, this book encourages readers to turn inward, to explore the vast inner landscape of their own biofield. By doing so, we can tap into a reservoir of healing, creativity, and spiritual insight that is far more potent than anything the external world can offer. Biofield reflects our inner state; by learning to cultivate and harmonize this energy, we can bring about profound changes in our external reality.

This book also addresses the importance of grounding and centering practices in 'Biofield Alchemy'. In an age of constant distraction and overstimulation, it is more important than ever to cultivate a sense of inner stability and calm. Techniques such as meditation, yoga, martial arts, breathwork and visualization are not just physical exercises; they are tools for aligning the biofield, for creating a coherent and balanced energy field that can withstand the challenges of modern life. Grounding practices help us stay connected to the Earth, while centering practices allow us to maintain our equilibrium in the face of life's inevitable ups and downs.

Another important aspect of 'Biofield Alchemy' is its focus on ancient rituals and traditions. Throughout history, cultures around the world have developed sophisticated systems for working with the biofield, from the use of mantras and meditation in Hinduism to the practice of Qi gong in Chinese Medicine. These traditions offer valuable insights into the nature of the biofield and provide a rich heritage of practices that can be adapted and integrated into modern life. Whether it is using sacred geometry, the application of precious metals and gemstones, or the performance of protective rituals, these ancient practices offer powerful tools for harmonizing the biofield and enhancing our overall well-being.

In conclusion, 'Biofield Alchemy' is not just a book; it is an invitation to explore the deeper dimensions of your being, to awaken to the subtle energies that shape your reality, and to embark on a journey of transformation and self-discovery. It is my hope that 'Biofield Alchemy' will serve as a guide and companion on your path, providing you with the knowledge, tools, and inspiration to harness the power of your biofield and create a life of health, harmony, and fulfillment.

As you read these pages, I encourage you to keep an open mind and a receptive heart. The concepts and practices discussed in this book may challenge your existing beliefs, but it is through this process of questioning and exploration that true growth occurs. Remember, the journey of alchemy is not about achieving perfection; it is about embracing the process of transformation, of becoming more fully and authentically yourself.

Welcome to the world of 'Biofield Alchemy'. May it inspire you to discover the alchemist within.

Love & Light
Dr. Namita Aggarwal

TABLE OF CONTENTS

PART 1
ESSENCE OF 'BIOFIELD ALCHEMY' 1

PART 1CHAPTER 0
THE PATH OF A 'BIOFIELD ALCHEMIST' - THE ALCHEMY OF SELF - DISCOVERY & THE JOURNEY OF BECOMING THE 'WHOLE' 2

ALCHEMIST'S JOURNEY: WALKING THE PATH OF EVOLUTION 3

PART 1
CHAPTER 1 INTRODUCTION 'BIOFIELD ALCHEMY'- UNLOCKING THE SECRETS OF ENERGY & MATTER 10

PART 1
CHAPTER 2 FOUNDATION 'BIOFIELD ALCHEMY' & IT'S FOUNDATION 23

PART 1
CHAPTER 3 PRINCIPLES PRINCIPLES OF 'BIOFIELD ALCHEMY' 32

PART 1
CHAPTER 4 ENERGETIC ANATOMY UNDERSTANDING THE SCIENCE OF HUMAN ENERGY FIELD IN 'BIOFIELD ALCHEMY' 39

PART 1
CHAPTER 5 50
THE QUANTUM FIELD THE CONNECTION BETWEEN THE BIOFIELD & THE QUANTUM FIELD 50

PART 1
CHAPTER 6 EPIGENETICS UNDERSTANDING
EPIGENETICS IN BIOFIELD ALCHEMY 55

PART 1
CHAPTER 7 ETHICS OF 'BIOFIELD ALCHEMY' - A
GUIDE TO RESPONSIBLE PRACTICE 61

PART 2
TOOLS & TECHNIQUES OF 'BIOFIELD ALCHEMY' -
DISCOVERING THE PHILOSOPHER'S STONE &
UNLOCKING THE RICHES OF GOLD WITHIN 67

PART 2
CHAPTER 1 SOUND & LIGHT BIOFIELD
ALCHEMY & THE ALCHEMICAL CIRCLE OF
VIBRATION & FREQUENCY & ENERGY 68

PART 2
CHAPTER 2 TIME & SPACE ALCHEMY OF TIME &
POTENCY OF SPACE - TURNING 'MOMENTS'
INTO 'MASTERPIECES' 79

PART 2
CHAPTER 3 THOUGHTS & INTENTION MAGIC OF
INVISIBLE THOUGHTS & INTENTION IN
CRAFTING REALITY 88

PART 2
CHAPTER 4 INTUITION & SIXTH SENSE - THE
ALCHEMIST'S EYE - SEEING POSSIBILITY IN THE
IMPOSSIBLE 94

PART 2
CHAPTER 5 LOVE & LIFE THE ALCHEMY OF
LOVE & LIFE & BIOFIELD 100

PART 2
CHAPTER 6 FIVE SENSES - ALCHEMIST'S LENSES

OF PERCEPTION -DISTILLING & DECODING THE ALCHEMICAL WISDOM 108

PART 2
CHAPTER 7 EMOTIONS 'BIOFIELD ALCHEMY' 114
& THE ALCHEMY OF EMOTIONAL ENERGY MAPPING 114

PART 2
CHAPTER 8 FIVE ELEMENTS - THE SACRED ALCHEMICAL ELIXIRS 121

PART 2
CHAPTER 9 BREATHWORK BREATH: THE GOLDEN THREAD OF LIFE - WEAVING ENERGY & MATTER TOGETHER 128

PART 2
CHAPTER 10 MEDITATION - THE MAGIC OF PRESENCE & CREATING ALCHEMY IN THE 'NOW' 135

PART 2
CHAPTER 11 BODYWORK & THE ALCHEMY OF MOVEMENT 141

PART 2
CHAPTER 12 GROUNDING & CENTRING BIOFIELD ALCHEMY & THE ART OF DISTILLING THE ESSENCE OF ENERGY WORK 146

PART 2
CHAPTER 13 PROTECTION OF BIOFIELD - SHIELDING THE INNER GOLD & FIXING THE ENERGY LEAKS 153

PART 2
CHAPTER 14 INITIATION OPENING THE BIOFIELD PORTAL FOR INSTANT ENERGY DOWNLOADS 159

PART 2
CHAPTER 15 SACRED GEOMETRY - THE COSMIC
ENERGY'S HELIPAD 165

PART 2
CHAPTER 16 NATURE- THE BIOFIELD
ENHANCER & THE ENERGY AMPLIFIER 170

PART 2
CHAPTER 17 DEITIES & ANGELS & THE
INFLUENCE OF CELESTIAL BEINGS IN
MANIFESTING MIRACLES 174

PART 2
CHAPTER 18 PLANT KINGDOM &,BIOFIELD
ALCHEMY - FROM DUST TO RADIANCE &
NURTURING THE INNER GARDEN 179

PART 2
CHAPTER 19 ANIMAL KINGDOM & THE RIPPLE
EFFECT OF THE LIFE FORCE ENERGY 185

PART 2
CHAPTER 20 MINERAL KINGDOM & 'BIOFIELD
ALCHEMY' - TAPPING INTO MOTHER EARTH'S
ENERGY 191

PART 2
CHAPTER 21 CLEANLINESS - THE ENERGY
HYGIENE - A STATE OF BEING FREE FROM
IMPURITIES 199

PART 3
'BIOFIELD ALCHEMY' & IT'S PRACTICAL
APPLICATIONS - APPLYING THE PHILOSOPHER'S
STONE WITH AN ALCHEMIST'S MINDSET 205

PART 3
CHAPTER 1 CREATIVITY & 'BIOFIELD

ALCHEMY' - DISTILLING KNOWLEDGE INTO INSIGHT 206

PART 3
CHAPTER 2 MANIFESTATION - THE ALCHEMY OF METAMORPHOSIS 213

PART 3
CHAPTER 3 PHYSICAL HEALTH & 'BIOFIELD ALCHEMY' ENERGISING THE SACRED VESSEL OF THE SOUL- THE HUMAN BODY 220

PART 3
CHAPTER 4 WEALTH MANIFESTATION & BIOFIELD ALCHEMY BIOFIELD: THE ULTIMATE WEALTH MAP - TURNING LEAD INTO GOLD ... 228

PART 3
CHAPTER 5 RELATIONSHIPS & BIOFIELD ALCHEMY ALCHEMICAL RELATIONSHIPS: BREWING THE ELIXIR OF 'PRESENCE' 235

PART 3
CHAPTER 6 TRAUMA TRAUMA HEALING - TURNING COALS INTO DIAMONDS 244

PART 3
CHAPTER 7 HEALING SELF & OTHERS THE GOLD OF COMPASSION & THE ALCHEMY OF ENERGY EXCHANGE 252

PART 3
CHAPTER 8 SPIRITUAL AWAKENING 'BIOFIELD ALCHEMY' & ACTIVATING THE PHILOSOPHER'S STONE 260

PART 4
INTEGRATING 'BIOFIELD ALCHEMY' IN REAL LIFE
.... 267

PART 4
CHAPTER 1 IN EDUCATION INTEGRATING 'BIOFIELD ALCHEMY' INTO EDUCATION INTEGRATING BIOFIELD ALCHEMY IN EDUCATION SYSTEM 269

PART 4
CHAPTER 2 IN HEALTHCARE INTEGRATING ... 274

BIOFIELD ALCHEMY IN HEALTH CARE 274

PART 4
CHAPTER 3 IN DIAGNOSTICS 'BIOFIELD ALCHEMY' & DIAGNOSTICS - THE SCIENCE OF BIOFIELD MEASUREMENT & INSTRUMENTATION 281

PART 4
CHAPTER 4 IN MODERN SCIENCE 'BIOFIELD ALCHEMY' - A MODERN SCIENCE EXPLORATION 286

PART 4
CHAPTER 5 IN TECHNOLOGY INTERSECTION . 293

OF 'BIOFIELD ALCHEMY' & MODERN TECHNOLOGY 293

PART 4
CHAPTER 6 BIOFIELD TECHNOLOGIES 'BIOFIELD ALCHEMY' &EMERGING BIOFIELD TECHNOLOGIES 299

PART 4
CHAPTER 7 GLOBAL HEALING BIOFIELD ALCHEMY & THE POWER OF GLOBAL HEALING 306

FINAL CONCLUSION 313

- THE FINAL TRANSMUTATION 313

- BECOMING THE 'PHILOSOPHER'S STONE' 313
  - FINAL CONCLUSION: CRAFTING A NEW CHAPTER OF LIFE 314
- 'ENDINGS' ARE THE 'NEW BEGINNINGS' 319
  - AUTHOR'S NOTE 325
- LIFE OF A 'BIOFIELD ALCHEMIST' - THE HERMETIC PATH OF AN UNDERCOVER YOGI . 329
- FEW NAMES OF ALTERNATIVE HEALING MODALITIES 342
- UPCOMING BOOK 364

PART 1

ESSENCE OF 'BIOFIELD ALCHEMY'

PART 1
CHAPTER 0

THE PATH OF A 'BIOFIELD ALCHEMIST'

- THE ALCHEMY OF SELF - DISCOVERY
&
THE JOURNEY OF BECOMING THE 'WHOLE'

ALCHEMIST'S JOURNEY: WALKING THE PATH OF EVOLUTION

'BIOFIELD ALCHEMY': UNLOCKING THE HIDDEN POTENTIAL OF HUMAN ENERGY

In the movie 'The Matrix', we are introduced to a world where reality is not as it seems. The iconic moment when Neo is offered the choice between the red pill and the blue pill represents a critical decision point: to continue living in an illusion or to awaken to a deeper, more profound reality. This concept parallels the journey of 'Biofield Alchemy', where individuals are given the tools to perceive and manipulate the subtle energies that constitute their true essence.

THE ILLUSION OF REALITY

Much like the simulated reality in 'The Matrix', our everyday perception of the world is limited by our five senses. These senses, while crucial for navigating the physical realm, only scratch the surface of the vast, interconnected web of energy that makes up our universe. 'Biofield Alchemy' teaches us to go beyond these limitations, to perceive the energy matrix that underlies all existence.

In the film, Morpheus explains to Neo, "The Matrix is everywhere. It is all around us. Even now, in this very room." Similarly, the biofield - the dynamic field of energy and information surrounding and interpenetrating the human body is omnipresent. This field interacts with everything, influencing our health, wealth emotions, and consciousness. By learning to sense and manipulate this field, we can unlock extraordinary capabilities that lie dormant within us.

THE AWAKENING

Neo's journey from ignorance to enlightenment mirrors the path of a 'Biofield Alchemist'. Initially, Neo is unaware of his true potential. He is a cog in the machine, living a life dictated by external forces. However, once he takes the red pill, he begins to see the world as it truly is; a construct that can be bent and shaped by those who understand its underlying code.

In 'Biofield Alchemy', this awakening involves tuning into the subtle vibrations that permeate our existence. Techniques such as creative visualization, meditation, breath work, sound work and other energy healing systems, allow practitioners to access deeper states of awareness. As we become more attuned to our biofield, we start to recognize patterns and disruptions within this energy matrix. Just as Neo learns to bend spoons and dodge bullets, 'Biofield Alchemist' can also influence their physical and emotional states, promoting healing and transformation.

MASTERING THE CODE

In 'The Matrix', once Neo understands the code, he gains the ability to manipulate the simulated environment. He can perform feats that defy the laws of physics because he grasps the fundamental nature of the matrix. 'Biofield Alchemist', too, can achieve seemingly miraculous outcomes by mastering the 'code' of their biofield.

This mastery involves cultivating a deep connection with the biofield and understanding its intricacies. Through the practice of energy healing modalities, individuals learn to harness and direct their 'life force energy' or 'prana' or 'chi'. This energy can be used to heal physical ailments, balance emotions, and even influence the environment around them.

Consider the scene where Neo stops bullets in mid-air. This represents a profound shift in perception and capability. In 'Biofield Alchemy', practitioners might not stop bullets, but they can achieve remarkable results, such as accelerated healing, heightened intuition, and a greater sense of harmony with the world. The key is recognizing that, like the matrix, our reality is malleable, and we have the power to shape it.

ALCHEMIST & THE ALCHEMICAL JOURNEY

The journey of a 'Biofield Alchemist' is one of continual growth and discovery. Just as Neo evolves from a reluctant hero to 'The One', individuals who commit to this path undergo profound transformations. This journey requires dedication, practice, and an open mind.

One of the most significant lessons from 'The Matrix' is the power of belief. When Neo finally believes in his true nature, he transcends the limitations of the matrix. Similarly, belief in one's ability to influence the biofield is crucial. Skepticism and doubt can hinder progress, while faith and openness can lead to breakthroughs.

'Biofield Alchemy' also emphasizes the interconnectedness of all things. In 'The Matrix', the idea that all beings are part of a larger system is a recurring theme. 'Biofield Alchemist' understand that their actions and intentions ripple through the energy matrix, affecting not only themselves but also others and the environment. This awareness fosters a sense of responsibility and compassion, guiding practitioners to use their abilities for the greater good.

CONCLUSION: EMBRACING THE INFINITE

'The Matrix' challenges us to question our reality and consider the infinite possibilities that lie beyond our current understanding. 'Biofield Alchemy' invites us to do the same, offering tools and techniques to explore the depths of our being and the vast energetic landscape that surrounds us.

By embracing the principles of 'Biofield Alchemy', we can transcend the limitations of our perceived reality, unlocking our true potential and experiencing the world in a profoundly new way. As we learn to navigate and influence our biofield, we become the architects of our destiny, capable of creating a life of balance, vitality, and infinite possibility.

Just as Neo's journey continues beyond the confines of 'The Matrix', so too does the journey of a 'Biofield Alchemist'. With each step, the alchemist move closer to a deeper understanding of self and the universe, guided by the knowledge that reality is not fixed but fluid, shaped by our consciousness and our connection to the energy matrix of life.

This journey of alchemy is deeply personal, unique to each individual, ever evolving and 'Biofield Alchemy' is not just a practice; it's a journey that begins within the depths of one's soul.

LESSONS TO BE LEARNED

The path of the 'Biofield Alchemist' is rich with lessons that transcend the physical and touch upon the spiritual, mental and emotional aspects of being. One of the most profound lessons is the realization that healing and growth is not a linear process. It requires patience, self-compassion, and openness to exploring the unknown.

A key lesson in 'Biofield Alchemy' is the importance of self-awareness. As practitioners delve into the nuances of energy healing, they learn to tune into their own biofields, recognizing the subtle fluctuations that signal imbalances. This heightened self-awareness extends beyond the individual, fostering a deeper connection with others and the environment. Through this practice, 'Biofield Alchemist' become more attuned to the energy exchanges that occur in daily interactions, leading to more harmonious relationships and a balanced life.

Another critical lesson is the power of intention. In 'Biofield Alchemy', intention serves as the catalyst for transformation. Practitioners learn that the focused intention behind their actions can significantly influence the outcome of healing sessions. This understanding empowers them to approach each session with clarity and purpose, enhancing the efficacy of their work. The realization that intention shapes reality encourages 'Biofield Alchemist' to cultivate positive thoughts and beliefs, not only for their clients but also in their own lives.

The journey of the 'Biofield Alchemist' also teaches the value of continuous learning. The field of energy healing is ever evolving, with new techniques and insights emerging regularly. Practitioners must remain open to expanding their knowledge and refining their skills. This commitment to lifelong learning ensures that they stay at the forefront of the field, offering the most effective and up-to-date healing modalities to their clients.

THE ONGOING JOURNEY OF DISCOVERY

The path of a 'Biofield Alchemist' is a continuous journey of discovery, marked by both personal growth and the advancement of the field itself. As practitioners deepen their understanding of the biofield, they often find that the boundaries of what they thought possible expand.

For many 'Biofield Alchemy' is an ongoing journey - which involves exploring the intersection of science and spirituality. Advances in quantum physics and biofield research provide new insights into the mechanics of energy healing, offering a bridge between the esoteric and the empirical. This convergence of science and spirituality enriches the practice of 'Biofield Alchemy', grounding it in a deeper understanding of the universe's fundamental principles.

The journey also includes a commitment to community and collaboration. 'Biofield Alchemist' recognize that healing and growth is a collective endeavor, benefiting from the shared wisdom and experiences of others. Practitioners often engage in networks and communities of like-minded individuals, participating in workshops, conferences, and study groups.

Moreover, the ongoing journey of discovery in 'Biofield Alchemy' involves a deepening relationship with the self. Practitioners continually refine their self-care practices, ensuring they maintain their energetic health while serving others. This balance is crucial, as the integrity and effectiveness of their work depend on their own well-being.

In conclusion, the path of the 'Biofield Alchemist' is a rich energy web - woven from personal stories, valuable lessons, and an unending quest for knowledge and growth. As 'Biofield Alchemists' continue to explore and expand the boundaries of energy healing, they contribute to a greater understanding of the interconnectedness of mind, body, and spirit, fostering a world where health, wealth, love and power is accessible to all.

PART 1
CHAPTER 1

INTRODUCTION

'BIOFIELD ALCHEMY' - UNLOCKING THE SECRETS OF ENERGY & MATTER

BIOFIELD ALCHEMY: AN INTRODUCTION

UNDERSTANDING 'BIOFIELD ALCHEMY'

In the quiet moments between our thoughts and the spaces between our cells, an intricate dance of energy is constantly at play. This subtle yet profound energy system, known as the biofield, encompasses and permeates our entire being. It is an ancient concept, recognized by various cultures and healing traditions across the globe, yet it is only now beginning to be understood and validated by modern science.

In an age where modern medicine and technology dominate the health and wellness landscape, a growing number of individuals are turning to ancient and holistic practices to restore balance and enhance their well-being. Among these practices, this book delves into the heart of 'Biofield Alchemy', offering a comprehensive exploration of its principles, history, and applications.

Welcome to 'Biofield Alchemy', a journey into the fascinating world of energy healing and transformation.

DEFINITION & OVERVIEW

The term 'biofield' refers to the complex and dynamic electromagnetic field that surrounds and permeates all living beings. This field is believed to be composed of various energy frequencies that interact with the physical, emotional, mental, and spiritual aspects of an individual. While the concept of the biofield has roots in ancient healing practices, it has gained recognition in modern science through disciplines such as quantum physics, biophysics, and integrative medicine.

THE ESSENCE OF THE BIOFIELD

Biofield - a complex and dynamic field of energy and information that surrounds and interpenetrates the human body. This field is not just a byproduct of our physical processes but an integral part of our being, influencing and being influenced by our thoughts, emotions, and environment. 'Biofield Alchemy' refers to the intricate and harmonious manipulation of the human biofield - an energy field that surrounds and permeates the body, influencing physical, emotional, and spiritual health. This field, often referred to in various traditions as the 'aura', 'qi' or 'prana', is considered a vital aspect of human existence. 'Biofield Alchemy' seeks to understand and optimize this energy, promoting healing, personal growth, and a deeper connection to the universe.

HISTORICAL BACKGROUND

The concept of the biofield is not new. It is rooted in ancient civilizations and spiritual traditions around the world. In Traditional Chinese Medicine, the concept of 'chi' or 'qi' represents the life force energy that flows through meridians in the body. Similarly, Ayurveda, the ancient Indian system of medicine, speaks of 'prana', the vital energy governing bodily functions and consciousness. Indigenous cultures worldwide have their own interpretations and practices related to the biofield, often involving rituals, ceremonies, and healing practices aimed at maintaining energetic balance.

Ancient healing traditions such as Ayurveda, Traditional Chinese Medicine, Martial Arts and Yoga practices have long recognized the importance of this energy field, although they may refer to it by different names - prana, qi, or spirit. Historically, many cultures have acknowledged the existence of an energy field surrounding the body.

In Traditional Chinese Medicine (TCM), it is known as 'Qi', while in Ayurveda, it is referred to as 'Prana'. Native American traditions speak of the 'Great Spirit', and ancient Egyptian texts mention the 'Ka' energy. Despite differing terminologies, these traditions share a common belief in the vital life force that sustains and animates all living things.

In recent years, scientific research has begun to explore the biofield, seeking to understand its properties and potential applications in healthcare. Instruments such as sensitive magnetometers and electroencephalographs are shedding light on the ways in which our biofield interacts with our physiological processes, offering new insights into health and disease. The modern understanding of the biofield began to take shape in the late 19th and early 20th centuries with the advent of bioelectricity research. Scientists like Nikola Tesla and Wilhelm Reich explored the idea of energy fields surrounding living organisms. However, it wasn't until the latter half of the 20th century that the term 'biofield' was coined, gaining recognition in both scientific and holistic health communities.

Moreover, research in bioenergetics has demonstrated that the biofield is a measurable and manipulable entity. For instance, experiments involving energy healers have shown that they can influence the biofield of their clients, leading to measurable changes in their physiological states. These findings challenge the conventional medical paradigm and open new possibilities for integrative and holistic approaches to health and healing.

Today, 'Biofield Alchemy' is recognized as an interdisciplinary field, integrating insights from quantum physics, biology, psychology, and spiritual traditions. It represents a convergence of ancient wisdom and modern science, offering a holistic framework for understanding and enhancing human energy.

THE SCIENCE BEHIND THE BIOFIELD

Modern science is catching up with what mystics and healers have known for centuries. Researchers are uncovering the ways in which the biofield can influence cellular function, genetic expression, and even the body's ability to heal itself. Studies on energy medicine modalities like Therapeutic Touch, Hypnosis, Yoga, Naturopathy and Acupuncture are demonstrating measurable effects on biological systems. These findings suggest that the biofield is not a mere abstraction but a critical aspect of our biology that holds immense potential for enhancing health and well-being.

The field of quantum biology is particularly promising in explaining how the biofield operates. Quantum mechanics, with its principles of non-locality and entanglement, provides a theoretical framework for understanding how distant healing and other energy-based practices might work. This intersection of ancient wisdom and cutting-edge science is forging a new paradigm in medicine, one that integrates the physical, emotional, and energetic dimensions of health.

THE PRACTICE OF 'BIOFIELD ALCHEMY'

'Biofield Alchemy' is more than just a concept; it is a practical approach to harnessing the power of our biofield for healing and transformation. At its core, 'Biofield Alchemy' involves techniques and practices designed to balance and optimize our energy field. These practices include meditation, visualization, breathwork, intention setting and energy healing. By learning to sense and manipulate the biofield, we can remove energy blockages, enhance vitality, and promote holistic well-being.

This book will guide you through a variety of techniques to harmonize and tune into your biofield. You will learn how to develop your sensitivity to subtle energies, use intention and visualization to direct healing energy, and apply specific methods to address physical, emotional, and spiritual imbalances. Whether you are a seasoned energy healer or a curious newcomer, the practices in this book will empower you to take charge of your own health and transformation.

UNDERSTANDING THE CONCEPT OF 'ALCHEMY'

The term 'alchemy' in this context is used metaphorically, drawing parallels to the ancient practice of transforming base metals into gold. Similarly, 'Biofield Alchemy' aims to transmute negative, stagnant energies into positive, dynamic forces, fostering holistic health and spiritual enlightenment. This practice encompasses a range of techniques, including energy healing, breathwork, sound therapy, creative visualization meditation, and more, each contributing to the harmonization and enhancement of the biofield.

'BIOFIELD ALCHEMY': AN ENERGETIC BLUEPRINT

As discussed, biofield, an intricate web of energy that surrounds and permeates the human body is believed to interact with physical, emotional, and spiritual aspects of a person, serving as a blueprint for overall well-being. 'Biofield Alchemy' focuses on understanding and manipulating this energetic matrix to foster holistic healing and transformation. Techniques such as Yoga, Pranayama, Naturopathy, Ayurveda, Martial Arts, Acupressure and other energy healing modalities are integrated within 'Biofield Alchemy' to clear blockages, balance energies, and enhance the flow of life.

'Biofield Alchemy's principles are to help individuals develop and enhance their energetic alignment. Whether through meditation, breathwork, visualization, sound therapy or specific energy exercises, the incorporation of disciplined practices fosters a daily engagement with one's biofield, promoting sustained transformation and growth.

The principle that is central to 'Biofield Alchemy' is to prioritize the importance of aligning one's heart to the universe and its signs. 'Biofield Alchemy' ensures that the process of transformation is not just about energetic adjustments but also about awakening to one's personal legend.

THE ALCHEMY OF 'INNER GOLD'

At its core, 'Biofield Alchemy' is about the transformation of the self - turning the lead of unfulfilled potential and unresolved emotions into the gold of enlightenment and self-actualization. This process mirrors the alchemical journey depicted in Coelho's 'The Alchemist', where the protagonist's external quest leads to an inner revelation. In the realm of 'Biofield Alchemy', the practitioner's journey through the layers of their biofield leads to a profound understanding and embodiment of their true self.

A UNIQUE PATH TO TRANSFORMATION

'Biofield Alchemy' represents an age-old ancient approach to personal growth and transformation. By merging the ancient wisdom of alchemy with modern understandings of the biofield ensuring that the transformation achieved is not only profound but also deeply resonant with one's true self. In this way, 'Biofield Alchemy' empowers individuals to uncover their inner gold and live a meaningful life of purpose, balance, and bliss.

THE JOURNEY OF SELF - DISCOVERY

Engaging with the biofield is not just about healing; it is also a profound journey of self-discovery. As we delve into our energy field, we uncover layers of our being that we may have forgotten or suppressed. The biofield holds the imprints of our experiences, emotions, and traumas, and by working with this energy, we can release old patterns and open ourselves to new possibilities.

This journey requires an open mind and a willingness to explore beyond the conventional boundaries of science and medicine. It invites us to embrace a holistic view of ourselves, recognizing that our health and wealth are intricately linked to our thoughts, emotions, and spiritual state. As we learn to navigate the biofield, we also deepen our connection to the world around us, fostering a sense of unity and interconnectedness.

THE POWER OF INTENTION

One of the key principles of 'Biofield Alchemy' is the power of intention. Intention is the focused direction of energy towards a specific outcome. In the context of energy healing, intention acts as a catalyst that directs the flow of energy in the biofield, facilitating healing and transformation. Studies have shown that intention can influence physical processes, such as the growth of plants or the healing of wounds, suggesting that our thoughts and intentions have tangible effects on the world around us.

This book will teach you how to harness the power of intention to shape your biofield and manifest your desired outcomes. You will learn how to set clear, focused intentions, and use them to guide your healing practices. By aligning your intentions with the universal laws, you can create a powerful synergy that enhances your journey towards health and wealth.

THE ROLE OF CONSCIOUSNESS

'Consciousness', is the foundation upon which 'Biofield Alchemy' is built. Our state of consciousness determines how we perceive and interact with the world, and it plays a crucial role in shaping our biofield. Practices that expand and elevate our consciousness such as mindfulness, meditation, and contemplative practices, are essential components of 'Biofield Alchemy'. These practices help us to attune to the subtle energies within and around us, fostering a deeper awareness of our true nature.

In this book, you will explore various practices to expand your consciousness and deepen your connection to the biofield. You will learn how to quiet the mind, cultivate inner stillness, and access higher states of awareness. These practices will not only enhance your ability to work with your biofield but also enrich your overall experience of life.

EMBRACING THE MYSTERY

While science is beginning to unravel the mysteries of the biofield, much remains unknown. 'Biofield Alchemy' invites us to embrace this mystery with curiosity and wonder. It encourages us to be open to new possibilities and to trust in the inherent wisdom of our energy field. As we engage with the biofield, we may encounter phenomena that challenge our conventional understanding of reality, prompting us to expand our horizons and rethink our assumptions.

This book is a call to adventure, an invitation to explore the uncharted territories of the biofield and discover the boundless potential that lies within us. It is a journey of healing, transformation, and self-discovery, one that promises to enrich your life in profound ways.

Beyond the scientific perspective, the biofield is also a gateway to understanding the deeper spiritual aspects of our existence. Many spiritual traditions recognize the biofield as the interface between the physical body and the higher realms of consciousness. Energy healing practices work directly with the biofield to harmonize and balance the flow of energy, promoting physical and spiritual healing.

A CALL TO TRANSFORMATION

'Biofield Alchemy' is more than just a guide to energy healing; it is a manifesto for personal and collective transformation. As we heal and harmonize our biofield, we contribute to the healing of our communities and the world at large. The ripple effects of our personal alchemy extend far beyond ourselves, creating a wave of positive change that can uplift humanity.

'Biofield Alchemy' explores the rich heritage of spiritual teachings that emphasize the importance of cultivating and maintaining a healthy biofield. By aligning our biofield with the universal energy, or life force, we can enhance our connection to the divine and unlock our innate healing potential.

In the pages that follow, you will find a wealth of knowledge, tools, and practices to help you master the art of 'Biofield Alchemy'. You will learn how to harness the power of your biofield, cultivate a deeper connection to yourself and the world, and embark on a transformative journey of healing and growth. Whether you are seeking to enhance your health, deepen your spiritual practice, or simply explore the mysteries of the human energy field. This book offers a comprehensive and practical roadmap.

PURPOSE & SCOPE OF THE BOOK

The purpose of this book is to provide a comprehensive and accessible guide to 'Biofield Alchemy', empowering readers to harness the transformative potential of their own biofields. Whether you are a seasoned practitioner or a curious newcomer, this book aims to offer valuable insights and practical tools for personal and collective healing.

Throughout the chapters, we will explore the fundamental principles of 'Biofield Alchemy', delving into the scientific basis of the biofield, as well as its metaphysical dimensions. We will examine various techniques and practices for cleansing, balancing, and amplifying the biofield, drawing on both ancient traditions and contemporary research. From energy healing modalities like Qigong and Pranayama to modern innovations in sound therapy and biofeedback, this book will present a diverse array of methods to suit different needs and preferences.

Additionally, we will consider the broader implications of 'Biofield Alchemy' for health, wealth and relationships and overall wellness. How can understanding and optimizing the biofield contribute to physical healing, wealthy mindset, emotional resilience, and spiritual growth? What role does the biofield play in our interactions with others and the environment? By addressing these questions, we aim to highlight the interconnectedness of all aspects of life and the profound impact of energetic balance on overall well-being.

Moreover, this book seeks to foster a deeper appreciation for the subtle yet powerful forces that shape our existence. Readers can cultivate greater self-awareness, intuition, and a sense of interconnectedness with the universe by learning to perceive and work with the biofield. This journey into 'Biofield Alchemy' is not just about healing your body and mind but it is about awakening to the true nature of our being and our potential for transformation.

'Biofield Alchemy' envisions a future where biofield healing is recognized as a fundamental aspect of healthcare, bridging the gap between science and spirituality. By embracing the wisdom of the biofield, we can create a more harmonious and balanced world, where healing is a holistic and transformative process.

SUMMARY

In summary, 'Biofield Alchemy' is an invitation to embark on a path of self-discovery and empowerment. By understanding and harnessing the biofield, we can unlock new dimensions of health, wealth, harmony, and spiritual fulfillment. This book is your guide to navigating this fascinating and transformative realm, offering insights, techniques, and inspiration to help you on your journey. Welcome to the world of 'Biofield Alchemy'- a world where science meets spirituality, and where the alchemy of energy can lead to profound and lasting change.

In the ever-evolving landscape of personal growth and spiritual enlightenment, 'Biofield Alchemy' emerges as a distinctive concept that harmonizes the ancient art of alchemy with contemporary practices of energy healing and self-transformation. Rooted in the timeless quest for inner gold, 'Biofield Alchemy' is not just a spiritual discipline but a personalized journey that adapts to the unique needs and aspirations of everyone. This holistic approach offers a tailored path towards self-realization and empowerment.

Welcome to 'Biofield Alchemy'. May this journey illuminate your path, awaken your inner alchemist and empower you to transform your life from lead to gold!

PART 1
CHAPTER 2

FOUNDATION

'BIOFIELD ALCHEMY'
&
IT'S FOUNDATION

FOUNDATION OF 'BIOFIELD ALCHEMY'

THE CONCEPT OF 'BIOFIELD'

'Biofield', is an energetic field that surrounds and permeates all living beings, acting as a matrix that connects and communicates with the physical, emotional, mental, and spiritual aspects of life. It is a complex, dynamic system that incorporates the body's electromagnetic field and other subtle energies, often described in various traditions as the 'Aura', 'Life Force', 'Prana', 'Qi' or 'Vital Energy'. Unlike the more commonly known physical systems, the biofield is not confined to the tangible. Instead, it encompasses the holistic essence of life, influencing and being influenced by the overall state of being.

Biofield represents an integrative framework where the energies of the mind, body, and spirit converge and interact. It is thought to serve as a blueprint for health, wealth and overall well-being, guiding physiological processes and maintaining the body's homeostasis. Disruptions or imbalances within this field are believed to precede and predict physical ailments and emotional disturbances, making the biofield a crucial element in both preventive and therapeutic practices.

SCIENTIFIC THEORIES & EVIDENCE

The scientific investigation into the biofield spans multiple disciplines, including physics, biology, and psychology. While mainstream science often views it with skepticism, a growing body of research offers intriguing insights that support its existence and relevance.

One foundational theory is rooted in biophotonics; the study of light and its interactions with biological systems. Research indicates that cells emit low levels of light, known as biophotons, which are thought to play a role in cellular communication and regulation. These biophotons form a part of the biofield, suggesting that our bodies communicate and maintain coherence through this light-based system.

Another important contribution comes from electromagnetic field (EMF) studies. It is well-established that the human body generates various EMFs, particularly around the heart and brain. Instruments like magnetoencephalography (MEG) and magnetocardiography (MCG) measure these fields and demonstrate their significance in bodily functions. These fields are dynamic, changing with emotional states, mental activities, and overall health, thus forming a key component of the biofield.

Quantum biology further enriches the understanding of the biofield. Quantum coherence, a principle where subatomic particles like electrons or photons are linked and act in unison, may extend to biological systems, suggesting that our bodies function through interconnected quantum processes. This coherence could underpin the unified field of energy that constitutes the biofield, making it more than just an abstract concept but a tangible aspect of our biological makeup.

Studies in psychoneuroimmunology, which explores the interactions between the nervous system, psyche, and immune system, also lend credence to the biofield.

Research shows that psychological states can influence physiological processes through neurochemical pathways, effectively suggesting a biofield-mediated interaction. Techniques like hypnosis, emotional freedom technique, therapeutic touch, and other energy-based healing modalities have shown promising results in clinical settings, supporting the idea that influencing the biofield can lead to significant health benefits.

ANCIENT & MODERN PERSPECTIVES

The concept of the biofield is deeply rooted in ancient traditions across different cultures, each offering a unique perspective on this vital energy system.

In Traditional Chinese Medicine (TCM), the biofield is understood as 'qi' (or 'chi'), the vital life force that flows through the body's meridians. Health is seen as a balance of qi, and practices such as Acupuncture, Tai Chi, and Qigong are designed to harmonize and enhance its flow. 'Qi' is believed to govern physical health, emotional balance, and spiritual well-being, integrating human experience into a cohesive energetic framework.

Similarly, in Ayurvedic medicine, the biofield is conceptualized as 'prana,' the life force that permeates all living entities. Prana flows through energy channels known as 'nadis' and converges at energy centers called 'chakras'. Ayurvedic practices, including Yoga, Pranayama, Acupressure, Hypnosis, aim to balance 'prana', ensuring optimal health and spiritual growth. This ancient understanding aligns closely with the modern concept of the biofield, emphasizing the interconnectedness of body, mind, and spirit.

Indigenous cultures worldwide also recognize the biofield, often referring to it in terms of 'Spirit' or 'Life Force'. Native American traditions, for example, speak of a 'Sacred Hoop' or an 'Energy Circle' that connects all life forms, reflecting a holistic view of health and existence. These cultural perspectives highlight the universality of the biofield concept, transcending geographical and temporal boundaries.

In the contemporary world, biofield science is gaining traction as a legitimate field of study. Integrative medicine increasingly incorporates biofield therapies, recognizing their potential to enhance conventional treatments. Techniques like Hypnosis, Healing Touch, Energy Psychology and other healing modalities are being validated through empirical research, showing significant benefits in reducing stress, alleviating pain, and improving overall quality of life. These modern approaches often draw on ancient wisdom, blending traditional knowledge with scientific inquiry to form a comprehensive understanding of the biofield.

Moreover, technological advancements are facilitating deeper explorations into the biofield. Tools like electroencephalograms (EEGs), functional magnetic resonance imaging (MRI), and biofield imaging technologies allow scientists to visualize and measure subtle energy changes, providing empirical evidence of the biofield's influence on health and disease. These innovations bridge the gap between ancient perspectives and modern science, offering a robust framework for understanding the biofield's role in human health.

In conclusion, the biofield represents a fundamental aspect of our existence, weaving together the physical, emotional, mental, and spiritual dimensions of life. Both ancient traditions and modern science acknowledge its significance, offering complementary insights that enrich our understanding of health and well-being. As research continues to uncover the mechanisms and effects of the biofield, its integration into mainstream healthcare promises to revolutionize our approach to healing, emphasizing a holistic and interconnected view of the human experience.

THE FOUNDATION OF ALCHEMY

'Alchemy', often regarded as the precursor to modern chemistry, is historically associated with the transmutation of base metals into noble ones, particularly gold. However, it's symbolic significance extends far beyond physical transformation. Alchemy is fundamentally a spiritual science, concerned with the transformation of the self. The pursuit of the 'Philosopher's Stone' and the 'Elixir of Life' in alchemical traditions symbolizes the quest for enlightenment and immortality. 'Biofield Alchemy' builds on this foundation, merging ancient principles with contemporary understandings of the human energy field, or biofield.

ART OF ALCHEMY

Alchemy, a term once shrouded in mystery and misconception, is reborn in the realm of 'Biofield Alchemy'. This ancient art, once associated with the quest for physical transmutation and material wealth, is revealed in its true essence: a timeless wisdom for spiritual transformation and self-actualization.

In 'Biofield Alchemy', alchemy represents the art of conscious evolution, where the lead of limitation is transmuted into the gold of higher potential. This evolutionary process unfolds within the crucible of the human biofield, where the forces of energy, intention, and awareness converge.

The alchemical journey in 'Biofield Alchemy' is a metaphor for the inner transformation that occurs when we awaken to our true nature.

'Biofield Alchemy' symbolizes the passage from:

A) DARKNESS TO LIGHT: Ignorance to awareness, unconsciousness to consciousness

B) SEPARATION TO UNITY: Duality to oneness, fragmentation to wholeness

C) DENSITY TO LIGHTNESS: Heavy energies to light, burdens to freedom through the lens of 'Biofield Alchemy', the ancient alchemical processes

ALCHEMICAL STAGES OF PERSONAL TRANSFORMATION:

1. CALCINATION: Burning away limiting beliefs and patterns

2. DISSOLUTION: Letting go of attachments and ego structures

3. SEPARATION: Discerning truth from illusion, wisdom from knowledge

4. CONJUCTION: Integrating opposites, balancing masculine and feminine

5. FERMENTATION: Incubating new insights, allowing growth and renewal

6. DISTILLATION: Refining essence, extracting wisdom from experiences

7. COAGULATION: Manifesting intentions, materializing desires in this context, the 'Philosopher's Stone' - the legendary alchemical treasure - represents the attainment of higher consciousness, where the individual's biofield is transmuted into a vessel for the divine.

BOUNDLESS POTENTIAL OF ALCHEMY IN 'BIOFIELD ALCHEMY' EMPOWERS INDIVIDUALS TO:

1. TRANSMUTE - emotional lead into golden wisdom

2. TRANSFORM - fear into courage, doubt into faith

3. ALCHEMIZE - limiting beliefs into liberating truths

4. ACTIVATE - dormant DNA, unlocking hidden potential

5. EMBODY - the Phoenix principle, rising from ashes anew

As we embrace the alchemical journey in 'Biofield Alchemy', we become the adepts of our own transformation, crafting a life of purpose, power, and wisdom. We discover that the 'Great Work' of alchemy is not a distant dream but a living reality, unfolding within us, through us, and as us.

In the following chapters, we will delve deeper into the practical applications and transformative potential of 'Biofield Alchemy', illuminating the path for those who seek to unlock the secrets of energy, matter, and human experience.

Let us embark on this extraordinary adventure, where the ancient art of alchemy is reborn in the fires of 'Biofield Alchemy', illuminating our journey towards self-mastery, and the realization of our highest potential.

PART 1
CHAPTER 3

PRINCIPLES

PRINCIPLES OF 'BIOFIELD ALCHEMY'

BIOFIELD ALCHEMY & THE PRINCIPLES OF ENERGY HEALING

Energy healing is an ancient practice rooted in the belief that the human body is composed of more than just physical matter. It also encompasses vital energy fields that influence health and well-being. By understanding and manipulating these energy fields, practitioners aim to promote healing, balance, and overall harmony within the body. This chapter delves into the principles of energy healing, exploring the mechanisms of energy healing and energy transfer, and their respective benefits and limitations.

PRINCIPLES OF 'BIOFIELD ALCHEMY':

'Biofield Alchemy' is founded on the understanding that the human biofield, an energetic field surrounding and permeating the body, holds the potential for profound transformation and healing. The principles of this practice are rooted in the belief that by consciously interacting with the biofield, one can influence physical, emotional, and spiritual well-being.

The core principles of 'Biofield Alchemy' include awareness, intention, and resonance.

AWARENESS: Awareness involves attuning to the subtle energies within and around oneself. This fosters a deeper connection with one's inner state, enhancing self-awareness and sensitivity to energetic changes.

INTENTION: It acts as a guiding force and directs the flow of energy towards desired outcomes, such as healing, personal growth, or transformation. It helps to focus and channel one's energetic efforts.

RESONANCE: It is the principle of harmonizing with the natural frequencies of the body and environment. This principle is crucial for achieving balance and coherence in the biofield, promoting overall well-being and energetic harmony.

Key aspects of 'Biofield Alchemy' encompass various techniques and practices aimed at cultivating and refining one's energetic field. These may include meditation, visualizations, breathwork, sound work and initiations and other energy modalities. The practice emphasizes self-awareness, encouraging individuals to recognize and release energetic blockages that may hinder their overall well-being.

In essence, 'Biofield Alchemy' is about harnessing the subtle energies that shape our existence, guiding them towards healing and transformation. By aligning with these principles and key aspects, practitioners can unlock the potential within their biofield, fostering a deeper connection to themselves and the world around them.

THE MECHANISM OF ENERGY TRANSFER

At the core of energy healing is the concept of energy transfer. This process involves the movement or manipulation of subtle energy fields within and around the body to promote physical, emotional, and spiritual well-being. Several mechanisms underpin this transfer:

1. ENERGY FIELDS & CHAKRAS

Many energy healing systems are based on the idea that the body has various energy centers, often referred to as chakras, and a surrounding energy field. These energy centers are believed to regulate the flow of vital life force, known as 'qi' (in Chinese Medicine) or 'prana' (in Ayurveda). Practitioners work to balance these centers, ensuring optimal energy flow.

2. BIOFIELD

The term 'biofield' refers to the complex electromagnetic field that surrounds and permeates the human body. This field is thought to interact with the body's cellular and molecular structures, influencing physiological processes. Energy healing techniques often aim to harmonize the biofield, addressing distortions or blockages that may contribute to illness or distress.

3. RESONANCE & ENTRAINMENT

Energy transfer can occur through resonance and entrainment. Resonance happens when the healer's energy field vibrates at a frequency that influences the recipient's field, promoting balance. Entrainment involves synchronizing the recipient's energy with the healer's, leading to a state of coherence and improved energy flow.

4. INTENTION & FOCUS

The practitioner's intention and focused attention are crucial in energy healing. Through meditation, visualization, and concentration, healers direct their energy to facilitate healing.

BENEFITS & LIMITATIONS

Energy healing offers numerous potential benefits, but it also has its limitations. Understanding both aspects is crucial for practitioners and recipients alike.

BENEFITS:

1. HOLISTIC HEALING: Energy healing addresses not just the physical symptoms but also the emotional, mental, and spiritual aspects of well-being. This holistic approach can lead to a profound, multidimensional healing.

2. STRESS REDUCTION: Many energy healing practices induce deep relaxation, helping to alleviate stress and anxiety. This relaxation response can enhance the body's natural healing processes.

3. COMPLEMENTARY THERAPY: Energy healing can be used alongside conventional medical treatments. It may enhance the effectiveness of medical care, speed up recovery times, and improve the overall quality of life.

4. NON - INVASIVE: Most energy healing modalities are non-invasive and gentle, making them suitable for individuals who may not tolerate more aggressive treatments. This characteristic also reduces the risk of adverse side effects.

5. SELF-EMPOWERMENT: Energy healing practices empower individuals to take an active role in their own healing process. This sense of empowerment can be a significant factor in achieving and maintaining health.

LIMITATIONS:

1. SCIENTIFIC VALIDATION: While many people report positive experiences with energy healing, scientific validation remains limited. The subjective nature of healing experiences and the challenge of measuring subtle energy fields make it difficult to produce robust, replicable research results.

2. PLACEBO EFFECT: Some benefits of energy healing may be attributed to the placebo effect - the belief in the treatment's efficacy leading to real improvements in symptoms. While the placebo effect is a powerful phenomenon, it does not negate the need for objective evidence.

3. PRACTITIONER VARIABILITY: The effectiveness of energy healing can vary significantly between practitioners. Differences in skill, experience, and personal energy can influence outcomes, making it crucial for recipients to find reputable and well-trained practitioners.

4. NOT A SUBSTITUTE FOR MEDICAL CARE: Energy healing should not replace conventional medical treatments, especially for serious or life-threatening conditions. It is best used as a complementary approach within a broader healthcare plan.

5. ETHICAL AND PROFESSIONAL CONCERNS: The field of energy healing is not uniformly regulated, which can lead to ethical and professional concerns. Recipients must exercise discernment in choosing

qualified practitioners who adhere to high ethical standards.

In conclusion, the principles of energy healing encompass a rich tapestry of traditions and techniques aimed at restoring balance and promoting health. By understanding the mechanisms of energy transfer, exploring common modalities, and acknowledging both benefits and limitations, individuals can make informed choices about incorporating energy healing into their wellness journeys. Whether seeking to enhance personal well-being or complement existing medical treatments, 'Biofield Alchemy' offers a unique and profound approach to holistic health, wealth and overall wellbeing.

PART 1
CHAPTER 4

ENERGETIC ANATOMY

UNDERSTANDING THE SCIENCE OF HUMAN ENERGY FIELD IN 'BIOFIELD ALCHEMY'

BIOFIELD ALCHEMY & THE ENERGY SYSTEM OF THE HUMAN BODY

The human body is a sophisticated and intricate system where various forms of energy interact seamlessly to maintain health, balance, and well-being. Understanding these energy systems provides profound insights into how we can enhance our physical, emotional, and spiritual health. This section delves into the key components of the body's energy systems, focusing on chakras and meridians, aura and electromagnetic fields, and the pivotal role of the nervous system.

CHAKRAS - THE ENERGY CENTRES

Chakras are the fundamental concepts in many traditional healing systems, such as Ayurveda, Yoga, Acupressure and Traditional Chinese Medicine (TCM). They represent pathways and centers of energy that influence our physical, mental and emotional states.

Chakras are energy centers located along the spine, each associated with specific physical, emotional, and spiritual functions. There are seven primary chakras:

1. ROOT CHAKRA (Muladhara): Located at the base of the spine, it is associated with survival, stability, and grounding.
2. SACRAL CHAKRA (Svadhisthana): Situated below the navel, it governs creativity, sexuality, and emotions.

3. SOLAR PLEXUS CHAKRA (Manipura): Found near the stomach area, it influences personal power, confidence, and self-esteem.
4. HEART CHAKRA (Anahata): Located in the center of the chest, it is the center of love, compassion, and relationships.
5. THROAT CHAKRA (Vishuddha): Positioned at the throat, it is linked to communication, expression, and truth.
6. THIRD EYE CHAKRA (Ajna): Located between the eyebrows, it is associated with intuition, insight, and wisdom.
7. CROWN CHAKRA (Sahasrara): At the top of the head, it connects us to higher consciousness and spiritual enlightenment.

When these chakras are balanced, energy flows freely, promoting health and harmony. Imbalances can lead to physical and emotional issues, which can often be alleviated through practices such as pranayama, meditation, yoga, and other energy healing modalities.

CHAKRAS IN ESSENCE, AS PER PATANJALI'S YOGA SUTRAS:

a. DESCRIBED - as energy centers within the human body

b. INFLUENCE - physical, mental emotional, and spiritual well-being

c. ACT - as conduits for prana, the vital life force

ROLE OF CHAKRAS IN YOGA & 'BIOFIELD ALCHEMY':

a) Integral to the practice of yoga, Pranayama provides a pathway for energy flow.
b) In 'Biofield Alchemy', chakras are used to harmonize and amplify one's life force energy.
c) Each chakra corresponds to specific physiological and psychological functions.

IMPACT OF CHAKRAS IN BALANCING AND ENHANCING THE BIOFIELD:

a) Understanding the unique attributes of each chakra, from Muladhara (root chakra) to Sahasrara (crown chakra), is essential.
b) Practitioners work to clear blockages and enhance the flow of energy throughout the biofield.
c) This process is likened to tuning an instrument, bringing the chakras into harmonious resonance.

TRANSFORMATIVE ASPECT OF CHAKRAS IN 'BIOFIELD ALCHEMY':

a) FOCUS on chakras helps transmute negative energies and break old outdated physical, mental, emotional patterns.
b) CULTIVATES a state of inner peace, balance and vitality.
c) COMBINES ancient wisdom with modern understanding for personal growth, material and spiritual evolution.

OUTCOME OF CHAKRA ALIGNMENT PRACTICE:

a) ACHIEVES a heightened state of awareness and well-being.
b) FOSTERS a deeper connection to the universal energy that flows through all living beings.
c) BALANCES material and spiritual realms.

MERIDIANS - THE ENERGY CHANNELS

Meridians play a crucial role in 'Biofield Alchemy', serving as channels that facilitate the flow of energy throughout the body. In Traditional Chinese Medicine, these pathways are believed to carry 'vital life force', or 'qi', which is essential for maintaining physical, emotional, and spiritual well-being. The concept of meridians aligns with the principles of 'Biofield Alchemy', where the focus is on harmonizing and balancing the body's energetic field.

In 'Biofield Alchemy', the meridians are seen as not just conduits for energy but also as intricate networks that connect various aspects of our being. They are considered bridges between the physical and subtle bodies, influencing everything from organ function to mental and emotional states. By understanding and working with these meridians, practitioners can identify and clear blockages, restore energy flow, and promote holistic healing.

Techniques such as breathwork, acupressure, acupuncture, sound work and other energy healing systems are often employed to stimulate and balance the meridians. These methods aim to release stagnation and allow for the free movement of energy, thereby enhancing the body's natural ability to heal and regenerate. Moreover, the meridians are thought to interact with the chakras, another key element in

'Biofield Alchemy', creating a dynamic interplay that influences overall health and vitality.

Incorporating the concept of meridians into 'Biofield Alchemy' offers a comprehensive approach to wellness, integrating ancient wisdom with modern understanding. This holistic perspective not only addresses physical ailments but also nurtures emotional and spiritual growth, providing a pathway to greater harmony and self-awareness.

KOSHAS - THE SHEATHS OF ENERGY

Koshas in Patanjali's Yoga: The concept of 'Koshas' or 'sheaths' provides a comprehensive understanding of human existence.

FIVE LAYERS:

1. ANNAMAYA (Physical): The outermost sheath, related to the physical body.
2. PRANAMAYA (Energy): The energy body, encompassing the life force or Prana.
3. MANOMAYA (Mental): The mental sheath, containing thoughts and emotions.
4. VIJNANAMAYA (Wisdom): The layer of wisdom and intuition.
5. ANANDAMAYA (Bliss): The innermost sheath, associated with bliss and the essence of being.

ROLE OF KOSHAS IN HUMAN EXPERIENCE & 'BIOFIELD ALCHEMY':

Each Kosh acts as a veil, covering the pure consciousness or Atman - The Soul, crucial for the journey toward self-realization. Understanding and balancing these Koshas through 'Biofield Alchemy' aligns physical, emotional, mental, and spiritual aspects, fostering overall well-being. Types of Koshas:

1. ANNAMAYA KOSH: Represents the physical body; influenced by nutrition, lifestyle, and health. It is the most tangible aspect of the biofield.
2. PRANAYAMA KOSH: Corresponds to the energy body, aligning with the concept of biofields. It reflects life force energy and is key concept in the practices like 'pranayama' and the ancient forms of martial arts.
3. MANOMAYA KOSH: Encompasses thoughts and emotions, affecting the biofield through mental and emotional states.
4. VIJNANAMAYA KOSH: Involves wisdom and intuition, impacting the clarity and coherence of the biofield.
5. ANANDAMAYA KOSH: Represents the state of bliss, reflecting inner peace and joy when aligned with the universe.

AURIC LAYERS - THE ENERGY FIELD

Beyond the physical body, each person is surrounded by an energy field known as the 'aura'. This multi-layered field extends beyond the skin and interacts with the environment and other beings. The aura consists of several layers, each corresponding to different aspects of our existence:

1. ETHERIC LAYER: Closest to the body, it mirrors our physical state and vitality.

2. EMOTIONAL LAYER: Reflects our emotions and feelings.
3. MENTAL LAYER: Represents our thoughts and mental processes.
4. ASTRAL LAYER: Connects the physical realm with higher spiritual planes.
5. ETHERIC TEMPLATE: Serves as a blueprint for the physical body.
6. CELESTIAL LAYER: Linked to our spiritual awareness and higher consciousness.
7. CAUSAL LAYER: Contains our soul's purpose and connection to the divine.

The aura can be influenced by our thoughts, emotions, and external factors, such as the environment and interactions with others. Practices like aura cleansing, hypnosis, sound work, meditation, and energy healing, can help maintain a healthy and balanced aura.

The body also generates its own electromagnetic field, which can be detected and measured. This field is produced by the electrical activity of the heart, brain, and other organs. Techniques like electrocardiograms (ECGs) and electroencephalograms (EEGs) measure these fields to provide insights into our physical and mental states. Maintaining a balanced electromagnetic field is essential for overall well-being and can be supported by grounding practices, spending time in nature, and reducing exposure to artificial electromagnetic radiation.

THE ROLE OF THE NERVOUS SYSTEM

The nervous system plays a crucial role in the body's energy systems by acting as a conduit for the transmission of electrical signals and coordinating bodily functions. It comprises two main parts: the central nervous system (CNS), consisting of the brain and spinal cord, and the peripheral nervous system (PNS), which includes all other neural elements.

The nervous system is responsible for:

1. SENSORY INPUT: Gathering information from the environment and internal body states.
2. INTEGRATION: Processing and interpreting sensory input.
3. MOTOR OUTPUT: Initiating and coordinating responses, such as muscle movements and glandular secretions.

The autonomic nervous system (ANS), a subdivision of the PNS, regulates involuntary bodily functions and is further divided into the sympathetic and parasympathetic nervous systems. The sympathetic nervous system prepares the body for 'fight or flight' responses during stressful situations, while the parasympathetic nervous system promotes 'rest and digest' functions, aiding relaxation and recovery.

The interplay between the nervous system and other energy systems is profound. For instance, the 'vagus nerve', a key component of the parasympathetic system, plays a significant role in regulating heart rate, digestion, and other vital functions. It also interacts with the gut-brain axis, influencing emotional and psychological states.

Energy practices such as sound work and meditation can have a significant impact on the nervous system by promoting relaxation, reducing stress, and enhancing the flow of energy throughout the body. Techniques like mindfulness and deep breathing activate the parasympathetic system, helping to restore balance and improve overall health.

INTEGRATIVE PERSPECTIVE

To achieve optimal health and well-being, it is essential to consider the intricate interactions between chakras, meridians, the aura, electromagnetic fields, and the nervous system. These energy systems do not function in isolation but rather in a dynamic interplay that affects every aspect of our lives.

Integrative approaches that combine traditional healing practices with modern scientific understanding offer powerful tools for balancing and enhancing the body's energy systems. For example:

1. CHAKRA BALANCING: Using visualisation, meditation and sound work to align and harmonize the chakras.
2. ACUPUNCTURE AND ACUPRESSURE: Stimulating meridian points to promote the flow of 'Qi' and alleviate blockages.
3. ENERGY HEALING: Practices like Yoga, Pranayama and Therapeutic Touch to cleanse and balance the aura.
4. MIND-BODY TECHNIQUES: Yoga, Pranayama and Qigong to integrate physical movement with energy flow and mental focus.
5. GROUNDING PRACTICES: Spending time in nature and engaging in activities that connect us with the Earth's natural electromagnetic field.

CONCLUSION

By understanding and working with the energy systems of the body, we can cultivate a deeper awareness of our physical, mental, emotional, and spiritual states. This holistic approach not only supports healing and balance but also empowers us to live more vibrant and fulfilling lives.

PART 1
CHAPTER 5

THE QUANTUM FIELD

THE CONNECTION BETWEEN THE BIOFIELD & THE QUANTUM FIELD

QUANTUM FIELD & 'BIOFIELD ALCHEMY'

UNVEILING THE QUANTUM FIELD

The concept of the quantum field has revolutionized our understanding of the universe, transforming the way we perceive reality. At its core, quantum field theory posits that the universe is a vast web of interconnected fields, each one representing different fundamental forces and particles. Renowned physicist John Wheeler encapsulated this idea succinctly, stating "Everything is information," highlighting the idea that at the quantum level, the universe is a complex interplay of informational fields.

QUANTUM FIELD THEORY & 'BIOFIELD ALCHEMY'

'Biofield Alchemy', a holistic approach to health, wealth and well-being, draws upon the principles of quantum field theory to explain the subtle energies that permeate the human body. According to 'Biofield Alchemy', the human biofield is an energetic matrix that extends beyond the physical body, encompassing various layers of subtle energies that influence our physical, mental emotional and spiritual health.

Dr. Deepak Chopra, a pioneer in integrative medicine, often refer quantum theory to explain the mind-body connection. He asserts, "We are not merely physical bodies; we are fields of consciousness - inextricably linked to the quantum field of the universe." This perspective aligns with the fundamental premise of 'Biofield Alchemy', which views the human biofield as an extension of the universal quantum field.

QUANTUM ENTANGLEMENT & 'BIOFIELD ALCHEMY'

One of the most intriguing aspects of quantum field theory is the phenomenon of quantum entanglement. This occurs when particles become entangled and their states remain interconnected, regardless of the distance separating them. Nobel laureate physicist Erwin Schrödinger described 'entanglement' as "the characteristic trait of quantum mechanics, the one that enforces its entire departure from classical lines of thought."

In the context of 'Biofield Alchemy', quantum entanglement suggests that our biofields are interconnected with the larger quantum field. This interconnectedness implies that changes in our biofield can influence and be influenced by the broader quantum field. Such a perspective opens possibilities for healing and transformation that transcend traditional boundaries.

THE ROLE OF CONSCIOUSNESS

Another cornerstone of quantum field theory is the role of the observer in shaping reality. The famous double-slit experiment demonstrated that particles behave differently when observed, implying that consciousness plays a pivotal role in the manifestation of reality. This concept is echoed by physicist Eugene Wigner, who argued that "it was not possible to formulate the laws of quantum mechanics in a fully consistent way without reference to the consciousness."

'Biofield Alchemy' leverages this principle by emphasizing the power of conscious intention in shaping our biofields. By cultivating positive thoughts and intentions, we can influence the subtle energies within and around us, promoting healing and well-being. Dr. Bruce Lipton, a cell biologist and author, supports this view, stating, "The moment you change your perception - is the moment you rewrite the chemistry of your body."

THE SCIENCE OF HEALING

The intersection of quantum field theory and 'Biofield Alchemy' offers a scientific basis for understanding energy healing practices. Various studies have explored the effects of intentional energy healing on the human biofield, yielding promising results. Dr. Beverly Rubik, a biophysicist and expert in biofield science, notes, "The biofield is a real, measurable energy field that can be influenced by various forms of healing, including intentionality and touch."

Quantum field theory provides a framework for understanding how subtle energies can influence physical health. It suggests that by tapping into the quantum field through practices such as hypnosis, meditation, visualization, affirmations, touch healing, and other forms of energy healing, we can harmonize our biofields and promote optimal health. This perspective aligns with the growing body of evidence supporting the efficacy of energy healing modalities.

BRIDGING SCIENCE & SPIRITUALITY

The exploration of the quantum field in relation to 'Biofield Alchemy' bridges the gap between science and spirituality.

While quantum field theory provides a scientific explanation for the existence of subtle energies and their interconnectedness, 'Biofield Alchemy' offers practical tools for harnessing these energies for healing and transformation.

Dr. Amit Goswami, a theoretical physicist and author, eloquently captures this synthesis: "The quantum world is not separate from us. We are part of this quantum world, and our consciousness is a fundamental aspect of it." By embracing this holistic view, 'Biofield Alchemy' empowers individuals to tap into the quantum field's potential for profound healing and personal growth.

CONCLUSION

The integration of quantum field theory into the framework of 'Biofield Alchemy' offers a powerful paradigm for understanding and working with the subtle energies that shape our existence. By recognizing the interconnectedness of our biofields with the universal quantum field, we open up to new possibilities for healing, transformation, and the realization of our highest potential. As we continue to explore the frontiers of science and spirituality, the wisdom of the quantum field will undoubtedly illuminate our path toward a deeper understanding of ourselves and the universe.

PART 1
CHAPTER 6

EPIGENETICS

UNDERSTANDING EPIGENETICS IN BIOFIELD ALCHEMY

EPIGENETICS & 'BIOFIELD ALCHEMY'

EPIGENETICS: AN INSIGHT

In the quest to understand the profound interplay between mind, body, and spirit, epigenetics emerges as a pivotal concept. Bruce Lipton, a pioneering cell biologist, has significantly contributed to this field, offering insights that fit together seamlessly with the principles of 'Biofield Alchemy'. This chapter explores the essence of epigenetics as elucidated by Bruce Lipton, and its implications for 'Biofield Alchemist', explaining how our thoughts, beliefs, and environments shape our biological reality.

Epigenetics, at its core, is the study of changes in gene expression that do not involve alterations to the underlying DNA sequence. These changes are influenced by various factors, including environmental stimuli, lifestyle choices, and even our mental states. Bruce Lipton's groundbreaking work has shown that our cells are not merely controlled by genetic code but are highly responsive to their environment. This responsiveness suggests a dynamic interaction between our external world and our internal biological processes.

BRUCE LIPTON'S CONTRIBUTION

Bruce Lipton's seminal book, "The Biology of Belief", posits that our beliefs and perceptions have a profound impact on our cellular function. He asserts that the cell membrane, rather than the nucleus, acts as the 'brain' of the cell, processing signals from the environment and translating them into biological responses. This paradigm shift challenges the traditional view of genetic determinism, emphasizing the role of the biofield - an energetic field that surrounds and permeates all living beings - in influencing our health, wealth and well-being.

Lipton's research underscores the importance of consciousness in shaping our biology. He argues that our thoughts and emotions can directly affect cellular activity through the biofield. This aligns with the principles of 'Biofield Alchemy', which posits that by harnessing and manipulating this energy field, we can influence our physical and emotional states.

THE BIOFIELD & CELLULAR COMMUNICATION

The biofield is a complex, dynamic energy field that encompasses the electromagnetic and subtle energy emanations of the body. It serves as a medium for information exchange between the mind and body. In the context of epigenetics, the biofield plays a crucial role in modulating gene expression.

When we experience positive emotions, such as love, joy, and gratitude, our biofield vibrates at a higher frequency, creating a harmonious environment for our cells. This harmony facilitates optimal gene expression, promoting health, wealth and vitality. Conversely, negative emotions like fear, anger, and stress generate low-frequency vibrations, leading to disharmony and potential disease.

Bruce Lipton's work highlights the influence of the biofield on cellular communication. He explains that cells use electromagnetic signals to communicate with each other, and these signals are affected by our emotional and mental states. Thus, by consciously cultivating positive emotions and thoughts, we can enhance the coherence of our biofield, thereby optimizing cellular function and overall health.

PRACTICAL APPLICATIONS IN 'BIOFIELD ALCHEMY'

'Biofield Alchemy' involves the intentional manipulation of the biofield to bring about desired changes in our physical and emotional states. By integrating the principles of epigenetics, practitioners of 'Biofield Alchemy' can enhance their ability to influence their biology. Here are some practical applications:

1. MEDITATION & MINDFULNESS

These practices help regulate the biofield by promoting relaxation and reducing stress. Research has shown that regular meditation can alter gene expression, enhancing immune function and reducing inflammation.

2. AFFIRMATION & POSITIVE THINKING

By consistently focusing on positive thoughts and beliefs, we can reprogram our subconscious mind and influence our biofield. This practice can lead to changes in gene expression that promote health, wealth and well-being.

3. ENERGY HEALING MODALITIES

Techniques such as Yoga, Pranayama, Hypnosis, Acupuncture, and Qigong work directly with the biofield to remove blockages and restore balance. These modalities can influence cellular communication and gene expression, facilitating healing and transformation.

4. ENVIRONMENTAL OPTIMIZATION

Creating a harmonious living environment by incorporating elements like nature, light, and sound can positively impact our biofield. By reducing exposure to toxins and electromagnetic pollution, we can create a supportive environment for optimal gene expression.

THE POWER OF PERCEPTION

One of Bruce Lipton's key insights is the power of perception in shaping our reality. He argues that our beliefs act as filters, influencing how we perceive and respond to our environment. These perceptions, in turn, affect our biofield and biological processes. By becoming aware of and transforming limiting beliefs, we can shift our perceptions and create a more supportive biofield for health, wealth and well-being.

For instance, if we hold a belief that we are vulnerable to illness, this belief can create a state of chronic stress, weakening our immune system and making us more susceptible to disease. However, by adopting empowering beliefs, such as the innate ability of our body to heal itself, we can create a biofield that supports health and vitality.

EPIGENETICS & CONSCIOUS EVOLUTION

Bruce Lipton's work in epigenetics also touches on the concept of conscious evolution. He suggests that by understanding and harnessing the principles of epigenetics, we can actively participate in our own evolution. This involves not only individual transformation but also a collective shift in consciousness.

'Biofield Alchemy', with its focus on energy and intention, provides a powerful framework for conscious evolution. By working with the biofield, we can align our individual and collective energies towards higher states of consciousness, fostering a more harmonious and sustainable world.

CONCLUSION

Epigenetics, as illuminated by Bruce Lipton, offers profound insights into the intricate relationship between mind, body, and spirit. By recognizing the power of our thoughts, beliefs, and environment in shaping our biology, we can harness the principles of 'Biofield Alchemy' to transform our health and well-being. Through practices such as pranayama, meditation, creative visualization positive thinking, affirmations and other energy healing modalities, we can optimize our biofield, influence gene expression, and participate in our conscious evolution. The synergy between epigenetics and 'Biofield Alchemy' opens new possibilities for healing and transformation, empowering us to create a vibrant and meaningful life.

PART 1
CHAPTER 7

ETHICS
OF
'BIOFIELD ALCHEMY'

- A GUIDE TO RESPONSIBLE PRACTICE

ETHICS OF PRACTISING & TEACHING 'BIOFIELD ALCHEMY'

'Biofield Alchemy', as a field intersecting the realms of science and spirituality, carries a profound ethical responsibility. Its practitioners and educators must navigate this complex landscape with a keen sense of moral integrity, as their work has the potential to deeply influence individuals' physical, mental, emotional and spiritual well-being. This chapter explores ethical considerations from both scientific and spiritual perspectives, offering a comprehensive understanding of how to ethically engage with 'Biofield Alchemy'.

A) SCIENTIFIC PERSPECTIVES ON ETHICS IN 'BIOFIELD ALCHEMY'

Scientists who delve into 'Biofield Alchemy' often emphasize the importance of rigorous ethical standards. The scientific community typically adheres to principles of transparency, accountability, and empirical validation.

1. TRANSPARENCY & INFORMED CONSENT

One of the cornerstones of ethical practice in the scientific realm is transparency. Practitioners must clearly communicate the nature of biofield interventions, including their potential benefits and limitations. This involves obtaining informed consent from clients or study participants, ensuring they fully understand what the practice entails and any associated risks.

2. EMPIRICAL VALIDATION & EFFICACY

From a scientific standpoint, it is crucial to base practices on empirical evidence. This means rigorously testing the effectiveness of biofield techniques through controlled studies and peer-reviewed research. Ethical practitioners must avoid making unfounded claims and ensure that their methods have been validated through scientific inquiry.

3. NON - MALEFICENCE & BENEFICENCE

The principles of non-maleficence (do no harm) and beneficence (act in the best interest of the client) are central to scientific ethics. Practitioners must prioritize the well-being of their clients, avoiding techniques that could cause harm and actively promoting those that have been shown to offer tangible benefits. This also includes being mindful of the psychological impact of biofield practices, as the mind-body connection is a critical aspect of overall health.

4. CONFIDENTIALITY & PROFESSIONALISM

Maintaining confidentiality is a fundamental ethical obligation. Practitioners must protect the privacy of their clients and handle personal information with the utmost care. Professionalism is also paramount, which involves continuous education, adherence to established protocols, and respectful interaction with clients and colleagues.

B) SPIRITUAL PERSPECTIVES ON ETHICS IN 'BIOFIELD ALCHEMY'

Spiritual masters bring a different, yet complementary, ethical framework to 'Biofield Alchemy'. Their approach is often rooted in ancient traditions and holistic principles, emphasizing the interconnectedness of all life and the pursuit of higher consciousness.

1. INTEGRITY & AUTHENTICITY

Spiritual ethics emphasize the importance of integrity and authenticity in practice. Practitioners are encouraged to live by the principles they teach, embodying the virtues of honesty, compassion, and humility. This authenticity helps to build trust and rapport with clients, fostering a safe and supportive healing environment.

2. COMPASSION & EMPATHY

Compassion is a central tenet in many spiritual traditions. Practitioners are urged to approach their work with empathy, genuinely caring for the well-being of their clients. This involves listening deeply, understanding the unique needs and experiences of each individual, and providing support that is both nurturing and empowering.

3. SERVICE & SELFLESSNESS

Many spiritual masters advocate for a service-oriented approach to 'Biofield Alchemy'. Practitioners are seen as conduits for healing energy, working selflessly for the benefit of others. This service mindset helps to mitigate ego-driven motives, ensuring that the primary focus remains on the client's healing journey rather than the practitioner's personal gain.

4. HOLISTIC RESPONSIBILITY

Spiritual ethics often extend beyond the individual to encompass a broader sense of responsibility towards the community and the environment. Practitioners are encouraged to consider the wider implications of their work, promoting practices that support ecological balance and social harmony. This holistic perspective underscores the interconnectedness of all life and the importance of living in alignment with natural and universal laws.

C) INTEGRATING SCIENTIFIC & SPIRITUAL ETHICS

In the practice and teaching of 'Biofield Alchemy', it is essential to integrate both scientific and spiritual ethical frameworks. This integration ensures a well-rounded, holistic approach that respects the best practices of empirical science while honoring the profound wisdom of spiritual traditions.

1. BALANCED APPROACH

Practitioners should strive for a balanced approach that values both scientific validation and spiritual insight. This means embracing evidence-based practices while also recognizing the importance of intuition and personal experience. Such balance helps to create a comprehensive and effective biofield practice that can cater to the diverse needs of clients.

2. CONTINUAL LEARNING & ADAPTATION

The field of 'Biofield Alchemy' is continually evolving. Ethical practitioners and teachers must commit to lifelong learning, staying abreast of the latest scientific research and spiritual teachings. This commitment to growth ensures that their practice remains relevant and effective, adapting to new insights and discoveries.

3. COMMUNITY & COLLABORATION

Building a community of ethical practice is vital. Practitioners should collaborate with peers, engage in ongoing dialogue, and participate in professional organizations that promote ethical standards. This sense of community helps to foster accountability, support, and shared learning, enhancing the overall integrity of the field.

4. CLIENT - CENTERED PRACTICE

Ultimately, the ethical practice of 'Biofield Alchemy' is client - centered. This means prioritizing the needs, goals, and well-being of clients above all else. Whether approaching from a scientific or spiritual perspective, the focus must remain on providing compassionate, effective, and respectful care.

CONCLUSION

The ethics of practicing and teaching 'Biofield Alchemy' are multifaceted, requiring a harmonious integration of scientific rigor and spiritual wisdom. By adhering to ethical principles from both domains, practitioners can ensure that their work is not only effective but also profoundly respectful of the individuals they serve and the larger interconnected web of life. This ethical foundation is essential for fostering trust, promoting healing, and advancing the field of 'Biofield Alchemy' in a way that honors its rich, multifaceted nature.

PART 2

TOOLS & TECHNIQUES OF 'BIOFIELD ALCHEMY'

- DISCOVERING THE PHILOSOPHER'S STONE & UNLOCKING THE RICHES OF GOLD WITHIN

PART 2
CHAPTER 1

SOUND & LIGHT

BIOFIELD ALCHEMY
&
THE ALCHEMICAL CIRCLE
OF
VIBRATION & FREQUENCY & ENERGY

THE UNIVERSE AS SOUND & LIGHT IN 'BIOFIELD ALCHEMY'

In the exploration of the universe through the lens of 'Biofield Alchemy', the concepts of sound and light take on profound significance. These elements are not just physical phenomena but are seen as fundamental aspects of existence, shaping the very fabric of reality. To understand this perspective, we must first delve into the definitions and key aspects of sound and light, and then explore their deeper implications within the framework of 'Biofield Alchemy'.

1. SOUND: A POTENT SEED OF ENERGY

In a conventional sense, sound is defined as vibrations that travel through a medium such as air, water, or solids and can be heard when they reach a living organism's ear. Scientifically, sound is characterized by properties such as frequency, wavelength, and amplitude. The frequency of sound waves determines the pitch, while the amplitude determines the volume.

2. LIGHT: A SYMBOL OF CONSCIOUSNESS

Light, on the other hand, is a form of electromagnetic radiation visible to the human eye. It behaves both as a wave and a particle (photon), a duality that is a cornerstone of quantum mechanics. Light waves are characterized by their wavelength and frequency, which determine the color of the light.

3. THE UNIVERSE AS SOUND & LIGHT

In 'Biofield Alchemy', the universe is conceptualized as a vast interplay of energies, with sound and light being two fundamental expressions of these energies. This perspective is deeply rooted in various spiritual and metaphysical traditions, which often describe the universe as being composed of vibrational frequencies.

4. SOUND AS A CREATIVE FORCE

According to many ancient philosophies, sound is not merely a byproduct of physical interactions but a primordial force that shapes reality. This idea is encapsulated in the concept of 'primordial sound' or 'cosmic vibration' often referred to as the "AUM" in Hinduism and Buddhism. In 'Biofield Alchemy', sound is seen as a tool for transformation and healing. The vibrations produced by sound can resonate with the biofield - the subtle energy field that surrounds and permeates all living beings - thereby influencing physical, mental, emotional, and spiritual states.

5. LIGHT AS A MANIFESTATION OF CONSCIOUSNESS

Light, within the context of 'Biofield Alchemy', is often equated with consciousness and awareness. The concept of 'light' is frequently used metaphorically to denote enlightenment, wisdom, and the expansion of consciousness. In this framework, light is not only a physical phenomenon but also a spiritual one. It represents the flow of energy and information throughout the universe, connecting all forms of life in a vast web of existence.

6. THE INTERPLAY OF SOUND & LIGHT

The interplay of sound and light in the universe is a central theme in 'Biofield Alchemy'. This interplay is not just metaphorical but is also considered a literal aspect of the universe's functioning. In modern science, there is an understanding that vibrations (sound) and electromagnetic waves (light) can influence each other. For example, sound waves can be converted into light waves through a process known as sonoluminescence, where tiny bubbles in a liquid emit light when subjected to intense sound waves.

In 'Biofield Alchemy', this interplay is viewed as a dynamic process that underlies all creation and transformation. Sound is seen as a carrier of intention and vibration, which can initiate change in the biofield. Light, as a manifestation of consciousness, illuminates and brings awareness to these changes, facilitating a higher understanding and integration of experiences.

7. THE TRANSFORMATIVE POWER OF SOUND & LIGHT

In essence, the 'Biofield Alchemy' perspective on the universe as being composed of sound and light offers a profound and holistic understanding of existence. It highlights the interconnectedness of all things and the continuous exchange of energy and information that shapes our reality. Sound and light are not merely passive elements but are active agents of transformation, capable of influencing our physical, mental emotional and spiritual states.

8. PRACTICAL APPLICATIONS IN 'BIOFIELD ALCHEMY'

The understanding of the universe as being composed of sound and light has practical applications in 'Biofield Alchemy', particularly in physical, mental, emotional and spiritual healing and personal transformation.

A) SOUND WORK

In the context of 'Biofield Alchemy', sound work is used to balance and harmonize the biofield by:

1. RESONATING with specific sound frequencies to release energy blockages
2. ALIGNING the biofield with harmonic vibrations
3. ENHANCING coherence and balance in the body's energy systems
4. SUPPORTING spiritual growth and higher states of consciousness
5. FACILITATING deep relaxation and meditation states

In the context of 'Biofield Alchemy', 'sound work' refers to the use of sound frequencies to influence and harmonize the body's biofield, an energetic field believed to surround and interpenetrate the human body. The term 'sound work' combines 'sound' indicating auditory vibrations, with 'work' signifying purposeful application. This practice involves the intentional use of sound to promote healing, balance, and transformation in the biofield.

SOUND HEALING: This practice involves the use of various sound-producing instruments, such as tuning forks, singing bowls, and gongs, to create specific frequencies that resonate with the body's energy centers (chakras). As per ancient traditions, repetition of specific mantras and affirmations are also believed to restore balance and promote healing at both physical and subtle levels.

Key aspects of sound work in 'Biofield Alchemy' include its basis in the understanding that everything in the universe, including the human body, is in a state of vibration. Sound work utilizes specific frequencies, tones, and rhythms to resonate with and influence these vibrations, aiming to restore harmony and coherence within the biofield. Instruments such as mantras, affirmations, guided meditations, classical music, sounds of nature, drums, tuning forks, singing bowl and many other musical instruments, and the human voice are often employed to deliver these frequencies.

Sound work is grounded in the principle that dissonance or imbalance in the biofield can manifest as physical, emotional, or mental ailments. By applying specific sound, 'Biofield Alchemist' believe they can clear energy blockages, align energy centers (chakras), and promote overall well-being. This approach is seen as complementary to other healing modalities, enhancing the body and mind's natural capacity for self-healing.

In 'Biofield Alchemy', sound work is not merely a passive experience but an interactive process, inviting participants to engage with the sounds and vibrations on a deep, intuitive level. This engagement is thought to facilitate profound physical, mental, emotional transformation and spiritual growth, making sound work a vital component of holistic health and wellness practices within the field of 'Biofield Alchemy'.

BASIC PRACTICE RITUALS

Sound healing is a cornerstone of 'Biofield Alchemy', harnessing the vibrational power of sound to harmonize and enhance the biofield. Daily rituals incorporating mantras, affirmations, and humming sounds can significantly impact your energetic health and overall well-being.

1. MANTRAS: ENERGETIC SEED SOUNDS THAT RAISES VIBRATION

Begin each morning with a focused mantra session. Choose a mantra that resonates with your current needs or intentions. For example, the Sanskrit mantra "AUM" is known for its universal vibration, aligning the mind, body, and spirit. Sit comfortably, close your eyes, and chant your chosen mantra aloud or silently for at least five minutes. Feel the vibrations permeate your being, clearing any stagnant energy and setting a harmonious tone for the day.

2. AFFIRMATIONS: THE POWER OF WORDS

Incorporate affirmations into your sound healing practice to reinforce positive intentions and beliefs. Affirmations are powerful statements that, when repeated, can reprogram your subconscious mind. Examples include "I am in perfect alignment with the universe," or "My biofield radiates vibrant energy and health." Recite these affirmations with conviction, either in front of a mirror or in nature to enhance their impact.

3. HUMMING SOUND: THE ACTIVATING & CATALYST SOUND WORK

The simple act of humming can also be profoundly healing. The vibrations produced by humming stimulate the 'vagus nerve', promoting relaxation and reducing stress. Spend a few minutes humming softly to yourself, focusing on the sensation of the sound within your body. Notice how the vibrations shift and balance your energy field.

Integrating these sound healing rituals into your daily routine can elevate your biofield, fostering a deeper connection to your inner self and the world around you. By consistently practicing these techniques, you align your biofield with higher frequencies, promoting overall harmony and well-being.

B) LIGHT WORK

In the context of 'Biofield Alchemy', light is seen as a multidimensional force that transcends physical properties, representing spiritual illumination, higher consciousness, and divine connection. It is viewed as a powerful tool for transformation, healing, and growth, and is often associated with the activation of the biofield's higher potential.

In the context of 'Biofield Alchemy', the term "light" transcends its common dictionary definition as a natural agent that stimulates sight and makes things visible. Within this field, light embodies a multifaceted concept encompassing both physical and metaphysical dimensions. Physically, light refers to the spectrum of electromagnetic radiation visible to the human eye, which plays a crucial role in biological processes and overall well-being. However, in 'Biofield Alchemy', light extends beyond the visible spectrum to include subtle energies that influence the body's biofield - a complex, dynamic energy system encompassing the physical, emotional, mental, and spiritual aspects of a being.

Key aspects of light in 'Biofield Alchemy' include its function as a medium for healing and transformation. Light is seen as a carrier of information and energy, capable of penetrating and affecting the biofield. It is believed to have the power to clear blockages, balance energies, and facilitate higher states of consciousness. This concept aligns with practices like chromotherapy, where different colors of light are used to heal and harmonize the body's energy centers, or chakras.

Furthermore, light in this context symbolizes awareness, enlightenment, and the manifestation of inner truths. It is associated with clarity, insight, and the ability to transcend limitations. In essence, light serves as both a literal and metaphorical tool in 'Biofield Alchemy', bridging the gap between the tangible and the intangible, the known and the unknown, guiding individuals towards greater harmony and self-realization.

BASIC PRACTICE RITUALS

Basic Practice Rituals for Sun, Moon and Fire in 'Biofield Alchemy'

Many ancient rituals were designed and practiced related to sun, moon and fire to harness the power of light .

Techniques such as color therapy, and light meditation are used to harmonize and balance the biofield.

1. COLOR THERAPY: In color and light therapy, different colors (each corresponding to specific wavelengths of light) are used to influence the energy field. Colors are thought to have unique vibrations that can affect mood, energy levels, and overall well-being. For instance, blue is often associated with calmness and tranquility, while red is linked to energy and vitality.

2. **LIGHT THERAPY:** In 'Biofield Alchemy', harnessing the energies of the sun, moon, and the fire is essential for balancing and enhancing one's biofield. Each element symbolizes a unique aspect of the universal energy, contributing to the practitioner's spiritual and physical well-being.

3. **SUN RITUALS:** The sun represents vitality, growth, and enlightenment. As per traditional yoga, 'Surya Namaskar' is one of the most potent practices to align and harness the power of sun. Daily practice of few minutes can increase vigor and vitality and biofield power.

   Basic exercise for the beginners: Begin at sunrise by facing the east, standing with your feet grounded, and arms raised. Visualize the sun's rays filling your biofield with vibrant energy. Chant affirmations of strength and clarity. This ritual enhances your aura with solar power, promoting confidence and vitality.

4. **MOON RITUALS:** The moon embodies intuition, reflection, and emotional balance. Under a full moon, find a serene outdoor spot. Sit comfortably and gaze at the moon. Breathe deeply, inhaling lunar energy and exhaling stress. Envision the moonlight cleansing your biofield, bringing calmness and heightened intuition. This practice aids in emotional healing and psychic awareness.

5. **FIRE RITUALS:** Fire represents transformation and purification. As per Vedic tradition, 'Havan' and 'Yagnas' are the most potent fire rituals.

Basic practice for beginners - Create a small, controlled fire in a safe environment. Write down any pressing thoughts or emotions on a piece of paper and burn it in the fire, visualizing these thoughts and emotions being transmuted into positive energy. Allow the warmth of the fire to energize your biofield, encouraging renewal and personal growth.

6. LAMP RITUALS: A lamp symbolizes inner light and wisdom. Light a lamp or candle during your meditation sessions. Focus on the flame, allowing it to guide you into a meditative state. Imagine the flame's light permeating your biofield, illuminating your inner wisdom and dispelling darkness. This ritual fosters mental clarity and spiritual insight.

Integrating these rituals into your practice enhances your biofield, aligning you with the natural rhythms and energies of the universe.

In essence - by recognizing and working with these fundamental forces, individuals can tap into a deeper level of consciousness and facilitate personal and collective evolution. Whether through sound healing, light therapy, or meditative practices, the integration of sound and light into our lives opens new pathways for growth, healing, and physical, mental, emotional and spiritual evolution. This holistic approach underscores the essence of 'Biofield Alchemy'; the art and science of harmonizing and transforming the subtle energies that permeate all aspects of existence.

PART 2
CHAPTER 2

TIME & SPACE

ALCHEMY OF TIME
&
POTENCY OF SPACE
- TURNING
'MOMENTS' INTO
'MASTERPIECES'

'BIOFIELD ALCHEMY' & TIME & SPACE

POWER OF 'WHEN' & 'WHERE'

In the context of 'Biofield Alchemy', time is seen as a multidimensional, fluid, and relative concept that influences the biofield and its dynamics. It encompasses linear time (past, present, future) and nonlinear time (sacred time, eternal time), and is viewed as a flexible and malleable force that can be worked with to achieve transformation and growth.

In the realm of 'Biofield Alchemy', the concept of 'time' transcends its conventional dictionary definition as a measurable period during which events occur. Here, time is perceived as a dynamic and fluid energy field that interacts with our biofield - a complex system of energy that surrounds and permeates the human body.

In traditional contexts, time is often seen as linear, moving from past to present to future. However, 'Biofield Alchemy' suggests that time is non-linear and multi-dimensional. It can be experienced and influenced in various ways, allowing for the manipulation of past traumas, present realities, and future possibilities. This perspective opens possibilities for healing and transformation, as practitioners believe that by altering the energetic patterns within one's biofield, they can affect their perception and experience of time.

Key aspects of time in 'Biofield Alchemy' include its role in the manifestation process and the healing of past wounds. Time is not merely a sequence of moments but a malleable resource that can be harnessed to align with one's highest intentions. By understanding and working with the biofield, individuals can access different timelines and potential futures, creating a more harmonious and fulfilling life path.

In essence, time in 'Biofield Alchemy' is both a medium and a tool. It is an integral part of the energetic landscape that influences our physical, emotional, and spiritual well-being. Understanding and mastering this concept allows for deeper insights into the nature of reality and one's place within it.

SPACE & BIOFIELD ALCHEMY: POWER OF 'WHERE'

In the context of 'Biofield Alchemy', space refers to the multidimensional expanse that includes the physical, emotional, mental, and spiritual realms. It encompasses the inner space of the self and the outer space of the environment, and is seen as a dynamic, interconnected web of energy and consciousness.

In the context of 'Biofield Alchemy', "space" transcends its conventional dictionary definition of a physical area or expanse. It is an intricate concept that encompasses the invisible realms of energy, consciousness, and intention. In this domain, space is not merely a container for objects or phenomena but dynamic fields where energies interact, resonate, and transform. 'Biofield Alchemy' recognizes space as a fundamental component in the practice of energy work, where the practitioner's awareness and intention shape and influence the energetic environment.

Key aspects of space in 'Biofield Alchemy' include its role as a conduit for energy flow and a medium for transformation. Space is seen as a living, breathing entity that can be infused with various energies, such as healing vibrations or intentions for manifestation. Practitioners often engage in creating sacred spaces, which are energetically cleansed and consecrated environments conducive to healing and spiritual work. These spaces amplify the practitioner's ability to access and manipulate subtle energies, facilitating deeper connections with the self and the universe.

Moreover, the concept of space in 'Biofield Alchemy' extends to the inner landscape of the individual. Inner space, or the mind's internal environment, is crucial in the alchemical process, where self-reflection and inner harmony are cultivated. This internal space is where personal transformation occurs, as the practitioner aligns their energies with higher frequencies and universal truths. In essence, space in 'Biofield Alchemy' is a multidimensional construct that plays a vital role in the manifestation of well-being, transformation, and spiritual growth.

ALCHEMIZING 'TIME' AS PER ASTROLOGY

Astrology, an ancient discipline observing celestial movements and their influence on human affairs, holds a profound significance in the context of time. In 'Biofield Alchemy', which explores the energetic interplay between mind, body, and the cosmos, astrology serves as a crucial tool for understanding and aligning with these energies. Time, as understood in astrology, is not merely linear but cyclical, marked by planetary transits and cosmic rhythms.

These cycles influence our biofield, the energetic aura surrounding everyone, and can affect our physical, mental emotional and spiritual states.

Key aspects of astrology, such as the positions of the planets at the time of one's birth (natal chart), transits, and progressions, offer insights into the energetic blueprint of an individual. This blueprint reveals inherent strengths, challenges, and opportunities for growth, acting as a guide in the alchemical process of transforming one's biofield. By understanding the astrological timing, individuals can harness the most potent periods for personal development, healing, growth and manifestation.

'MUHURTA' - POWER OF 'THE MOMENT'

In Vedic tradition, the concept of "muhurta" - a specific period deemed auspicious or inauspicious for various activities - is a critical aspect of the "panchang", an ancient almanac that guides daily life. In 'Biofield Alchemy', which explores the subtle energies surrounding and influencing human beings, the concept of muhurta plays a pivotal role. It emphasizes the importance of timing in harnessing and aligning these energies for optimal outcomes.

The 'Panchang' considers planetary positions, lunar phases, and other celestial factors to determine the most favorable times for actions ranging from daily rituals to significant life events. Similarly, in 'Biofield Alchemy', the alignment of one's biofield with cosmic energies is essential for manifestation and healing. By choosing an auspicious muhurta, individuals can synchronize their biofield with universal rhythms, enhancing the efficacy of their practices.

This synergy between Vedic wisdom and 'Biofield Alchemy' underscores the profound influence of time on our energetic state. It suggests that not only the 'what' and 'how' of our actions matter, but also the 'when,' making 'time' a critical component in achieving harmony and balance within the biofield.

Incorporating the principles of 'muhurta' and Astrology into biofield activities ensures that these practices are not only personally attuned but also cosmically aligned, maximizing their transformative potential.

SPACE: RESERVOIR OF ALL POTENTIAL ENERGIES

Energy power places hold immense significance in the practice of 'Biofield Alchemy'. These locations, often referred to as sacred sites, are believed to possess potent energetic frequencies that can enhance spiritual practices, promote healing, and facilitate profound personal transformation. The alignment of natural energies at these sites creates an ideal environment for 'Biofield Alchemy' to deepen their connection with the biofield, the subtle energy field that surrounds and interpenetrates the human body.

In 'Biofield Alchemy', energy power places serve as amplifiers of intention and catalysts for energetic shifts. When a practitioner engages in specific rituals or meditative practices at these sites, the inherent energies of the location interact with their personal biofield, fostering a state of heightened awareness and receptivity. This interaction can lead to profound insights, emotional release, and a greater alignment with one's higher self.

SACRED SITES: BIOFIELD CHARGING STATIONS

Historically, many cultures have recognized and revered energy power places, building temples, monuments, and sanctuaries at these sites.

Here are the top ten most powerful energy places

1. KAMAKHYA TEMPLE (Assam, India) - Located in Guwahati, this temple is one of the most revered Shakti Peethas. It is associated with the reproductive organs of Goddess Sati, symbolizing feminine power and fertility. The temple is known for its unique annual Ambubachi Mela.
2. VARANASI (Kashi) - Known as the spiritual capital of India, Varanasi is a center for Hindu rituals and pilgrimage, believed to be a place where one can attain moksha (liberation).
3. AMARNATH CAVE (India) - Located in Jammu and Kashmir, this sacred cave is a major pilgrimage site dedicated to Lord Shiva, famous for its naturally occurring ice lingam.
4. MOUNT KAILASH - Revered in Hinduism, Buddhism, Jainism, Mount Kailash in Tibet is considered the abode of Lord Shiva and a significant spiritual site.
5. MACHU PICCHU (Peru) - Known for its breathtaking beauty and spiritual energy, Machu Picchu is often referred to as the "Lost City of the Incas."
6. STONEHENGE (England) - This ancient stone circle has been a site of pilgrimage and mystery

for centuries, believed to be an astronomical calendar and a spiritual center.
7. SEDONA (Arizona) USA - Famous for its red rock formations and vortex sites, Sedona is considered a place of healing and spiritual renewal.
8. THE GREAT PYRAMIDS (Egypt) - These ancient structures are not only architectural marvels but also believed to be sources of powerful energy.
9. MOUNT FUJI (Japan) - A sacred mountain in Shinto and Buddhist traditions, Mount Fuji is a symbol of beauty and spiritual power.

These locations have long been associated with spiritual and energetic practices. In modern 'Biofield Alchemy', visiting such sites can provide a powerful means of attuning to the Earth's natural energies, facilitating a deeper understanding of one's energetic anatomy and enhancing the efficacy of alchemical practices.

Every city and place possesses its unique energy power space, an invisible force that shapes our experiences and well-being. In the practice of 'Biofield Alchemy', aligning with this local energy enhances our personal energy fields, amplifying positivity and growth. By attuning to the vibrational essence of our surroundings, we can harmonize our biofields, fostering a deeper connection to the environment and unlocking greater potential within ourselves. This alignment not only elevates our own energies but also contributes to the collective energetic harmony of the community, creating a powerful synergy for holistic development and transformation.

Engaging with these sites, either physically or through visualization, allows 'Biofield Alchemist' to tap into ancient wisdom and universal energies, ultimately supporting their journey of transformation and self-discovery.

PART 2
CHAPTER 3

THOUGHTS & INTENTION

MAGIC OF INVISIBLE THOUGHTS & INTENTION IN CRAFTING REALITY

THOUGHTS & INTENTION: THE INVISIBLE ARCHITECTS OF REALITY

IMPORTANCE OF THOUGHTS IN 'BIOFIELD ALCHEMY'

In the realm of 'Biofield Alchemy', thoughts are considered as the subtle, invisible currents that shape our energetic landscape. The term 'thoughts' refers to the mental processes and conscious considerations that influence our emotions, actions, and overall state of being. According to the Oxford English Dictionary, a thought is "an idea or opinion produced by thinking, occurring suddenly in the mind." However, in the context of 'Biofield Alchemy', thoughts transcend mere mental activity; they are seen as vibrational frequencies that interact with and modify the biofield - the energetic field surrounding and permeating the human body.

Key aspects of thoughts in 'Biofield Alchemy' include their frequency, intention, and alignment with one's inner truth. Every thought carries a specific vibrational signature that can either harmonize or disrupt the biofield. Positive, constructive thoughts are believed to elevate the vibrational state of the biofield, promoting well-being and balance. Conversely, negative or discordant thoughts can create energy blockages, leading to physical, emotional, or spiritual dissonance.

In 'Biofield Alchemy', practitioners emphasize the importance of cultivating awareness and mindfulness in thought patterns. By consciously selecting thoughts that resonate with desired outcomes, individuals can harness their mental energy to manifest positive changes in their lives. This process, often referred to as mental alchemy, underscores the transformative power of thoughts in shaping not only one's internal world but also the external reality. Thus, thoughts are not merely fleeting mental events but foundational elements in the alchemical journey of personal and spiritual growth.

POWER OF INTENTION IN 'BIOFIELD ALCHEMY'

In the context of 'Biofield Alchemy', intention is seen as a powerful force that shapes the biofield and influences its dynamics. Clear and focused intentions can help balance and align the biofield, while unclear or conflicting intentions can create disharmony. By setting conscious intentions, individuals can harness the power of their biofield to manifest positive change and transformation in their lives.

In the context of 'Biofield Alchemy', the term 'intention' refers to a conscious and deliberate mental state or focus that directs energy towards a specific outcome or goal. Derived from the Latin word "intentio," which means "stretching toward" or "aim," intention in 'Biofield Alchemy' goes beyond mere wishful thinking; it involves a focused, purposeful alignment of thoughts, emotions, and energy to manifest desired changes within the biofield.

Intention is a foundational concept in 'Biofield Alchemy', where it serves as the catalyst for transformation and healing. It operates under the principle that energy follows thought, meaning that the nature and quality of one's intentions can directly influence the biofield - a complex, dynamic energy system that surrounds and permeates the human body. Key aspects of intention in this practice include clarity, emotional resonance, and consistency.

'SANKALPAM' - THE ALCHEMICAL RITUAL - OF BREWING THOUGHTS, WORDS AND ACTION TO MAKE LIFE OF GOLD

In the context of 'Biofield Alchemy', the term 'power' refers to the intrinsic energy that individuals harness and direct to influence their physical, mental, and spiritual states. This concept transcends mere physical strength, encompassing the subtle, yet profound energies within and around us - The "Biofield."

A key aspect of power in this context is the idea of 'sankalpa,' a Sanskrit term that means a firm resolve or intention. In Indian philosophy, particularly among 'Sages' and 'Rishis', 'sankalpa' is seen as a powerful tool for manifesting desires and achieving spiritual growth. It is more than just a wish or desire; it is a focused and determined intention that aligns the mind, body, and spirit towards a specific goal.

The ancient 'Sages' and 'Rishis' of India recognized the importance of 'sankalpam' in harnessing the power of the biofield. Through practices such as meditation, mantra chanting, and breath work. They cultivated their biofields and used the power of 'sankalpam' to direct their energies towards enlightenment and self-realization. This deep connection between intention and energy transformation is a cornerstone of 'Biofield Alchemy', illustrating how ancient wisdom can be applied to modern spiritual practices. By understanding and practicing these concepts, individuals can tap into their own inherent power, transforming their lives and achieving a greater sense of harmony and well-being.

Clarity involves having a precise and well-defined goal or desired outcome. The more specific the intention, the more effectively it can guide the flow of energy. Emotional resonance refers to the alignment of one's emotions with the intention, as emotions are powerful amplifiers of energy. Consistency involves maintaining a steady focus on the intention over time, which helps to reinforce and stabilize the energy patterns within the biofield.

INTENTION EXPERIMENT IN 'BIOFIELD ALCHEMY'

The essence of the Intention Experiment in 'Biofield Alchemy' lies in harnessing the power of focused intent to influence and transform the biofield, the subtle energy field surrounding and permeating the human body. Intention is a powerful tool, capable of shaping reality and manifesting desired outcomes. In the context of 'Biofield Alchemy', the Intention Experiment explores the profound connection between conscious thought, energy, and matter.

Central to this experiment is the premise that our thoughts and intentions have a tangible impact on the biofield. By consciously directing our intentions, we can alter the energetic patterns within and around us, promoting healing, balance, and transformation. This process involves deepening our awareness of our own biofield, understanding its interactions with external energies, and learning to consciously manipulate these energies through focused intent.

The Intention Experiment draws on ancient wisdom and modern science, blending esoteric knowledge with empirical research. One key contributor to this field is Lynne McTaggart, whose groundbreaking work has shown how collective intention can produce measurable effects on physical reality. Studies in the realm of quantum physics and consciousness research, such as those conducted by the Institute of Noetic Sciences, further support the idea that our thoughts can influence matter and energy.

This experiment involves practices such as meditation, creative visualization, and energy healing techniques, all aimed at refining our ability to focus and direct intention. Participants in this experiment learn to cultivate a state of coherent consciousness, where their thoughts are clear, aligned, and purposeful.

The ultimate goal of the Intention Experiment in 'Biofield Alchemy' is to empower individuals to take an active role in their own energy evolution. By mastering the art of intention, we can unlock new levels of personal transformation, enhance our well-being, and contribute to the collective healing of humanity. This journey is not just about individual growth but also about fostering a deeper connection with the universal energy that binds us all, revealing the true potential of human consciousness.

PART 2
CHAPTER 4

INTUITION & SIXTH SENSE

- THE ALCHEMIST'S EYE
- SEEING POSSIBILITY IN THE IMPOSSIBLE

INTUITION & SIXTH SENSE - THE ALCHEMIST'S TRUE COMPASS

ROLE OF INTUITION IN BIOFIELD ALCHEMY

In the context of 'Biofield Alchemy', intuition is seen as a powerful tool for accessing and navigating the biofield, allowing individuals to tap into their inner wisdom and gain deeper insights into themselves and their environment. By cultivating intuition, individuals can enhance their ability to sense and balance the biofield, leading to greater harmony, balance, and transformation.

In the context of 'Biofield Alchemy', intuition can be defined as an innate ability to perceive and understand information without the use of conscious reasoning. It is often described as a 'gut feeling' or an inner knowing that transcends the analytical mind. In traditional dictionaries, intuition is defined as "the ability to understand something immediately, without the need for conscious reasoning."

Within 'Biofield Alchemy', intuition is considered a vital component, acting as a bridge between the conscious mind and the subtle energy fields that surround and permeate all living beings. This practice acknowledges that intuition is not merely a mystical or abstract concept but a practical skill that can be cultivated and refined. It is seen as a form of inner wisdom that guides alchemists toward understanding the energetic imbalances and potentials within themselves and others.

Key aspects of intuition in 'Biofield Alchemy' include the ability to sense energy patterns, recognize subtle shifts in one's own biofield and attune to the energetic states of others. Intuition also plays a crucial role in decision-making processes, especially in discerning the most beneficial paths for personal growth and healing. Practitioners often engage in mindfulness and meditative practices to enhance their intuitive abilities, enabling them to connect more deeply with their biofield and the universal energies that influence it.

Intuition in 'Biofield Alchemy' is not only a natural human faculty but also a skill that can be developed to enhance one's ability to perceive and work with subtle energies, leading to greater self-awareness and transformation.

Although there are many books written on intuition but one of the most notable books on intuition by a medical doctor and scientist is "The Intuitive Mind: Profiting from the Power of Your Sixth Sense" by Dr. Eugene Sadler-Smith. Dr. Sadler-Smith is a professor of organizational behavior with extensive research in the field of intuition in decision-making.

In his book, Dr. Sadler-Smith combines his academic research with practical insights to explore how intuition operates in the human mind, particularly in the context of business and leadership. He delves into scientific studies and experiments that validate the role of intuition in effective decision-making, highlighting the balance between intuitive and analytical thinking.

IMPORTANCE OF SIXTH SENSE

In the context of 'Biofield Alchemy', the sixth sense is seen as a key to unlocking the secre ts of the biofield, allowing individuals to tap into its subtle energies and access higher states of consciousness. By developing the sixth sense, individuals can enhance their ability to sense and balance the biofield, leading to greater self-awareness, spiritual growth, and transformation.

In the realm of 'Biofield Alchemy', the concept of the "sixth sense" transcends traditional sensory perception, embodying an awareness beyond the five physical senses. This term, often associated with extrasensory perception (ESP), encompasses abilities like precognition, and telepathy. Within 'Biofield Alchemy', the sixth sense is understood as a heightened sensitivity to the subtle energies and vibrations that exist beyond the ordinary sensory spectrum.

The sixth sense, in this context, is not merely a mystical or supernatural phenomenon; it is considered a natural extension of human consciousness. Practitioners of 'Biofield Alchemy' view it as an intrinsic part of the biofield - the energetic blueprint of the human being, which interacts with and influences the physical, mental, and emotional aspects of existence. This perception allows individuals to tap into deeper layers of reality, gaining insights and understanding that are inaccessible through conventional means.

Key aspects of the sixth sense in 'Biofield Alchemy' include the development of intuitive faculties, the ability to sense and interpret subtle energy shifts, and the cultivation of a heightened awareness of interconnectedness. This expanded perception aids in personal transformation, healing, and the manifestation of one's desires by aligning the biofield with higher vibrational frequencies.

In essence, the sixth sense within 'Biofield Alchemy' serves as a bridge to a more profound understanding of the self and the universe, fostering a deeper connection with the unseen forces that shape our reality.

ROLE OF ANCIENT TECHNIQUES IN ENHANCING INTUITION & SIXTH SENSE

The integration of ancient techniques such as 'yoga', 'pranayama', 'mantras', 'vipassana', and 'trataka' plays a pivotal role in enhancing intuition and sixth sense. These time-honored methods offer profound benefits in enhancing and sharpening the intuition and sixth sense, essential components of 'Biofield Alchemy'.

1. PRANAYAMA: Specific breathing techniques in 'pranayama' are used to regulate and enhance the 'pranic' flow, thereby revitalizing and creating a heightened state of awareness which sharpens the sixth sense, allowing practitioners to perceive and interpret energetic information more accurately.

2. MANTRAS: The chanting of 'mantras' generates vibrational frequencies that attune the mind to higher states of consciousness, enhancing intuitive perception and sensitivity to subtle energies.

3. VIPASSANA: This ancient meditation technique fosters deep self-awareness and mental purification. The deep introspective nature of vipassana strengthens the inner vision, enhancing the practitioner's intuitive insights and connection to the sixth sense.

4. TRATAKA: The practice of fixed gazing, or 'trataka', sharpens mental focus and enhances the

flow of energy through concentrated attention. Trataka's intense focus not only stabilizes the mind but also opens channels for deeper intuitive insights, making it a powerful tool for developing the sixth sense.

Incorporating these ancient techniques into 'Biofield Alchemy' not only enriches the practitioner's energetic environment but also aligns the body, mind, and spirit, paving the way for profound transformation, holistic well-being, and heightened intuitive abilities.

PART 2
CHAPTER 5

LOVE & LIFE

THE ALCHEMY OF

LOVE & LIFE & BIOFIELD

LOVE & LIFE & BIOFIELD ALCHEMY

VALUE OF TRUE LOVE IN 'BIOFIELD ALCHEMY'

True love, often defined as an intense and enduring affection between individuals, transcends mere emotional connection, embodying a profound resonance with another's being. In the context of 'Biofield Alchemy', true love is seen not just as a romantic ideal but as a state of energetic harmony and alignment. It is the vibrational synergy between individuals that fosters deep understanding, unconditional acceptance, and mutual growth.

Key aspects of true love in 'Biofield Alchemy' include authenticity, empathy, and balance. Authenticity refers to the genuine expression of one's true self, free from masks or pretenses, which allows for a deeper connection. 'Empathy' involves the capacity to intuitively sense and resonate with the emotions and energies of another, facilitating a compassionate and supportive bond. 'Balance' - crucial in this energetic framework, signifies the equilibrium between giving and receiving, ensuring that the relationship nurtures both partners equally.

True love, in this alchemical perspective, is also about the transformative power of such connections. It serves as a catalyst for personal and spiritual growth, encouraging individuals to evolve and realize their highest potential. The biofield, an energy field that surrounds and permeates the body, is influenced by these loving interactions, becoming more vibrant and harmonious.

In summary, true love in 'Biofield Alchemy' is not only a profound emotional and energetic connection but also a dynamic force that enhances the well-being and growth of individuals, reflecting the deeper alchemical principles of transformation and unity.

LIFE AS THE 'LIFE FORCE ENERGY'

In the context of 'Biofield Alchemy', life force refers to the dynamic, multidimensional energy that permeates and sustains the biofield, connecting it to the universal life force. It is seen as a powerful, transformative energy that can be harnessed and balanced to enhance well-being, vitality, and spiritual growth.

LIFE FORCE ENERGY IN 'BIOFIELD ALCHEMY'

In the realm of 'Biofield Alchemy', the concept of 'life force' holds a central and profound significance. Traditionally, the term 'life force' refers to the vital energy or animating principle that sustains all living beings - known by various names across cultures - such as 'prana' in Hindu philosophy, 'chi' in Chinese Medicine, and 'qi' in Taoism. This 'energy' is believed to flow through all living organisms, providing vitality and the capacity for growth and healing.

Within 'Biofield Alchemy', life force is not merely an abstract concept but a dynamic and tangible phenomenon. It is the foundational element that 'Biofield Alchemy's work with to transform and enhance well-being. The practice involves understanding and manipulating this energy to bring about balance and harmony in the body, mind, and spirit. The key aspects of life force in this context include its flow, balance, and interaction with the biofield - the electromagnetic field that surrounds and permeates the human body.

'Biofield Alchemy' posits that disruptions or blockages in the flow of life force can lead to physical, mental emotional or spiritual imbalances. Therefore, techniques such as energy healing, bodywork, meditation, and breathwork are employed to clear these blockages, restore the natural flow of energy, and enhance the individual's overall vitality. This practice recognizes that by attuning to the life force, one can access a deeper state of awareness, facilitate self-healing, and achieve a harmonious state of being.

In essence, life force in 'Biofield Alchemy' is both the medium and the message - an essential element that underscores the interconnectedness of all life and the potential for transformation within each individual.

LOVE AS A HIGH FREQUENCY STATE

The Essence of 'True Unconditional Love' in 'Biofield Alchemy'

In the intricate tapestry of life, the concept of 'True Unconditional Love' stands as a profound cornerstone, particularly within the realm of 'Biofield Alchemy'. This form of love transcends the ordinary understanding of affection and attachment; it is a pure, all-encompassing energy that nurtures and sustains life itself. In the practice of 'Biofield Alchemy', which involves the conscious manipulation and transformation of the human energy field, this 'unconditional love' is not merely a philosophical ideal but a vital force that animates and heals.

PURE UNCONDITIONAL LOVE = PURE LIFE ENERGY

'True Unconditional Love' is an energy that is infinite and unbounded, characterized by its selfless nature. It is the love that exists beyond conditions and judgments, embracing all beings and aspects of existence without discrimination. In the context of 'Biofield Alchemy', this love is considered the fundamental frequency that underpins all energetic processes. It is the essence that fuels the 'life force energy', or 'prana', within and around us, harmonizing the biofield and promoting balance and well-being.

ROLE OF LOVE IN 'BIOFIELD ALCHEMY'

The biofield, an intricate matrix of energy that surrounds and interpenetrates the physical body, is highly responsive to emotions and thoughts. Emotions like fear, anger, and sadness can create distortions in the biofield, leading to blockages that may manifest as physical or emotional ailments. Conversely, the presence of 'True Unconditional Love' within the biofield acts as a harmonizing agent. It raises the vibrational frequency of the biofield, dissolving blockages and restoring the natural flow of energy.

'Biofield Alchemy' utilizes this understanding by consciously channeling 'unconditional love' into the energy field. This practice can be as simple as setting an intention to embody love or as complex as engaging in specific energetic techniques to align one's frequency with this universal force. Practitioners often report a profound sense of peace and interconnectedness when they align with this love, which not only enhances personal well-being but also radiates outward, influencing the surrounding environment.

HISTORICAL PERSPECTIVES & SPIRITUAL CONTEXT

Throughout history, spiritual traditions across the world have recognized the power of 'unconditional love'. In many Eastern philosophies, such as Buddhism and Hinduism, love is seen as a universal principle that connects all beings. Similarly, in Western traditions, the concept of 'agape' in Christianity refers to a selfless, divine love that transcends human understanding. These traditions often describe 'unconditional love' as the ultimate reality or the highest state of being, a state in which the ego dissolves and the true nature of existence is revealed.

In 'Biofield Alchemy', this spiritual perspective is integrated into the understanding of the human energy system. The practitioner recognizes that the biofield is not isolated but interconnected with the larger web of life. By cultivating 'true unconditional love', individuals align themselves with this web, promoting healing and transformation on both personal and collective levels.

PRACTICAL APPLICATION IN 'BIOFIELD ALCHEMY'

In practical terms, cultivating 'True Unconditional Love' involves several key practices:

1. SELF - ACCEPTANCE AND COMPASSION: Before one can extend love to others, it is essential to cultivate it within oneself. This involves accepting all aspects of oneself, including flaws and imperfections, and treating oneself with kindness and compassion. This self-love raises the personal vibrational

frequency, making it easier to channel unconditional love outward.

2. MINDFULNESS AND PRESENCE: Being present in the moment and mindful of one's thoughts and emotions helps in identifying and releasing negative patterns that may disrupt the flow of love in the biofield. Practicing mindfulness fosters a deeper connection with the self and the surrounding world, enhancing the ability to give and receive love.

3. ENERGY HEALING TECHNIQUES: Techniques such as touch healing or initiations or simple meditative visualization can be used to channel 'unconditional love' into the biofield. These practices involve visualizing oneself as a conduit for 'divine love', allowing this energy to flow through the hands and into the energy field, promoting healing and balance.

4. AFFIRMATIONS AND INTENTIONS: Regularly affirming one's commitment to embodying 'True Unconditional Love' helps reinforce this state of being. Intentions set with love are powerful catalysts for change, influencing not only the individual but also the collective consciousness.

THE ALCHEMICAL POWER OF LOVE

The impact of 'True Unconditional Love' in 'Biofield Alchemy' extends beyond personal healing. As individuals cultivate this love within themselves, they contribute to a larger shift in the collective energy field. This collective upliftment has the potential to bring about positive changes in society, fostering a culture of compassion, empathy, and interconnectedness.

Moreover, the practice of embodying this love serves as a reminder of our true nature and purpose. It encourages individuals to live authentically, guided by love rather than fear or ego-driven desires. In doing so, they align with the natural rhythms of the universe, experiencing a sense of harmony and fulfillment that transcends ordinary existence.

CONCLUSION

'True Unconditional Love' is more than an abstract concept; it is the very essence of life itself. In the practice of 'Biofield Alchemy', this love serves as a powerful force for healing and transformation, harmonizing the human energy field and fostering a deeper connection with all of existence. By cultivating this love within us, we not only enhance our own well-being but also contribute to the collective healing and evolution of humanity. As we align with this universal force, we remember our true nature as beings of love and light, interconnected with the vast web of life.

PART 2
CHAPTER 6

FIVE SENSES

- ALCHEMIST'S LENSES OF PERCEPTION

-DISTILLING & DECODING THE ALCHEMICAL WISDOM

FIVE SENSES: DOORWAYS TO PERCEPTION

FIVE SENSES - THE REALITY SHIFTERS

The five fundamental ways that humans perceive and interpret the world around them:

1. SIGHT (vision): the ability to perceive light, color, and shape
2. HEARING (audition): the ability to perceive sound waves.
3. TASTE (gustation): the ability to perceive flavors and textures through the tongue.
4. SMELL (olfaction): the ability to perceive odors and scents.
5. TOUCH (tactician): the ability to perceive sensations of pressure, temperature, and texture through the skin.

The five senses are the primary means by which humans gather information about their environment and experience reality.

In the context of 'Biofield Alchemy', the five senses are seen as doorways to perception and awareness and are often used as a framework for exploring and balancing the biofield. By cultivating awareness of the senses, individuals can deepen their connection to their inner world and the world around them.

In 'Biofield Alchemy', the concept of the 'Five Senses' extends beyond traditional definitions, exploring their profound role in shaping our energetic and physical realities. Traditionally, the five senses - sight, hearing, taste, smell, and touch - are understood as faculties that enable us to perceive and interact with the physical world. However, in the context of 'Biofield Alchemy', these senses are viewed as powerful tools for tuning into and influencing our subtle energy fields.

Sight, in 'Biofield Alchemy', is not merely about visual perception but involves the ability to perceive the energetic auras and vibrations that surround all living beings. Hearing transcends the auditory range, encompassing the subtle vibrations and frequencies that can influence our emotional and mental states. Taste and smell, while often seen as purely physical, are recognized for their ability to trigger memories and emotions, serving as gateways to deeper emotional and energetic layers. Touch, perhaps the most tangible of the senses, is reinterpreted as a conduit for energy exchange, allowing practitioners to sense and manipulate the biofield.

NEURO - LINGUISTIC PROGRAMMING & FIVE SENSES IN 'BIOFIELD ALCHEMY'

Neuro-Linguistic Programming (NLP) is a psychological approach that explores the connections between neurological processes, language, and behavioral patterns acquired through experience. In the context of 'Biofield Alchemy', NLP plays a pivotal role in enhancing the harmony and balance of one's biofield, which is the energy field surrounding and interpenetrating the human body.

NLP emphasizes the positive influence it can have on the five senses: sight, sound, touch, taste, and smell. By understanding and manipulating these sensory inputs, individuals can create more empowering and enriching experiences. For instance, visualizations (sight) can be used to project desired outcomes, reinforcing the biofield with positive energy. Auditory techniques (sound), such as affirmations and mantras, can harmonize the biofield's vibrational frequency. Tactile feedback (touch), like tapping or physical anchors, helps in grounding and stabilizing the energy field. Engaging taste and smell with specific aromas or flavors can trigger beneficial emotional states, further aligning the biofield with desired states of being.

Key aspects of NLP include the identification and alteration of limiting beliefs, the use of language to reshape perception and reality, and the development of new, positive behavioral patterns. In 'Biofield Alchemy', these elements are integral in transforming one's energetic blueprint. By utilizing NLP techniques, practitioners can recalibrate their biofield, fostering greater emotional resilience, mental clarity, and overall well-being.

Incorporating NLP into 'Biofield Alchemy' provides a comprehensive toolkit for personal transformation, leveraging the profound impact of sensory experiences and language on the human energy field. This synergy not only enhances individual energy alignment but also promotes a holistic approach to health, wealth, love, power and personal development.

'PRATYAHARA' & FIVE SENSES IN 'BIOFIELD ALCHEMY'

Pratyahara, a key component of Patanjali's Ashtanga Yoga, plays a crucial role in 'Biofield Alchemy'. Derived from the Sanskrit words 'prati' meaning 'against' or 'away' and 'ahara' meaning "food" or "anything we take into ourselves from the outside," pratyahara signifies the withdrawal of the senses from external objects and distractions. This practice serves as the fifth limb of Ashtanga Yoga, bridging the external practices of 'yama', 'niyama', 'asana', and 'pranayama' with the internal practices of 'dharana', 'dhyana', and 'samadhi'.

In 'Biofield Alchemy', 'pratyahara' is essential for harmonizing and refining the biofield, the energy field that surrounds and interpenetrates the human body. By turning inward and detaching from sensory stimuli, practitioners can conserve and direct their energy more effectively. This inward focus allows for a deeper connection to the subtle energies within and around them, facilitating profound transformations and healing.

The powerful impact of pratyahara on the five senses - sight, sound, smell, taste, and touch - lies in its ability to quiet the mind and reduce sensory overload. This withdrawal helps to calm the nervous system, reduce stress, and enhance mental clarity. By minimizing external distractions, individuals can access heightened states of awareness and tap into their innate intuitive abilities. This sensory refinement is crucial for 'Biofield Alchemist', as it enables practitioners to perceive and manipulate the subtle energies with greater precision and sensitivity.

Key aspects of 'pratyahara' include disciplined practice, self-awareness, and mindfulness. Regular practice fosters a state of inner peace and balance, essential for advanced biofield alchemical work. By mastering 'pratyahara', individuals can create a serene internal environment conducive to deep meditation, self-healing, and the manifestation of their highest potential.

The key aspects of the five senses in 'Biofield Alchemy' involve their use as tools for energetic attunement and healing. Practitioners learn to refine these senses to detect imbalances in the biofield and employ them to restore harmony and flow. This expanded understanding of the 5 senses transforms them from mere biological functions into potent instruments for personal and spiritual transformation, bridging the gap between the physical and energetic realms. In 'Biofield Alchemy', the five senses are pathways to deeper awareness and mastery of the subtle energies that influence our lives.

PART 2
CHAPTER 7

EMOTIONS

'BIOFIELD ALCHEMY'
&
THE ALCHEMY
OF
EMOTIONAL
ENERGY MAPPING

EMOTIONAL INTELLIGENCE: THE TRUE ENERGY COMPASS

IMPORTANCE OF EMOTION MANAGEMENT

In the context of 'Biofield Alchemy', emotions are seen as powerful energies that shape the biofield and influence its dynamics. Emotions can either harmonize or disrupt the biofield, depending on their quality and intensity. By becoming aware of and balancing one's emotions, individuals can align their biofield, leading to greater well-being, resilience, and spiritual growth.

In the context of 'Biofield Alchemy', 'emotions' refer to the complex interplay of feelings that arise within an individual, often influencing their energy field or biofield. Traditionally, emotions are defined as intense feelings that result from one's circumstances, mood, or relationships. They encompass a wide range of human experiences, including joy, sorrow, anger, love, and fear.

In 'Biofield Alchemy', emotions are considered vital components of an individual's energetic makeup. They are not merely psychological states but are also seen as vibrations or frequencies that can affect one's physical and energetic health. Key aspects of emotions in this field include their dual role as both indicators and influencers of biofield balance. Positive emotions, such as love and gratitude, are believed to enhance the biofield, fostering harmony and well-being. In contrast, negative emotions, such as anger and resentment, can disrupt the biofield, leading to disharmony and potential physical ailments

EMOTIONAL INTELLIGENCE IN 'BIOFIELD ALCHEMY'

Emotional intelligence (EI) is defined as the ability to perceive, understand, manage, and utilize emotions effectively in oneself and others. Coined by psychologists Peter Salovey and John D. Mayer, and popularized by Daniel Goleman, EI has gained significant attention in both scientific and medical communities. It encompasses self-awareness, self-regulation, motivation, empathy, and social skills. These components are integral in the practice of 'Biofield Alchemy', a holistic approach to health and well-being that involves balancing and harmonizing the body's energy fields.

In 'Biofield Alchemy', emotional intelligence is paramount as it directly influences the energy flow within the biofield. Emotions are seen as energy that can either block or facilitate the smooth circulation of 'life force energy' or 'prana' throughout the body. High emotional intelligence allows practitioners to recognize and release negative emotions, which are often the root cause of energy blockages. By doing so, they can maintain a balanced biofield, which is essential for physical, mental, and spiritual health.

Prominent scientists and doctors have emphasized the role of EI in health and healing. Dr. Candace Pert, a neuroscientist known for her work on the mind-body connection, highlighted the biochemical basis of emotions and their impact on health. Similarly, Dr. Goleman's research demonstrates that individuals with high EI are better equipped to handle stress, build stronger relationships, and achieve overall well-being.

Key aspects of EI in 'Biofield Alchemy' include the ability to identify and process emotions, maintain emotional balance, and develop empathy and compassion. These skills enhance one's ability to connect with and influence their biofield, leading to a harmonious and energized state of being. Thus, cultivating emotional intelligence is a crucial practice for anyone seeking to master 'Biofield Alchemy' and achieve holistic health.

CONCEPT OF 'SHADRIPUS' IN 'BIOFIELD ALCHEMY' SHADRIPUS:

1. Derived from Sanskrit, meaning 'six enemies' or inner foes.

2. Impede spiritual growth and self-realization.

3. According to the Vedas, these six enemies are:

   1. KAMA (lust)

   2. KRODHA (anger)

   3. LOBHA (greed)

   4. MOHA (delusion)

   5. MADA (pride)

   6. MATSARYA (jealousy)

Seen as obstacles that distort one's biofield. Affect overall well-being and spiritual evolution.

In the context of 'Biofield Alchemy', understanding and overcoming 'Shadripus' is crucial for achieving balance and harmony within the energy field. Each of these inner foes corresponds to specific vibrations and energetic disruptions within the biofield. For instance, "Kama" can lead to excessive attachment and energy blockages, while "Krodha" generates negative energy that disrupts the flow of life force.

Addressing 'Shadripus' involves various practices aimed at purification and transformation. Techniques such as fasting, donations, celibacy, selfless service, meditation, breathwork, and mindfulness and other specific rituals can help in recognizing and mitigating these negative traits. By fostering self-awareness, one can identify the presence of these enemies and work towards neutralizing their effects.

In 'Biofield Alchemy', the transformation of 'Shadripus' is not just about suppression but about transmutation. This means converting the energy of these negative traits into positive attributes. For example, transforming 'Kama' into unconditional love, 'Krodha' into righteous action, and 'Lobha' into generosity.

Ancient texts suggest that mastery over 'Shadripus' leads to a purified biofield, which enhances one's ability to connect with higher states of consciousness and spiritual dimensions. In essence, the journey through 'Biofield Alchemy', guided by the wisdom of the Vedas, involves recognizing and overcoming 'Shadripus', thereby achieving a state of inner harmony and spiritual fulfillment.

'Biofield Alchemy' posits that by consciously cultivating positive emotions and releasing negative ones, individuals can transform their energetic state. Techniques such as meditation, energy healing, and intentional focus on positive thoughts are often employed to realign the biofield with a more balanced and harmonious state. Thus, emotions are not only responses to external stimuli but are also tools for self-transformation and healing within the practice of

'Biofield Alchemy'. This holistic approach underscores the interconnectivity of mind, body, and spirit, highlighting the power of emotions in shaping one's energy reality.

EMOTIONAL FREEDOM TECHNIQUE (EFT) & 'BIOFIELD ALCHEMY'

Emotional Freedom Technique, commonly known as EFT or tapping, is a therapeutic method that involves tapping on specific meridian points on the body while focusing on emotional distress or physical pain. This practice combines elements of acupuncture, psychology, and neurology to address the underlying causes of emotional and physical issues. Key aspects of EFT include its simplicity, accessibility, and the ability to provide rapid relief from emotional distress.

EFT & EMOTION MANAGEMENT

EFT's power in emotion management lies in its ability to quickly and effectively reduce the intensity of negative emotions. By tapping on specific points while voicing specific thoughts or feelings, individuals can release blocked energy and emotional pain, leading to a sense of calm and emotional balance. This technique is particularly powerful because it empowers individuals to self-manage their emotions, offering a practical tool that can be used anytime and anywhere.

In the context of 'Biofield Alchemy', EFT plays a crucial role in maintaining and enhancing the energetic balance of the biofield. Emotional disturbances often manifest as disruptions in the biofield, affecting overall well-being. By integrating EFT into 'Biofield Alchemy' practices, individuals can clear these disruptions, promoting a harmonious flow of energy. This alignment of the emotional and energetic bodies not only fosters emotional resilience but also enhances physical health and spiritual growth.

EFT's ability to address the root causes of emotional issues aligns with the holistic principles of 'Biofield Alchemy', where the goal is to achieve comprehensive wellness by balancing the mind, body, and spirit. As a powerful tool for emotion management, EFT supports the journey of self-discovery and transformation, making it an invaluable component of 'Biofield Alchemy' practices.

PART 2
CHAPTER 8

FIVE ELEMENTS

- THE SACRED ALCHEMICAL ELIXIRS

FIVE ELEMENTS: THE FIVE PILLARS OF 'LIFE ENERGY'

FIVE ELEMENTS & 'BIOFIELD ALCHEMY'

In ancient philosophy and science, the five fundamental substances that comprise the universe are:

1. EARTH (solid, stable, and dense)

2. WATER (liquid, flowing, and adaptable)

3. AIR (gaseous, intangible, and mobile)

4. FIRE (energetic, transformative, and consuming)

5. ETHER (ethereal, divine, and celestial)

The 'five elements' are often seen as interconnected, interdependent, and cyclical, representing the harmony and balance found in nature.

In the context of 'Biofield Alchemy', the 'five elements' are seen as a framework for understanding the dynamic interplay of energies within the biofield, and for achieving balance, harmony, and transformation.

In the context of 'Biofield Alchemy', the 'five elements' refer to foundational forces that compose and influence the universe and human existence. These elements - traditionally Earth, Water, Fire, Air, and Ether (or Space) - serve as metaphysical building blocks that shape the physical and energetic dimensions of life. Each element embodies distinct qualities and energies, playing a crucial role in balancing the biofield, the subtle energy system surrounding and permeating the body.

FIVE ELEMENTS & THE HUMAN BODY

The human body, according to ancient wisdom and modern holistic practices, is comprised of five essential elements – earth, water, fire, air, and ether. This elemental composition forms the foundation of 'Biofield Alchemy', a practice that leverages these elements to facilitate healing and balance within the human system. Understanding and harnessing the power of these elements is crucial for achieving optimal health and spiritual well-being.

KEY ASPECTS OF THE FIVE ELEMENTS

1. EARTH

Symbolizing stability, grounding and the physical structure of the body, the earth element is associated with health aspects related to bones, muscles, and overall physical endurance.

In 'Biofield Alchemy', grounding techniques, such as spending time in nature or practicing grounding breathwork and meditations can help restore balance and enhance the body's inherent healing capabilities.

2. WATER

Representing fluidity and adaptability, water is linked to bodily fluids, emotions, and intuition. Influences bodily fluids, intuition, and the flow of energy within the biofield.

Healing practices involving water, such as hydrotherapy or consuming pure, energized water, can cleanse and rejuvenate the body, promoting emotional and physical health.

3. FIRE

Fire embodies transformation and metabolism. It is associated with the body's digestive and metabolic processes. Governs energy production and the inner drive that fuels personal growth.

Techniques such as sun gazing, fire rituals and consuming warm foods can invigorate the body's energy and foster inner transformation.

4. AIR

Air signifies movement and communication. It is connected to the respiratory system and the mind.

Relating to intellect and breath, air affects mental clarity, respiratory functions, and the free movement of energy.

'Pranayama' (breath work), spending time in fresh air, and mindfulness practices can enhance mental clarity, respiratory health, and overall vitality.

5. ETHER (Space)

The most subtle element, encompassing the essence of the potential of emptiness. Linked to spiritual awareness, creativity, and the expansiveness of consciousness. Ether, or space, represents the most subtle realms of consciousness and it is the most refined element, associated with the mind and spirit.

Practices like meditation, sound healing, and visualization tap into the ether element, facilitating profound healing and spiritual growth.

In 'Biofield Alchemy', the integration of these five elements is essential for holistic healing. By aligning with the natural balance of these elements, individuals can achieve physical, mental, emotional, and spiritual harmony, unlocking their full potential for health and well-being.

NATUROPATHY: HEALING THROUGH FIVE ELEMENTS

Naturopathy, championed by Dr. Benedict Lust, emphasizes the healing power of nature and the body's intrinsic ability to restore balance. It aligns with 'Biofield Alchemy' through its focus on the five elements; Earth, Water, Fire, Air, and Ether. Each element corresponds to physical, emotional, and energy aspects of our being. Naturopathic practices, such as dietary recommendations, hydrotherapy, detoxification, and breathing exercises, help maintain the balance of these elements. This integrative approach provides a comprehensive framework for holistic health, highlighting naturopathy's foundational role in 'Biofield Alchemy'.

Dr. Benedict Lust advocated for a holistic approach to health that mirrors the principles of 'Biofield Alchemy'. In his work, he emphasized the significance of balancing the five elements, viewing them as fundamental to human well-being. Each element in naturopathy corresponds to specific physical, mental and emotional, and energetic aspects of our being

1. EARTH: Earth is associated with stability, structure, and physical health. Naturopathy helps balance the Earth element through healthy diet and nutrition, herbal remedies, and grounding practices. Consuming whole, organic foods rich in minerals supports the body's structural integrity. Herbal remedies of consuming specific plant roots, leaves and barks, enhance body's immune and nervous system and also supports in grounding and stability.

Practices like walking barefoot on earth's natural surfaces and spending time in nature strengthen the Earth element, promoting a sense of security and well-being.

2. WATER: Water governs emotions, intuition, and fluidity. Naturopathic approaches like hydrotherapy and herbal teas facilitate the flow of the Water element. Hydrotherapy techniques, such as hot and cold baths and compresses, soothe the nervous system and promote emotional release. Specific Herbs aid in emotional balance and fluid digestion. Encouraging regular physical activity and mindfulness practices ensures the free flow of energy, balancing the Water element.

3. FIRE: Fire represents metabolism, energy, and transformation. Naturopathy ignites and balances the Fire element through detoxification, metabolic support, and energy-enhancing practices. Detox protocols, such as fasting and the use of liver-supportive herbs cleanse the body and rejuvenate its metabolic processes. Techniques like sun exposure, specific breathwork, and the use of warming herbs stimulate the inner fire, enhancing vitality and transformative energy.

4. AIR: Air relates to breath, intellect, and communication. Naturopathy balances the 'Air' element with practices that enhance respiratory health and mental clarity. 'Pranayama' (breathing exercises) and aerobic activities increase oxygen flow, supporting mental and physical vitality. Herbal remedies improve cognitive function and communication. Incorporating mindfulness and

meditation practices also fosters mental clarity and emotional balance.

5. ETHER: Ether signifies space, consciousness, and spiritual connection. Naturopathic approaches to balancing Ether include meditation, sound healing, and energy work. Meditation and mindfulness practices create space for inner reflection and spiritual growth. Sound healing, using mantras and affirmations and instruments like singing bowls and tuning forks, harmonizes the biofield and enhances spiritual awareness. Practicing different forms of energy healing modalities open and balance the 'Ether' element, fostering a deeper connection to the self and the universe.

By employing a variety of techniques including nutrition, herbal remedies, hydrotherapy, mud therapy, detoxification, fasting and specific exercises and lifestyle modifications, naturopathy provides a comprehensive framework for balancing these five elements. This alignment with the principles of 'Biofield Alchemy' underscores naturopathy's role as a foundational base in achieving holistic health and well-being.

In 'Biofield Alchemy', understanding and harmonizing these five elements is essential for achieving holistic well-being. By aligning the biofield with the natural balance of these elements, individuals can enhance physical health, emotional resilience, mental clarity, and spiritual growth. This alignment fosters a deeper connection to the universe, promoting a state of inner harmony, peace, bliss and self-realization.

PART 2
CHAPTER 9

BREATHWORK

BREATH: THE GOLDEN THREAD OF LIFE - WEAVING ENERGY & MATTER TOGETHER

BREATH- THE COSMIC CONNECTOR

BREATHWORK & THE BIOFIELD EXPANSION

In the context of 'Biofield Alchemy', breathwork is used to balance and harmonize the biofield by regulating the flow of 'life-force energy' ('prana' or 'chi') in the body. Conscious breathing practices can help to:

1. RELEASE energetic blockages and tension
2. CULTIVATE inner calm and relaxation
3. ENHANCE spiritual connection and awareness
4. BALANCE and align the biofield
5. SUPPORT overall physical, emotional, and mental well-being

In the context of 'Biofield Alchemy', breathwork is a fundamental practice that involves conscious control and manipulation of the breath to influence one's biofield - the subtle energy field that surrounds and permeates the body. The term 'breathwork' broadly refers to a range of breathing techniques and exercises designed to promote physical, emotional, and spiritual well-being. This practice is rooted in the understanding that breath is not just a physiological process but a vital energy conduit that can harmonize the mind, body, and spirit.

Key aspects of breathwork in 'Biofield Alchemy' include its role in energy modulation, emotional release, and spiritual awakening. By consciously regulating the breath, individuals can alter their biofield's vibrational frequency, facilitating the release of stagnant or negative energies. This process can lead to profound emotional healing, helping to overcome mental, emotional and energy blockages.

Moreover, breathwork is considered a gateway to expanded states of consciousness, enhancing one's intuitive abilities and connection to the higher self. In 'Biofield Alchemy', these practices are seen as tools for transmuting dense energies into higher vibrational states, thus contributing to personal transformation and spiritual growth.

'PRANAYAMA': HARNESSING THE POWER OF 'LIFE FORCE ENERGY'

Pranayama, derived from the Sanskrit words "prana" (life force) and "ayama" (extension), refers to the ancient practice of breath control. This technique, a cornerstone of yogic traditions, involves regulating the breath to enhance mental, physical, and spiritual well-being. Pranayama is more than mere breathwork; it is a vital aspect of 'Biofield Alchemy', focusing on the flow of energy within and around the body.

'Pranayama' encompasses various techniques, each designed to influence the biofield in distinct ways. 'Nadi Shodhana' (alternate nostril breathing) balances the body's energy channels, promoting harmony between the left and right hemispheres of the brain. 'Kapalabhati' (skull shining breath) invigorates the mind and purges toxins, clearing the biofield of negative energies. 'Bhramari' (bee breath) soothes the nervous system, fostering a state of inner peace that reflects in a calm biofield.

The importance of 'pranayama' in 'Biofield Alchemy' lies in its ability to regulate the 'prana', or 'life force energy', directly influencing the biofield. Through controlled breathing, practitioners can enhance their vitality, reduce stress, and achieve heightened states of consciousness. This alignment of breath and biofield fosters holistic healing, allowing individuals to tap into deeper reservoirs of energy and awareness.

In the context of 'Biofield Alchemy', 'pranayama' serves as a powerful tool for breathwork, helping to clear energetic blockages and promote a free flow of prana. This not only supports physical health but also enhances mental clarity and spiritual growth. By integrating 'pranayama' into daily practice, individuals can cultivate a balanced biofield, leading to overall well-being and a harmonious connection with the universe.

Thus, 'pranayama', with its profound impact on breathwork, is essential in the practice of 'Biofield Alchemy', offering a pathway to transformative healing and inner alchemy.

'Pranayama' is one of the most powerful tools for 'Biofield Alchemy' due to its direct influence on the body's energy systems and its ability to harmonize the mind, body, and spirit. Here's how:

1. ENERGY REGULATION: 'Pranayama' techniques control the flow of 'prana', or 'life force energy', which is crucial for maintaining a balanced biofield. By regulating the breath, 'pranayama' helps ensure a smooth and steady flow of energy throughout the body, clearing blockages and enhancing vitality.
2. STRESS REDUCTION: Stress and negative emotions can disrupt the biofield, leading to imbalances and health issues. 'Pranayama' reduces stress by activating the

parasympathetic nervous system, promoting relaxation and reducing the production of stress hormones. This creates a calm and stable biofield.
3. ENHANCED MENTAL CLARITY: 'Pranayama' practices, such as 'Nadi Shodhana' (alternate nostril breathing), help balance the hemispheres of the brain, improving mental clarity and focus. A clear and focused mind supports a coherent and well-structured biofield, essential for effective 'Biofield Alchemy'.
2. EMOTIONAL HEALING: Techniques like 'Bhramari' (bee breath) have a soothing effect on the nervous system, aiding in the release of pent-up emotions and trauma. This emotional release is reflected in the biofield as a more harmonious and balanced energy pattern.
3. SPIRITUAL CONNECTION: 'Pranayama' facilitates deeper meditation and spiritual experiences by increasing the flow of prana to higher energy centers (chakras). This enhanced energy flow fosters a stronger connection to the spiritual realm, aligning the biofield with higher states of consciousness and spiritual insights.
4. PHYSICAL HEALTH: By improving oxygenation and detoxification, pranayama supports overall physical health. A healthy body reflects a balanced biofield, free from toxins and energetic imbalances.
5. SELF-AWARENESS: Regular practice of 'pranayama' increases self-awareness and

mindfulness. This heightened awareness allows individuals to sense and correct imbalances in their biofield, making 'pranayama' an essential tool for ongoing biofield maintenance and alchemical transformation.

In summary, 'Pranayama's' ability to regulate energy, reduce stress, enhance mental clarity, facilitate emotional healing, strengthen spiritual connections, and improve physical health makes it the most powerful tool in 'Biofield Alchemy'. It's holistic impact ensures a balanced and harmonious biofield, paving the way for profound transformation and healing.

REBIRTHING TECHNIQUES- BIRTHING A NEW 'YOU'

Leonard Orr, a pioneer in the field of conscious breathing, introduced the world to the transformative practice of 'Rebirthing'. In his seminal works, Orr delves into techniques that harness the breath to release suppressed emotions and traumas, thus fostering spiritual and personal growth. 'Rebirthing', or 'conscious energy breathing', involves a rhythmic, connected breathing pattern that integrates the physical, mental, and spiritual aspects of an individual, paving the way for profound healing and self-discovery.

In the context of 'Biofield Alchemy', Orr's techniques can be aligned with the empowerment of the five elements - earth, water, fire, air, and ether. Each element corresponds to different aspects of the human experience and the biofield, the subtle energy field that surrounds and permeates the body. By consciously engaging with the breath, individuals can harmonize these elements within their biofield, promoting balance and well-being.

REBIRTHING: A therapeutic breathing technique aimed at releasing suppressed emotions and achieving holistic healing through controlled, continuous breath cycles.

Key Aspects:

1. BREATHWORK: Central to 'Rebirthing', this involves deep, connected breathing patterns to facilitate emotional and energetic release.
2. INTEGRATION OF ELEMENTS: 'Rebirthing' aids in the alignment and empowerment of the five elements within the biofield, enhancing overall energy balance.
3. EMOTIONAL RELEASE: The process helps in surfacing and resolving past traumas and emotional blockages.
2. SPIRITUAL GROWTH: By purifying the biofield and harmonizing the elements, 'Rebirthing' supports spiritual development and self-awareness.
3. HOLISTIC HEALING: Emphasizes the interconnectedness of mind, body, and spirit, promoting comprehensive health and well-being.

Leonard Orr's rebirthing techniques offer a profound method for 'Biofield Alchemy', providing tools for elemental empowerment and deep, transformative healing.

Overall, breathwork in 'Biofield Alchemy' is not just a technique for relaxation or stress relief but a holistic practice that integrates the physical, emotional, and spiritual dimensions of being. It empowers individuals to take an active role in their healing journey, aligning their biofield with their highest potential and the universal energy flow.

PART 2
CHAPTER 10

MEDITATION

- THE MAGIC OF PRESENCE
&
CREATING ALCHEMY IN THE 'NOW'

MEDITATION: ALCHEMY IN MOTION

MEDITATION: PREPARING MIND AS A CONTAINER FOR PURE ENERGY

In the context of 'Biofield Alchemy', meditation is used to:

1. QUIET the mind and access deeper states of consciousness
2. CONNECT with the biofield and balance its energies
3. CULTIVATE awareness of thoughts, emotions, and bodily sensations
4. ENHANCE spiritual growth and self-awareness
5. SUPPORT overall well-being and resilience

Regular meditation practice can help to harmonize and balance the biofield, leading to greater coherence, clarity, and inner peace.

MEDITATION & 'BIOFIELD ALCHEMY'

Meditation, often defined as a practice where an individual uses techniques such as mindfulness, focusing the mind on a particular object, thought, or activity, aims to achieve a mentally clear and emotionally calm state. In the context of 'Biofield Alchemy', meditation serves as a pivotal practice for tuning into and harmonizing one's energy field, also known as the 'biofield'. This subtle energy body, encompassing and permeating the physical body, is thought to play a crucial role in our overall well-being.

Key aspects of meditation in 'Biofield Alchemy' include intention, focus, and resonance. "Intention" refers to the conscious aim of the practitioner, such as healing, insight, or balance. By setting a clear intention, one aligns their mental and energetic focus, enhancing the effectiveness of the practice. "Focus" involves directing attention towards a specific aspect of the biofield, such as a chakra or meridian, facilitating deeper awareness and potential shifts in energy patterns. "Resonance" denotes the vibrational harmony achieved through meditation, allowing for a more coherent and balanced biofield.

Meditation in this context is not merely a relaxation technique but a transformative tool for accessing deeper states of consciousness and subtle energy. It aids in clearing energy blockages, promoting physical healing, and fostering emotional and spiritual growth. Thus, meditation becomes an integral practice within 'Biofield Alchemy', empowering individuals to attune to their energetic nature and catalyze profound personal transformation.

CONCEPT OF 'DHYAN' & 'DHARNA'

In the realm of 'Biofield Alchemy', 'Dhyan' and 'Dharna', or focused meditation, holds a transformative power. Defined as the practice of profound concentration and contemplation, 'Dhyan' and 'Dharna' is derived from ancient Sanskrit, where 'Dhyan' means meditation and 'Dharna' signifies concentration or holding. This practice is a cornerstone of meditation, emphasizing the union of the mind and soul to transcend ordinary consciousness and access deeper states of awareness and spiritual insight.

The importance of 'Dhyan' and 'Dharna' in 'Biofield Alchemy' cannot be overstated. It acts as a conduit for harmonizing the body's energy fields, aligning them with the universal life force. By engaging in focused meditation, practitioners can refine their inner vibrations, clear energy blockages, and elevate their spiritual frequency. This process not only enhances mental clarity and emotional stability but also fosters a profound sense of inner peace and balance.

Key aspects of 'Dhyan' and 'Dharna' include sustained attention, intentional focus on a single point or concept, and the cultivation of inner stillness. Practitioners often use breath control, mantras, or visualizations to anchor their concentration. The ability to maintain this focused state is essential for deepening one's meditative practice and unlocking the full potential of 'Biofield Alchemy'.

In 'Biofield Alchemy', 'Dhyan' and 'Dharna' serve as powerful tools for self-transformation. They facilitate the purification of the mind, body, and spirit, allowing practitioners to access higher states of consciousness and tap into the subtle energies that govern their existence. By mastering 'Dhyan' and 'Dharna', individuals can enhance their ability to manifest intentions, heal from within, and achieve a harmonious balance with the cosmos, ultimately leading to a more enlightened and empowered state of being.

SILVA METHOD & 'BIOFIELD ALCHEMY'

The 'Silva Method', developed by José Silva in the 1960s, is a self-help program designed to enhance an individual's mind-body connection. It employs techniques like visualization, guided imagery, and controlled relaxation to tap into higher states of consciousness and intuitive abilities. In the context of 'Biofield Alchemy', the 'Silva

Method' aligns seamlessly with the practice of influencing and enhancing one's energy field for healing and personal transformation.

'Biofield Alchemy' revolves around the concept that our thoughts, emotions, and intentions influence our energy fields. The 'Silva Method' provides practical tools to harness these elements, offering a structured approach to entering deep meditative states, specifically alpha, beta, theta, and delta brainwave states. Each state of mind has distinct characteristics and benefits, which can be leveraged in 'Biofield Alchemy'.

1. ALPHA STATE (8-12 Hz): This state is associated with relaxation and light meditation. Techniques such as creative visualization and guided imagery are used in the 'Silva Method' to access the alpha state, promoting calmness, enhanced creativity, and problem-solving abilities.
2. BETA STATE (12-30 Hz): The beta state is linked to normal waking consciousness and active thinking. While not the primary focus in deep meditative practices, maintaining a healthy beta state is essential for everyday cognitive functions and alertness.
3. THETA STATE (4-8 Hz): Deep relaxation and meditation are achieved in the theta state. 'Silva Method' techniques, like deep relaxation exercises and focused meditation, help practitioners reach this state, which is ideal for programming the mind for healing, emotional balance, and intuition.

4. DELTA STATE (0.5-4 Hz): This is the state of deep sleep and profound meditation. Advanced 'Silva Method' practitioners use techniques to access delta brainwaves, facilitating deep healing and regeneration at the cellular level.

Meditation, a cornerstone of the 'Silva Method', is paramount in 'Biofield Alchemy'. It acts as a conduit for accessing and amplifying the subtle energies that constitute the biofield. Regular meditation practices help in harmonizing the mind and body, reducing stress, and fostering a state of inner peace. This state is crucial for biofield practitioners to maintain clarity, focus, and the ability to influence their biofield positively.

Key aspects of meditation in this context include mindfulness, creative visualization, and breath control. Mindfulness fosters awareness of the present moment, allowing practitioners to tune into their biofield's current state. Visualization techniques enable the projection of positive intentions into the biofield, shaping it towards desired outcomes. Breath control aids in regulating the flow of energy, ensuring a balanced and vibrant biofield.

Incorporating the 'Silva Method' into 'Biofield Alchemy' not only enhances the efficacy of the practice but also empowers individuals to harness their innate potential for holistic well-being and transformation.

PART 2
CHAPTER 11

BODYWORK
&

THE ALCHEMY OF
MOVEMENT

BODY WORK: PREPARING BODY AS A CONTAINER FOR PURE ENERGY

'BODY WORK' & 'BIOFIELD ALCHEMY'

In the context of 'Biofield Alchemy', bodywork refers to the use of manual therapies and techniques to balance and align the biofield, release energy blockages, and promote harmony and coherence in the body's energy systems. By working directly with the body, practitioner can help restore balance and flow to the biofield, leading to improved physical, mental, emotional, and spiritual well-being.

BODY WORK: MOVEMENT AS MEDICINE

A therapeutic practice involving the manipulation of the body's muscles and tissues, often incorporating techniques to influence the energy fields, with the goal of promoting physical, emotional, and energetic well-being.

Key Aspects:

1. THERAPEUTIC TOUCH: Involves hands-on techniques to manipulate muscles, fascia, and energy fields.
2. ENERGY FLOW: Aims to enhance the free flow of life force energy throughout the body.
3. HOLISTIC APPROACH: Addresses the interconnectedness of body, mind, and spirit.
4. HEALING: Promotes natural healing processes and overall well-being.

5. CUSTOMIZATION: Tailored to individual needs and energy constitutions.

In the realm of 'Biofield Alchemy', 'bodywork' encompasses a variety of therapeutic practices aimed at enhancing the body's natural energy flow and promoting holistic well-being. At its core, 'bodywork' refers to techniques that manipulate the physical structure of the body - such as muscles and bones - to facilitate the free movement of energy. This is achieved through methods like naturopathy, yoga, martial arts, body stretching, ayurvedic massages, acupressure and other healing practices.

The primary definition of 'bodywork' focuses on these manual therapies designed to improve physical health. However, within the context of 'Biofield Alchemy', the term takes on a broader meaning. Here, 'bodywork' is not just about physical manipulation but also about understanding and influencing the body's subtle energy systems. Alchemists believe that by releasing physical blockages and aligning the body, one can also harmonize the biofield, which is the energetic blueprint that surrounds and interpenetrates the physical body.

Key aspects of 'bodywork' in 'Biofield Alchemy' include it's emphasis on the interconnectedness of the body, mind, and spirit. Techniques are chosen and applied not only for their physical benefits but also for their potential to transform energy patterns, enhance emotional well-being, and support spiritual growth. This holistic approach views the body as a complex, dynamic system where physical and energetic health are intertwined. Therefore, 'bodywork' serves as a vital tool in 'Biofield Alchemy', offering pathways to healing that are both deeply physical and profoundly subtle.

POWERFUL 'BODY WORK' INCLUDES:

1. MARTIAL ARTS

2. YOGA ASANAS

3. AYURVEDIC MASSAGES

1. MARTIAL ARTS

Martial arts, such as 'Kalarippayattu', 'Tai Chi', 'Qigong', and 'Aikido', are revered in 'Biofield Alchemy' for their ability to cultivate and enhance 'life force energy'. These practices involve precise movements, breath control, and mental focus, which collectively work to ground and center the practitioner. Martial arts teach the art of harnessing and directing internal 'energy', or 'qi', for self-defense and personal empowerment. The discipline and focus required in martial arts training enhance one's awareness and control over their biofield. By integrating martial arts into 'Biofield Alchemy', practitioners can achieve a higher state of physical and energetic alignment, fostering a profound connection between mind, body, and spirit.

2. YOGA ASANAS

'Yoga Asanas', or postures, are foundational practices in 'Biofield Alchemy'. These physical exercises are designed to align the body, mind, and spirit, facilitating the free flow of 'prana', or 'life force energy'. Each asana stimulates different energy centers, or 'chakras', enhancing the overall vitality and balance of the biofield. The practice of yoga asanas not only increases flexibility and strength but also purifies the energy channels, or 'nadis', thereby promoting a harmonious energy flow. This purification process is essential in 'Biofield Alchemy' as it prepares the body to hold and sustain higher vibrations of energy.

3. AYURVEDIC MASSAGES

'Ayurvedic Massages' play a significant role in 'Biofield Alchemy' by harmonizing the body's energy. Rooted in ancient Indian medicine, these massages utilize specific oils and techniques tailored to an individual's dosha (body constitution). The therapeutic touch in Ayurvedic massages helps in removing energy blockages, reducing stress, and enhancing the body's natural healing processes. This practice ensures that the biofield remains clear and vibrant. The incorporation of herbal oils not only nourishes the skin but also infuses the body with medicinal properties that strengthen the immune system and promote overall well-being. In 'Biofield Alchemy', Ayurvedic massages are considered a vital tool for maintaining energetic balance and facilitating deep healing.

In 'Biofield Alchemy', the integration of yoga asanas, ayurvedic massages, and martial arts serves as a comprehensive approach to cultivating and enhancing the body's energy system. These practices not only foster physical health but also elevate the practitioner's vibrational frequency, facilitating a deeper connection to universal energy. By understanding and utilizing these ancient techniques, individuals can achieve a state of energetic harmony and transformation, embodying the essence of 'Biofield Alchemy'.

PART 2
CHAPTER 12

GROUNDING & CENTRING

BIOFIELD ALCHEMY
&
THE ART OF DISTILLING THE ESSENCE OF ENERGY WORK

GROUNDING & CENTERING: THE ART OF TUNING THE BIOFIELD

ART OF GROUNDING

Grounding is act of connecting with Earth's energy to promote balance, stability, and harmony in the body, mind, and spirit.

In the context of 'Biofield Alchemy', grounding is used to:

1. BALANCE and harmonize the biofield
2. CONNECT with the Earth's energy to reduce stress and promote calmness
3. INCREASE feelings of safety and security
4. FOCUS one's attention and energy back to the present moment
5. SUPPORT overall well-being and resilience

Grounding techniques may include walking barefoot, specific breathwork, mild body stretching in nature, including some household chores in daily activities, gardening, farming, hugging trees and domestic animals or simply focusing on the sensation of one's feet on the ground. Regular grounding practice can help to stabilize and balance the biofield, leading to greater overall well-being.

In the context of 'Biofield Alchemy', grounding refers to the practice of creating a balanced and stable connection between the physical body and the Earth's energy. This connection is crucial for maintaining a harmonious flow of energy within the human biofield, which is the field of energy that surrounds and permeates the body, often referred to as the energy field.

Grounding is essential in 'Biofield Alchemy' because it helps individuals stay centered and present, preventing the dispersion of energy that can lead to feelings of anxiety, disorientation, or emotional instability. This practice involves various techniques, such as walking barefoot on natural surfaces, engaging in mindful breathing, and visualizing roots extending from the body into the Earth.

The key aspects of grounding in 'Biofield Alchemy' include its role in enhancing physical and emotional well-being, improving mental clarity, and facilitating spiritual growth. By establishing a strong connection with the Earth, individuals can release excess or negative energies, replenish their vitality, and enhance their intuitive abilities. Grounding also supports the body's natural healing processes, making it a foundational practice for those seeking to harmonize their biofield.

ART OF CENTERING

Centering is an act of focusing one's attention and energy on a central point, such as the heart, 'hara', or third eye, to promote balance, harmony, and inner alignment.

In the context of 'Biofield Alchemy', centering is practiced to:

    1. BALANCE and harmonize the biofield

    2. CONNECT with one's central, core energy

    3. REDUCE stress and promote calm and clarity

    4. INCREASE feelings of inner peace and alignment

5. SUPPORT spiritual growth and self-awareness

Centering techniques may include visualization, breathwork, or simply focusing on a central point in the body. Regular centering practice can help to align and balance the biofield, leading to greater overall well-being and spiritual connection.

In the realm of 'Biofield Alchemy', 'centering' is a pivotal concept that refers to aligning one's physical, emotional, mental, and spiritual energies into a cohesive state of harmony. This process is crucial for achieving a balanced and effective practice in energy work. In the dictionary, 'centering' typically means to bring or focus on a central point. However, in 'Biofield Alchemy', it takes on a more nuanced meaning, encompassing both an inward journey and an outward manifestation of balanced energies.

Key aspects of centering in 'Biofield Alchemy' include grounding, mindfulness, and intention. Grounding is the foundational step, connecting oneself with Earth's energies to stabilize the biofield. Mindfulness involves becoming fully present in the moment, aware of one's thoughts, emotions, and physical sensations without judgment. This awareness allows practitioners to detect and address any imbalances within their energy fields.

Intention plays a crucial role in centering. By consciously setting an intention to align and balance one's energies, practitioners can focus their efforts and direct their biofield towards desired outcomes, such as healing, clarity, or transformation. Centering is not a one-time action but a continual practice that enhances sensitivity to subtle energy shifts and strengthens one's ability to navigate life's challenges with resilience and grace.

ROLE OF YOGA & MARTIAL ARTS IN GROUNDING & CENTERING

'Grounding' and 'centering' are fundamental concepts in 'Biofield Alchemy', vital for maintaining balance and stability within one's energy field. According to the dictionary, grounding refers to the process of achieving emotional and psychological stability, while centering involves focusing one's attention and energy inward to achieve a state of equilibrium.

Yoga and Martial arts, with their rich traditions and disciplined practices, offer potent methods for achieving both grounding and centering. These practices emphasize the connection between mind, body, and spirit, which is essential in 'Biofield Alchemy'.

'Grounding' in yoga and martial arts involves techniques that connect the practitioner to the Earth, fostering a sense of stability and security. Stances such as the 'horse stance' in 'kung-fu' or the 'rooted stance' in 'tai chi' encourage practitioners to feel the earth beneath them, providing a physical and energetic anchor. This connection helps to discharge negative energy and stress, promoting a calm and balanced state.

'Centering' in yoga and martial arts is achieved through focused breathing, meditation, and mindful movement. Practices such as Qigong and Aikido emphasize the flow of 'life force energy' ('qi') within the body, aligning it with the universe's natural rhythms. By concentrating on breath and movement, practitioners can align their energy centers ('chakras') and cultivate an inner sense of peace and clarity.

In 'Biofield Alchemy', the integration of yoga and martial arts practices enhances one's ability to manipulate and harmonize their energy field. The discipline and mindfulness required in martial arts training not only strengthens the physical body but also refine the subtle energy body, making it an invaluable tool for grounding and centering in the journey of 'Biofield Alchemy'.

ROLE OF PERFORMING DAILY HOUSEHOLD CHORES

In 'Biofield Alchemy', grounding and centering are essential practices that connect individuals to their physical bodies and the present moment. The term 'grounding' refers to establishing a stable connection with the Earth, while 'centering' involves bringing one's awareness to a calm and focused state. These concepts are crucial for maintaining balance and harmony in one's biofield, the energy field that surrounds and permeates the human body.

Daily household chores such as cleaning, washing, gardening and cooking - play a significant role in grounding and centering. Engaging in these activities requires physical movement, attention to detail, and mindfulness. When one cleans, washes, or cooks, they become fully present in the task at hand, promoting a sense of physical and mental stability. The repetitive nature of these activities can also induce a meditative state, allowing for the release of stress and the cultivation of inner peace.

Cleaning, for instance, involves physical contact with surfaces and objects, which enhances the connection to the physical environment. Washing dishes or laundry incorporates water, a natural grounding element, facilitating the release of negative energy and the absorption of positive vibrations. Cooking, on the other hand, involves handling food, a vital source of nourishment, which reinforces the connection to life-sustaining forces.

Incorporating these domestic activities into daily routines can significantly enhance grounding and centering practices in 'Biofield Alchemy'. By approaching household chores with intention and awareness, individuals can transform mundane tasks into powerful rituals that support their energetic well-being.

In summary, daily household chores are not just necessary for maintaining a clean and organized living space; they also serve as practical tools for grounding and centering, integral to the practice of 'Biofield Alchemy'. Through mindful engagement in these activities, one can foster a balanced and harmonious biofield, promoting overall health and vitality.

In essence, grounding is a preventive measure against energy imbalances and can be particularly beneficial for those who engage in practices that elevate their energy levels, such as yoga, meditation, martial arts , energy work, or other energy healing modalities. In 'Biofield Alchemy', grounding is seen as a continuous process that helps maintain equilibrium, enabling individuals to navigate life's challenges with resilience and grace.

Ultimately, centering is about finding and maintaining a state of equilibrium, where the practitioner's energies are harmoniously integrated, allowing for a more profound and transformative engagement with the world. This balanced state is essential for effective 'Biofield Alchemy', enabling the alchemist to harness and direct their energies with precision and clarity.

PART 2
CHAPTER 13

PROTECTION OF BIOFIELD

- SHIELDING

THE INNER GOLD & FIXING THE ENERGY LEAKS

BUILDING BIOFIELD'S DEFENCE SYSTEM

SECURING BIOFIELD'S ENERGY

In the context of 'Biofield Alchemy', 'protection' refers to the creation of a safe and secure energetic environment that shields the biofield from negative influences, harmful energies, or external interference. This can involve techniques such as setting boundaries, creating energy shields, or using protective symbols and geometry to maintain the integrity and balance.

'Protection', in 'Biofield Alchemy', refers to the energetic safeguarding of one's biofield, the subtle energy body that surrounds and permeates the physical form. This concept extends beyond physical safety, encompassing emotional, mental, and spiritual well-being. Protection, as a fundamental aspect of 'Biofield Alchemy', involves creating and maintaining a resilient and harmonious energy field, capable of deflecting or transforming negative influences and promoting overall vitality.

Key aspects of protection in 'Biofield Alchemy' include awareness, boundary setting, and energy purification.

> 1. AWARENESS: This involves being conscious of one's energy and the influences that may affect it, whether from people, environment, or thoughts. This mindfulness allows individuals to identify and address potential disruptions to their energy field.

2. BOUNDARY SETTING: This is another crucial aspect, where individuals establish clear energetic limits to prevent external negativity from penetrating their biofield. This can be achieved through various practices such as visualization techniques, affirmations, or using protective symbols and talismans.

3. ENERGY PURIFICATION: This is the process of cleansing the biofield of accumulated negative energies or blockages. Techniques such as smudging with herbs, sound work (using specific mantras and sounds), or using ritually energized plant, animal and mineral materials to purify and restore balance to the biofield.

ALCHEMICAL TRADITIONAL ANCIENT RITUALS

In the realm of 'Biofield Alchemy', ancient protection rituals hold a significant place, acting as energy shields that harmonize and strengthen the human biofield. Hindu traditions offer profound insights into these practices, with rituals such as 'Raksha Kavach' (protective shield) and the chanting of protective mantras and sounds. These practices are believed to create a protective energy field around individuals, safeguarding them from negative influences. The application of 'Vermillion' and 'Vibhuti' (sacred ash) on the forehead and the use of 'Yantras' (mystical diagrams) further reinforce this protective aura, aligning the biofield with higher vibrations.

Globally, ancient civilizations also embraced protection rituals to enhance the biofield. In Egypt, the 'Ankh' symbol was often used as a talisman for protection and vitality, while in Native American traditions, the creation of 'medicine wheels' and the use of smudging rituals were integral to maintaining spiritual and energetic protection. In Chinese culture, the practice of Feng Shui involved the strategic placement of objects to harmonize energy and protect against harmful forces, a concept closely tied to the cultivation of a balanced biofield.

These ancient rituals, while diverse in form, share a common purpose: to fortify the biofield against negative energies and promote a state of equilibrium. By integrating these time-honored practices into modern 'Biofield Alchemy', practitioners can tap into the wisdom of the ancients, creating a resilient energy shield that supports overall well-being.

SETTING HEALTHY BOUNDARIES

In the context of 'Biofield Alchemy', the term "boundaries" refers to the energetic and psychological limits that define the space of an individual's personal energy field. Boundaries in 'Biofield Alchemy' are crucial as they determine how we interact with others and our environment, affecting our well-being and spiritual development. A dictionary definition might describe boundaries as "the dividing line or limit between two areas." However, in 'Biofield Alchemy', boundaries are more than physical demarcations; they are dynamic and permeable, allowing for the flow of energy while maintaining a sense of self.

In the context of 'Biofield Alchemy', boundaries refer to the energetic limits and definitions that separate the individual biofield from the external environment, other people, and their energies. Healthy boundaries are essential for maintaining the integrity, balance, and harmony of the biofield, and can be established and reinforced through techniques such as energy shielding, visualization, and intention-setting.

BOUNDARIES IN 'BIOFIELD ALCHEMY' INCLUDE:

1. ENERGY BOUNDARIES: These are the unseen lines that delineate where one's energy ends, and another's begins. Healthy energetic boundaries help prevent the absorption of negative energies and emotions from others, maintaining energetic integrity.
2. PSYCHOLOGICAL BOUNDARIES: These involve mental and emotional limits that protect our thoughts, feelings, and beliefs. They enable individuals to express themselves authentically without fear of intrusion or judgment.
2. PHYSICAL BOUNDARIES: Though not the primary focus in 'Biofield Alchemy', physical boundaries still play a role, as they pertain to one's comfort with physical space and touch, influencing how we interact with our surroundings.
3. SPIRITUAL BOUNDARIES: These refer to the limits we set in our spiritual practices and beliefs, ensuring that we maintain our spiritual autonomy while respecting others' paths.

In 'Biofield Alchemy', cultivating strong and flexible boundaries is essential for personal growth, healing, and maintaining a balanced and harmonious energy field.

Overall, protection in 'Biofield Alchemy' is about cultivating a state of inner strength and stability, enabling individuals to navigate life's challenges with greater ease and resilience. It is a proactive and ongoing practice, integral to maintaining a healthy and vibrant energy system.

PART 2
CHAPTER 14

INITIATION

OPENING THE BIOFIELD PORTAL
FOR INSTANT ENERGY DOWNLOADS

ALCHEMY OF INITIATION RITUALS

UNDERSTANDING THE INITIATION PROCESS

In the context of 'Biofield Alchemy', initiation may involve:

1. A FORMAL ceremony or ritual to mark a new level of understanding or attainment
2. A TRANSMISSION of knowledge or energy from a teacher or mentor
3. A PERSONAL ritual or ceremony to mark a new phase of life or spiritual journey
4. A SYMBOLIC death and rebirth, marking a transformation or new beginning.

In the context of 'Biofield Alchemy', 'initiation' is a transformative process marking the beginning of an individual's deepened engagement with the energetic and spiritual realms. Traditionally, initiation is defined as the act of beginning something new or the formal admission into a group or practice. In 'Biofield Alchemy', however, it encompasses more than just an entry point; it is a rite of passage that signifies a conscious awakening to one's innate healing abilities and spiritual potential.

Key aspects of initiation in 'Biofield Alchemy' include the conscious opening of one's energy field to higher frequencies, the release of limiting beliefs, and the activation of dormant energetic pathways. This process often involves guidance from a mentor or spiritual teacher who facilitates the initiate's journey through practices such as traditional rituals, meditation, energy work, and sacred ceremonies. Initiation serves as a catalyst for personal growth, fostering a deeper connection with the universal life force and enhancing the individual's capacity to channel healing energies.

The experience of initiation can vary widely among individuals, influenced by their unique energy makeup, past experiences, and spiritual readiness. However, common themes include a heightened sense of awareness, increased intuitive abilities, and a profound sense of interconnectedness with all life. Ultimately, initiation in 'Biofield Alchemy' is not just a beginning, but a continuous unfolding of one's spiritual journey, leading to greater self-realization and mastery in working with the biofield. It is both a personal and universal experience, reflecting the timeless quest for knowledge, healing, and transformation.

ALCHEMY OF ANCIENT INITIATION RITUALS

Initiation rituals have played a vital role in various ancient traditions, marking significant spiritual transformations and the deepening of one's connection with the universe. In Hindu tradition, these rites, known as 'Diksha', signify a sacred transmission of energy and knowledge from the 'Guru' to the disciple, often involving mantras, meditation, and specific rites that align the disciple's biofield with higher spiritual frequencies. This alignment is critical in 'Biofield Alchemy' as it sets the foundation for profound energetic transformations.

ANCIENT TRADITIONAL INITIATION PROCESSES

Initiation processes in ancient traditions are deeply intertwined with the activation and transformation of the human biofield. These rites of passage serve as powerful gateways to spiritual enlightenment, aligning the individual's energy with universal forces. In 'Biofield Alchemy', few popular ancient initiation processes stand out for their profound impact on the human energy system.

1. DIKSHA (Hindu Tradition): A sacred initiation often given by a 'Guru'; 'Diksha' marks the spiritual rebirth of the individual. It involves the transmission of divine energy from the teacher to the student, awakening the latent spiritual potential within the disciple's biofield.
2. THE ELEUSINIAN MYSTERIES (Ancient Greek Tradition): This secretive initiation was dedicated to Demeter and Persephone, and involved a series of rites and ceremonies that symbolizes death and rebirth. The initiate's biofield was believed to be cleansed and transformed through direct interaction with the divine, facilitating a deep connection with the mysteries of life and death.
3. SHAKTIPAT (Tantric Tradition): This initiation involves the direct transmission of spiritual energy from a master to a disciple. It is a key process in Tantric practices, where the biofield of the initiate is profoundly altered, often resulting in a kundalini awakening, which ignites the transformation of consciousness.
4. THE RITE OF OSIRIS (Ancient Egyptian Tradition): This initiation mirrored the death and resurrection of Osiris, focusing on the soul's journey through the afterlife. The process was designed to purify and empower the initiate's biofield, ensuring their successful passage into the divine realms.

5. SOMA SACRAMENT (Vedic Tradition): This initiation involved the ritual consumption of Soma, a sacred plant, believed to confer immortality. It altered the biofield by elevating consciousness, allowing initiates to experience higher states of being and connect with the cosmic order.

These initiation processes exemplify the profound connection between ancient traditions and the transformative potential of 'Biofield Alchemy'.

Beyond the widely known initiation practices, there are numerous other ancient traditions that have employed initiation rites to unlock the deeper layers of the human biofield, fostering spiritual growth and energetic alignment. Here are five more significant initiation processes:

1. VISION QUEST (Native American Tradition):

A rite of passage involving solitary meditation in nature, often without food or water, the 'Vision Quest' initiates a deep connection with spiritual guides. The isolation and austerity intensify the initiate's biofield sensitivity, allowing visions and insights that guide their spiritual path.

2. KACHINA INITIATION (Hopi Tradition):

The Hopi people of North America engage in Kachina initiation, where young initiates are introduced to 'Kachinas', spirit beings that influence the natural world. Through ceremonial dances and teachings, the initiate's biofield is harmonized with these spiritual forces, fostering a deep connection with the sacred.

3. BUDDHIST MONASTIC SORDINATION (Theravada Tradition):

In this process, novices shave their heads, don robes, and take vows of celibacy, renunciation, and moral conduct. The ordination ceremony aligns the initiate's biofield with the teachings of the Buddha, purifying their energy and setting them on the path to enlightenment.

4. MAYA BLOODLETTING RITUAL (Mesoamerican Tradition):

In ancient Maya culture, bloodletting was an initiation rite believed to communicate with the gods. By offering their blood, initiates activated their biofield, opening portals to the divine and receiving spiritual insights and empowerment.

5. MIKVEH (Jewish Tradition):

The Mikveh is a ritual bath that serves as an initiation for spiritual purification and renewal. Immersing in the Mikveh is believed to cleanse the biofield of impurities, symbolizing a rebirth and heightened spiritual awareness, aligning the individual with divine energies.

Ancient rituals, though varied in form, share a common goal: the transformation and elevation of the individual's energy, making initiation a cornerstone in the practice of 'Biofield Alchemy'

Each of these initiation processes highlights the intricate ways in which ancient traditions have harnessed 'Biofield Alchemy' to cultivate spiritual awareness, energy alignment, and profound personal transformation.

PART 2
CHAPTER 15

SACRED GEOMETRY

- THE COSMIC ENERGY'S HELIPAD

SACRED GEOMETRY: THE ENERGY MAGNETIZING FIELD

SACRED GEOMETRY & BIOFIELD ALCHEMY

In the context of 'Biofield Alchemy', sacred geometry is seen as a powerful tool for understanding and balancing the biofield, as geometric patterns and shapes can influence the flow of energy and consciousness. By applying sacred geometric principles, individuals can harmonize their biofield, align with universal forces, and access higher states of awareness.

Sacred geometry refers to the symbolic and sacred meanings assigned to certain geometric shapes and proportions, believed to reflect the fundamental blueprint of the universe. These forms, including the circle, square, triangle, and more complex patterns like the Flower of Life and Metatron's Cube, are considered sacred because they represent the underlying principles of creation and the interconnectedness of all things. In the context of 'Biofield Alchemy', sacred geometry plays a crucial role in understanding how energy patterns and vibrations influence the human biofield.

In 'Biofield Alchemy', sacred geometry is used as a tool to harmonize and align the energy body with universal energies. 'Biofield Alchemist' believe that by engaging with these geometric forms, whether through visualization, physical representation, or meditation, individuals can tap into the intrinsic order of the cosmos, promoting healing and spiritual growth.

Key aspects of sacred geometry in this practice include its use in creating energetic fields that support balance and healing, its role in the visualization techniques to enhance meditative states, and its symbolic representation of the unity and diversity of life. Understanding and working with these patterns allows practitioners to access deeper states of consciousness and align their biofield with the natural harmonies of the universe, fostering a state of holistic well-being and spiritual awakening.

SACRED SYMBOLS: THE SYMBOLS OF THE SUBCONSCIOUS

Sacred symbols in ancient traditions hold profound power in 'Biofield Alchemy', acting as energetic conduits that harmonize the body's subtle energies. Symbols like the 'Swastik', 'Aum', 'Sri Yantra' and 'Ankh' have been revered for their ability to tap into universal forces, aligning the individual with cosmic rhythms. In 'Biofield Alchemy', these symbols are not mere icons but potent tools for transformation, helping to unlock latent potential and enhance spiritual growth. By integrating these ancient symbols, practitioners can amplify their biofield, fostering deeper healing and a stronger connection to the divine.

CONCEPT OF YANTRA

'Yantras', sacred geometric diagrams in Hindu traditions, hold profound importance in 'Biofield Alchemy'. These intricate designs are believed to harness and amplify cosmic energies, aligning the practitioner's biofield with universal forces. Each 'yantra' serves as a visual tool for meditation, aiding in focusing intent and manifesting specific energies. The power of 'yantras' lies in their precise geometric patterns, which resonate with the frequencies of the universe, facilitating spiritual awakening, protection, and transformation. In 'Biofield Alchemy', 'yantras' are essential for channeling energy, harmonizing the mind and body, and unlocking higher states of consciousness.

CONCEPT OF RANGOLI

In 'Biofield Alchemy', auspicious 'rangoli' designs serve as powerful tools within sacred geometry, resonating with the subtle energies of the biofield. These intricate patterns, often created using natural materials like rice or flower petals, embody geometric principles that harmonize the surrounding energy. 'Rangoli' acts as a symbolic gateway, inviting positive vibrations and aligning space with cosmic forces. Its symmetrical forms and vibrant colors create a protective, uplifting aura, facilitating spiritual connection and energy balance. By integrating these ancient designs, one can enhance the biofield, fostering a profound sense of harmony and well-being.

ANCIENT ARCHITECTURE & THE SACRED GEOMETRY

Ancient architecture and 'sacred geometry' form the foundation of 'Biofield Alchemy', linking physical spaces with energetic harmony. Structures like the temples, pyramids and cathedrals were designed using sacred geometric principles, such as the 'Golden Ratio' and the 'Flower of Life', to resonate with the Earth's energy grid. These patterns align with the natural order, amplifying the biofield and facilitating spiritual transformation. In 'Biofield Alchemy', these ancient designs serve as blueprints for creating environments that enhance energy flow, promote healing, and connect individuals with the cosmic order, bridging the physical and metaphysical realms.

In essence, the sacred geometry serves as a bridge, linking the physical and metaphysical realms, and acts as a conduit for transformative energies.

PART 2
CHAPTER 16

NATURE

- THE BIOFIELD ENHANCER & THE ENERGY AMPLIFIER

ALCHEMY OF NATURE'S SUPERNATURAL POWERS

NATURAL WORLD & BIOFIELD ALCHEMY

In the context of 'Biofield Alchemy', the natural world is seen as a vast, interconnected web of life, where every living being, and element is part of a larger, holistic system. The natural world is considered a source of wisdom, guidance, and healing, and is often used as a reference point for balancing and harmonizing the biofield.

By connecting with the natural world, individuals can:

1. ALIGN with the rhythms and cycles of nature

2. ACCESS ancient wisdom and knowledge

3. FIND balance and harmony within themselves and with the environment

4. CULTIVATE a sense of awe, wonder, and reverence for life

5. SUPPORT their own healing and growth, as well as that of the planet.

In the realm of 'Biofield Alchemy', the term 'natural world' refers to the inherent essence and interconnectedness of all living things. According to dictionary definitions, the 'natural world encompasses the physical universe, including plants, animals, landscapes, and other features and products of the Earth, as opposed to humans and human creations. However, in 'Biofield Alchemy', the natural world is understood as more than just the physical environment; it is a dynamic system of energy and consciousness that interacts with all life forms.

Key aspects of the natural world in 'Biofield Alchemy' include its role as a foundational source of energy and healing. This perspective acknowledges that everything in the natural world possesses a biofield - an energetic signature that interacts with other biofields. Practitioners believe that these interactions can influence health, well-being, and spiritual growth. The natural world is also seen as a mirror reflecting the internal states of individuals, offering insights into their emotional and spiritual conditions.

Another critical aspect is the idea of resonance, where the energies of the natural world can harmonize with human biofields. This resonance is thought to facilitate healing, balance, and alignment with one's true nature. 'Biofield Alchemy' encourages a deep, respectful connection with the natural world, viewing it as a partner in the journey towards self-discovery and transformation. Through this lens, the natural world is not merely a backdrop for human activity but an active participant in the alchemical process of growth and evolution.

ENVIRONMENT: THE NATURE'S MATRIX FOR BIOFIELD

In the context of 'Biofield Alchemy', environment refers to the multidimensional space that surrounds and interacts with the individual's biofield, including physical, emotional, mental, and spiritual factors. It encompasses the external world and the internal landscape, and is seen as a dynamic, interconnected web of energy and consciousness.

In the context of 'Biofield Alchemy', the term 'environment' extends beyond its conventional dictionary definition of the surrounding conditions in which a person, animal, or plant lives or operates. It encompasses the subtle energy fields that interact with and influence the human biofield. The environment includes not only the physical space and its elements (such as air, water, and fire), but also the invisible energies, like electromagnetic fields, sound frequencies, and even the collective emotional and mental atmosphere of a place.

Key aspects of the environment in 'Biofield Alchemy' involve understanding how these external and internal energies interact with our personal biofield. The quality of the physical environment, including factors like cleanliness, order, and natural elements, can directly impact the biofield's harmony. Moreover, the emotional and psychological environment - shaped by the thoughts, feelings, and intentions of the people around us - can influence our energetic state. This highlights the importance of cultivating positive interpersonal dynamics and fostering environments that support energetic well-being.

'Biofield Alchemy' emphasizes the practice of aligning one's internal environment, which includes thoughts, emotions, and beliefs, with the external environment to achieve energetic balance and harmony. This alignment can enhance personal health, emotional resilience, and spiritual growth. Therefore, in 'Biofield Alchemy', the environment is not just a backdrop but a dynamic, interactive field that plays a crucial role in shaping our energetic reality and overall well-being.

PART 2
CHAPTER 17

DEITIES & ANGELS
&

THE INFLUENCE OF CELESTIAL BEINGS IN MANIFESTING MIRACLES

DEITIES & ANGELS: THE SUPERNATURAL DIVINE BEINGS

'DEITIES' - THE DIVINE BEINGS

- A) BEINGS or entities considered to be gods or goddesses, often worshipped or revered in religious or spiritual contexts.
- B) SUPERNATURAL or divine beings with powers or attributes beyond those of humans.

In various spiritual or esoteric contexts, deities may be seen as:

1. ASPECTS of the divine or ultimate reality
2. INTERMEDIARIES between humans and the divine
3. EMBODIMENTS of natural forces or principles
4. GUARDIANS of knowledge, wisdom, or spiritual growth
5. SYMBOLS or archetypes representing human qualities or experiences

In 'Biofield Alchemy', deities may be invoked or worked with to:

1. ACCESS higher states of consciousness
2. CONNECT with divine guidance or wisdom
3. BALANCE and align the biofield
4. AMPLIFY intentions and manifestations

5. SUPPORT personal growth and transformation

In the context of 'Biofield Alchemy', the term 'deities' refers to divine beings or spiritual entities that are often revered and invoked for their perceived powers and wisdom. According to traditional dictionaries, a deity is defined as a 'God' or 'Goddess', a 'Supreme Being', or a 'Supernatural Entity'. However, in 'Biofield Alchemy', deities transcend their traditional religious connotations, embodying various aspects of universal energy and consciousness.

Key aspects of deities in 'Biofield Alchemy' include their role as archetypal energies that represent fundamental aspects of existence, such as creation, destruction, love, wisdom, and transformation. These archetypes can be invoked or meditated upon to facilitate personal growth, healing, and spiritual evolution. In this framework, deities are not external figures to be worshipped but are seen as symbolic representations of inner states and potentials.

'Biofield Alchemy' emphasizes the interactive nature of deities, suggesting that engaging with these energies can lead to profound changes in one's biofield - the energetic field surrounding and interpenetrating the human body. By aligning with the vibrational frequencies associated with specific deities, practitioners believe they can harmonize their own energy fields, leading to greater well-being and spiritual awakening.

Thus, in 'Biofield Alchemy', deities are considered crucial guides and allies on the path to self-realization and healing, offering unique insights and energies that help individuals navigate their spiritual journeys. They are both symbols and catalysts for transformation, inviting practitioners to explore deeper dimensions of their consciousness and connect with the divine essence within.

'ANGELS': THE COSMIC CARETAKERS

In various spiritual or esoteric contexts, angels may be seen as:

1. MESSENGERS of divine guidance or wisdom
2. PROTECTORS or guardians of individuals or groups
3. AGENTS of healing, comfort, or support
4. EMBODIMENTS of divine love or light
5. INTERMEDIARIES between humans and the divine

In 'Biofield Alchemy', angels may be invoked or worked with to:

1. ACCESS divine guidance or wisdom
2. CONNECT with divine love or light
3. BALANCE and align the biofield
4. SUPPORT personal growth and transformation
5. ENHANCE spiritual connection and awareness

The concept of angels can vary widely across cultures and belief systems.

In the realm of 'Biofield Alchemy', "angels" are often understood as 'energy beings' or spiritual guides that exist in higher vibrational frequencies. Traditionally, angels are seen as messengers or intermediaries between the divine and human realms. Within 'Biofield Alchemy', this definition extends to viewing angels as entities that influence and interact with the subtle energies surrounding and permeating the human body, often referred to as the biofield.

Key aspects of angels in this context include their roles as protectors, healers, and guides. They are believed to assist in the healing process by helping to clear, balance, and harmonize the biofield. This is thought to enhance physical, emotional, and spiritual well-being. Angels are also seen as facilitators of spiritual growth, offering guidance and support during times of transition or challenge. Their presence is often invoked in various energy healing practices, meditations, and rituals within 'Biofield Alchemy' to bring clarity, peace, and comfort.

Furthermore, angels are non-denominational, transcending specific religious or cultural beliefs. They are accessible to anyone regardless of their spiritual or religious background. This universal aspect underscores their role in 'Biofield Alchemy' as embodiments of unconditional love and wisdom, accessible to all who seek to connect with them.

In summary, within the framework of 'Biofield Alchemy', angels are viewed as divine energies that support and enhance the holistic health and spiritual evolution of individuals by interacting with their biofield.

PART 2
CHAPTER 18

PLANT KINGDOM
&
BIOFIELD ALCHEMY

- FROM DUST TO RADIANCE
&
NURTURING THE INNER GARDEN

PLANT KINGDOM & THE ALCHEMY OF PHOTOSYNTHESIS & GROWTH

'Biofield Alchemy', the practice of harmonizing and enhancing the subtle energy fields surrounding all living beings, extends beyond human interactions to the natural world, particularly plants and trees. By understanding and nurturing these biofields, we can cultivate a deeper connection with nature, enhancing both the health of our environment and our own well-being.

BIOFIELDS OF PLANTS & TREES

Plants and trees, like all living organisms, emit biofields - subtle energy fields that reflect their vitality and health. These biofields are integral to their growth, reproduction, and interactions with their surroundings. In 'Biofield Alchemy', we recognize that these energy fields are not isolated; they are interconnected with the biofields of other plants, animals, and humans, forming a vast web of life energy.

ROLE OF PLANTS & TREES IN HUMAN'S 'BIOFIELD ALCHEMY'

Plants and trees play a crucial role in human 'Biofield Alchemy'. They function as natural purifiers, transforming sunlight into energy, absorbing carbon dioxide, and releasing oxygen. This process not only sustains human life but also revitalizes the biofields of all organisms within their vicinity. By nurturing plants and trees, we contribute to the overall harmony and balance of the human biofield and the entire ecosystem.

TECHNIQUES FOR SERVING & LOVING PLANTS & TREES:

1. MINDFUL INTERACTION

Engaging with plants and trees mindfully enhances their biofields and our connection with them. Spend time observing their growth, touching their leaves, and appreciating their beauty. This mindful interaction strengthens the energy bond between humans and the plants, promoting mutual healing and growth.

2. ENERGY HEALING PRACTICES

Techniques like touch healing, sound healing, pranic healing and holographic healing can be applied to plants and trees. By channeling healing energy into their biofields, you can boost their vitality and resilience. Place your hands near their leaves or trunk, visualize a flow of healing energy, and sense their response to your touch.

3. GROUNDING & EARTHING

Connecting with the Earth is fundamental in 'Biofield Alchemy'. Walk barefoot on the soil near plants and trees to ground yourself and align your biofield with Earth's energy. This practice helps in balancing your biofield while nourishing the plants with your presence.

4. COMMUNICATION & INTENTION SETTING

Plants and trees respond to positive intentions and communication. Speak to them, express gratitude for their presence, and set intentions for their growth and health. Your words and thoughts carry vibrations that can enhance their biofields.

5. ENVIRONMENTAL CONSERVATION

Protecting and caring for the environment is essential in 'Biofield Alchemy'. Engage in sustainable practices, avoid harmful chemicals, and create habitats that support diverse plant life. A healthy environment strengthens the biofields of all living beings.

SCIENTIFIC PERSPECTIVE ON PLANT'S BIOFIELD

Recent studies have begun to explore the scientific basis of plant biofields. Research in bioelectromagnetic and biophotonics suggests that plants emit low levels of light and electromagnetic fields, which may play a role in their growth and communication. These findings align with the principles of 'Biofield Alchemy', highlighting the interconnectedness of all life forms through subtle energy fields.

THE SPIRITUAL CONNECTION

Beyond the scientific perspective, there is a profound spiritual dimension to serving and loving plants and trees in 'Biofield Alchemy'. Many ancient cultures revered trees as sacred beings, recognizing their role in connecting the physical and spiritual realms. By honoring plants and trees, we tap into this ancient wisdom and align ourselves with the natural rhythms of the earth.

PRACTICAL APPLICATIONS OF PLANT KINGDOM IN 'BIOFIELD ALCHEMY':

1. CREATING HEALING GARDENS

Design spaces that promote healing and tranquility by incorporating a variety of plants and trees. Use plants with known biofield - enhancing properties, such as Basil, lavender, and rosemary. These gardens can serve as sanctuaries for meditation, relaxation, and biofield alignment.

2. FOREST BATHING (Shinrin-Yoku)

This Japanese practice involves immersing oneself in a forest environment to absorb its healing energies. Forest bathing enhances biofields by reducing stress, improving mood, and boosting overall health. Spend time in forests, breathe deeply, and connect with the trees to experience these benefits.

3. PERMACULTURE & SUSTAINABLE AGRICULTURE

Implementing permaculture principles in gardening and farming fosters a harmonious relationship between humans and nature. Sustainable practices such as companion planting, crop rotation, and organic farming enhance the biofields of plants and trees, leading to healthier ecosystems.

4. URBAN GREENING

In urban environments, integrating plants and trees into cityscapes can mitigate pollution, reduce heat, and improve the quality of life. Urban greening projects, such as rooftop gardens and green walls, support the biofields of city dwellers and promote ecological balance.

CONCLUSION: THE PATH FORWARD

Human Biofield Enhancement: Serving and loving plants and trees through the lens of 'Biofield Alchemy' offers a transformative approach to interacting with the natural world. By recognizing the subtle energies that connect all life forms, we can foster a deeper appreciation for the environment and our place within it. As we cultivate these practices, we not only enhance the biofields of plants and trees but also contribute to a more balanced, harmonious, and vibrant world.

In embracing 'Biofield Alchemy', we become the alchemist of the Earth, nurturing the delicate web of life that sustains us all. Through mindful interaction, energy healing, grounding, communication, and sustainable practices, we can honor and support the vital role of plants and trees in our lives. This holistic approach invites us to live in harmony with nature, recognizing the profound interconnectedness of all beings and the limitless potential for mutual healing and growth.

PART 2
CHAPTER 19

ANIMAL KINGDOM
&

THE RIPPLE EFFECT
OF
THE LIFE FORCE ENERGY

ANIMAL KINGDOM & 'BIOFIELD ALCHEMY'

BIOFIELD ENHANCEMENT BY SERVING ANIMALS

In the intricate dance of life, humans and animals share an unspoken bond that transcends the physical realm. This connection is deeply rooted in the biofield, an energetic matrix that envelops all living beings. 'Biofield Alchemy', an emerging field that explores the interactions between these energy fields, reveals profound insights into how serving and loving animals can enhance our biofields as humans, creating a harmonious symphony of well-being.

UNDERSTANDING THE BIOFIELD OF ANIMALS

As discussed in previous chapters, the biofield, also known as the energy field - a complex network of electromagnetic energies that emanate from and interact with the body. Since it is influenced by thoughts, emotions, and environmental factors; it plays a crucial role in maintaining physical, mental, emotional, and spiritual health. Just like humans, Animals, too, possess their own biofields, which are similarly dynamic and responsive to their surroundings.

THE ROLE OF ANIMALS IN HUMAN'S 'BIOFIELD ALCHEMY'

Animals, with their pure and untainted energy, serve as powerful catalysts for 'Biofield Alchemy'. Their presence can significantly influence the human biofield, promoting healing, reducing stress, and enhancing emotional well-being. This interplay between human's and animal's biofields can be harnessed through intentional practices of service and love.

SERVING ANIMALS: A PATHWAY TO MUTUAL HEALING

Serving animals, whether through food sharing, caregiving, rehabilitation, or simply providing companionship, creates a reciprocal flow of energy that benefits both the giver and the receiver. When humans care for animals, they engage in acts of kindness that elevate their own energetic vibrations. This altruistic behavior can lead to a heightened state of coherence in the biofield, fostering physical and emotional resilience.

1. ANIMAL CARE & REHABILITATION

Volunteering at animal shelters or participating in wildlife conservation efforts are profound ways to serve animals. The act of nurturing and healing animals in distress not only aids their recovery but also invokes a deep sense of purpose and fulfillment in the caregiver. This sense of purpose can harmonize the caregiver's biofield, creating a state of balance and alignment.

2. PROVIDING COMPANIONSHIP

Pets, particularly dogs and cats, offer unconditional love and companionship that can profoundly impact the human biofield. Studies have shown that petting a dog or cat can lower blood pressure, reduce anxiety, and increase the release of oxytocin, a hormone associated with bonding and affection. These interactions foster a positive energetic exchange, enhancing both human and animal biofields.

3. ADVOCATING FOR ANIMAL RIGHTS

Advocacy and activism for animal welfare also play a crucial role in 'Biofield Alchemy'. By standing up for the rights of animals, individuals engage in compassionate action that resonates with high-frequency vibrations. This form of service not only helps create a more compassionate world but also strengthens the advocate's biofield, promoting a sense of empowerment and interconnectedness.

LOVING ANIMALS: ENHANCING BIOFIELD COHERENCE

Loving animals, whether they are pets, wildlife, or farm animals, fosters a deep emotional bond that enhances biofield coherence. This love, characterized by empathy, compassion, and respect, generates high-frequency vibrations that permeate the biofield, creating a state of harmony and balance.

1. EMOTIONAL BONDING

The emotional bond between humans and animals is a powerful force in 'Biofield Alchemy'. This bond, rooted in love and mutual respect, creates a coherent energy field that supports physical and emotional health. Spending time with animals, engaging in play, and expressing affection can elevate mood, reduce stress, and enhance overall well-being.

2. MINDFULNESS & PRESENCE

Animals live in the present moment, and their ability to fully engage with their surroundings can teach humans the value of mindfulness. Mindful interactions with animals, such as observing their behavior, appreciating their uniqueness, and being fully present in their company, can help align the human biofield with the present moment. This alignment promotes a state of inner peace and tranquility.

3. HEALING THROUGH LOVE

Love is a powerful healing force that can transform both the giver and the receiver. When humans express love towards animals, they emit positive vibrations that can help heal emotional wounds and traumas in both parties. This healing process is facilitated by the biofield, which responds to the high-frequency energy of love, promoting overall well-being and harmony.

INTEGRATING ANIMAL'S 'BIOFIELD ALCHEMY' INTO DAILY LIFE

Integrating 'Biofield Alchemy' into daily life involves intentional practices that cultivate a deep connection with animals. Here are a few practical ways to incorporate these principles:

1. DAILY INTERACTIONS

Make time each day to interact with animals, whether they are pets or wildlife. Simple acts such as feeding birds and animals, walking a dog, or observing animals in nature can create positive energetic exchanges that enhance the biofield.

2. MEDITATION & VISUALIZATION

Incorporate animals into your meditation or visualization practices. Imagine yourself surrounded by animals, sharing a space of mutual love and respect. Visualize the exchange of positive energy and the harmonization of your biofield with theirs.

3. GRATITUDE & APPRECIATION

Practice gratitude for the presence of animals in your life. Acknowledge the joy, companionship, and lessons they bring. This practice of gratitude can elevate your energetic vibrations and promote a state of coherence in your biofield.

4. COMPASSIONATE LIVING

Adopt a lifestyle that reflects compassion and respect for all living beings. This can include choosing cruelty-free products, supporting animal-friendly organizations, and educating others about the importance of animal welfare. Compassionate living aligns your biofield with high-frequency energies, fostering a state of harmony and well-being.

CONCLUSION

Serving and loving animals through the lens of 'Biofield Alchemy' reveals a profound interconnectedness that enhances the well-being of both humans and animals. By engaging in acts of service and expressing love towards animals, we create a harmonious exchange of energy that promotes healing, balance, and coherence in the biofield. This symbiotic relationship not only enriches our lives but also contributes to a more compassionate and harmonious world. As we continue to explore and understand the principles of 'Biofield Alchemy', we uncover the transformative power of serving and loving animals, fostering a deeper connection with all living beings.

PART 2
CHAPTER 20

MINERAL KINGDOM & 'BIOFIELD ALCHEMY'

- TAPPING INTO MOTHER EARTH'S ENERGY

MINERAL KINGDOM: ACTIVATING THE ENERGY OF 'MOTHER EARTH'

MINERAL KINGDOM:

CATALYST FOR ACTIVATING THE INNER GOLD OF PURE ENERGY

In the context of 'Biofield Alchemy', the mineral kingdom is seen as a source of powerful energetic and vibrational properties that can be used for healing, balance, and transformation. Minerals are believed to hold ancient wisdom and knowledge, and are often used in various rituals, sacred ceremonies, energy grids, geometric layouts, and meditation practices to:

1. PROTECT: Integrating mineral kingdom helps in the protection of the biofield and its energies.
2. CONNECT: Incorporating mineral kingdom supports in connecting with Mother Earth's energy
3. BALANCE: Proper use of minerals helps in balancing and aligning the biofield
2. AMPLIFY: Specific minerals support in amplifying intentions and manifestations
3. ACCESS: Mineral kingdom can help access ancient wisdom and knowledge
4. HEALING: Mineral kingdom can support physical, emotional, and spiritual healing.

By working with the mineral kingdom, individuals can tap into the transformative power of minerals and harness their energies for personal growth and mental clarity and transformation.

In the realm of 'Biofield Alchemy', the 'Mineral Kingdom', refers to a category of natural substances comprising minerals, rocks, and crystals, each possessing unique vibrational frequencies. The dictionary defines the 'Mineral Kingdom', as the collective group of naturally occurring inorganic substances with a definite chemical composition and crystalline structure. In the context of 'Biofield Alchemy', these minerals are not merely inert objects; they are viewed as reservoirs of Earth's energies, capable of interacting with and influencing the human biofield.

Key aspects of the Mineral Kingdom in 'Biofield Alchemy' include their role in energy healing, grounding, and transformation. Minerals are believed to emit specific vibrational frequencies that can resonate with and harmonize the human biofield, aiding in the alignment of physical, emotional, and spiritual energies. For instance, crystals such as quartz and amethyst are commonly used in practices to cleanse, balance, and amplify the energy flow within the body.

Another crucial aspect is the use of minerals in grounding practices. 'Grounding', or 'Earthing', involves using the Earth's natural energies to stabilize and reconnect one's energy to the Earth's frequency, providing a sense of balance and centeredness. Minerals like hematite and black tourmaline are known for their grounding properties, helping individuals anchor their energies and dispel negativity.

Thus, the Mineral Kingdom serves as a bridge between the physical and energetic realms, facilitating healing, transformation, and connection to the Earth in the practice of 'Biofield Alchemy'.

POWER OF MINERAL KINGDOM

Importance of Precious Metals, Gemstones, and Crystals in 'Biofield Alchemy':

A) ENERGETIC RESONANCE & FREQUENCY

Precious metals, gemstones, and crystals have unique vibrational frequencies that influence the biofield. For instance:

1. METALS

a) GOLD: Associated with the sun; amplifies personal energy, warmth, and vitality.

b) SILVER: Linked to the moon; offers calming and protective qualities, balancing emotional energies.

c) COPPER: Revered for its conductive properties; enhances energy flow and healing.

d) PLATINUM: Symbolizes strength and endurance; aids in spiritual transformation.

e) PALLADIUM: With its rare and powerful energy, it supports detoxification and purification.

Each metal uniquely contributes to harmonizing and amplifying one's energetic resonance.

2. CRYSTALS

a) AMETHYST

1. Resonates with the crown chakra.

2. Enhances spiritual awareness and intuition.

3. Supports meditation and promotes a sense of calm.

b) ROSE QUARTZ

1. Connected to the heart chakra

2. Fosters love, compassion, and emotional healing.

3. Helps in opening the heart to both self-love and love for others.

c) CLEAR QUARTZ

1. Amplifies energy and thought, harmonizing all chakras.

2. Acts as an expert healer, enhancing spiritual growth.

3. Used to cleanse and energize other crystals.

d) CITRINE

1. Resonates with the solar plexus chakra.

2. Attracts abundance, prosperity, and success.

3. Promotes positivity and dispels negativity.

e) BLACK TOURMALINE

1. Associated with the root chakra.

2. Offers protection and grounding, shielding against negative energies.

3. Stabilizes the biofield by neutralizing harmful vibrations

3. GEMSTONES

Gemstones harmonize and stabilize the biofield, promoting overall well-being, balance, and spiritual growth. For instance:

a) EMERALD

1. Linked to the heart chakra.

2. Symbolizes rebirth, renewal, and growth.

3. Encourages truthfulness and enhances memory.

b) RUBY

1. Resonates with the root and heart chakras.

2. Invokes passion, vitality, and courage.

3. Strengthens the biofield by energizing the body and spirit.

c) MOONSTONE

1. Associated with the sacral and crown chakras.

2. Enhances intuition and emotional stability.

3. Fosters new beginnings and encourages inner growth.

d) YELLOW SAPPHIRE

1. Resonates with the solar plexus chakra.

2. Attracts wealth, success, and wisdom.

3. Encourages mental clarity and boosts confidence.

e) DIAMOND

1. Associated with the crown chakra.

2. Symbolizes purity, clarity, and invincibility.

3. Amplifies energy, clears the aura, and aligns the chakras.

B) HISTORICAL & CULTURAL SIGNIFICANCE

Precious metals, gemstones, and crystals have been used in rituals and ceremonies for centuries.

a) ANCIENT EGYPTIANS: Used gold and precious stones for protection and guidance in the afterlife.

b) HINDU TRADITION: The Navaratna (nine gemstones) correspond to the nine planets, each offering specific protective and healing qualities. These historical practices underscore the enduring power of these materials in influencing the human energy field.

c) CHINESE CULTURE: Jade has been revered in Chinese culture for thousands of years, symbolizing purity, protection, and immortality. It was often used in burials and worn as talismans for good luck and spiritual well-being.

d) NATIVE AMERICAN TRADITIONS: Turquoise, commonly used by Native American tribes, is believed to bring protection, strength, and healing. It was used in both jewellery and ceremonial objects to connect with the spiritual world.

e) MEDIEVAL EUROPE: Amethyst was highly valued during the middle ages, believed to protect against intoxication and evil thoughts. Royalty and religious figures often wore amethyst jewelry to symbolize power, wisdom, and spiritual clarity.

C) PRACTICAL APPLICATIONS OF MINERAL KINGDOM IN 'BIOFIELD ALCHEMY'

a) Can be worn as jewellery to provide continuous energetic support.

b) Used in meditation to deepen connection with specific energies.

c) Placed in the environment to create a harmonious and protective space.

d) Serve as focal points in rituals, amplifying intention and directing energy towards desired outcomes.

e) Often used with other practices like sound healing and aromatherapy for enhanced vibrational alignment.

D) SCIENTIFIC PERSPECTIVES

a) METAPHYSICAL PROPERTIES: Are widely acknowledged; scientific exploration is ongoing.

b) PIEZOELECTRIC PROPERTIES OF CRYSTALS: May play a role in influencing the human energy field.

c) CONDUCTIVE PROPERTIES OF METALS: Gold and silver may interact with the body's electromagnetic field, supporting their use in 'Biofield Alchemy'.

CONCLUSION

The power and importance of these materials lie in their ability to resonate with and influence the biofield. By harnessing their unique vibrational frequencies, practitioners can enhance spiritual and energetic practices. These elements serve as tools for healing, protection, and empowerment, drawing on both ancient wisdom and emerging scientific insights.

PART 2
CHAPTER 21

CLEANLINESS

- THE ENERGY HYGIENE

- A STATE OF BEING FREE FROM IMPURITIES

CLEANLINESS: THE ART OF PURIFICATION & REFINING THE SOUL

POWER OF CLEANLINESS

Cleanliness, in its most basic form, refers to the state of being free from dirt, impurities, and anything that might be considered unclean or unhealthy. However, the concept of cleanliness extends beyond the physical realm, encompassing mental, emotional, and spiritual dimensions. Each aspect plays a critical role in maintaining the harmony and balance of an individual's biofield, which is the energetic field surrounding and interpenetrating the human body.

In 'Biofield Alchemy', cleanliness in all its forms - physical, mental, emotional, and spiritual, serves as a foundation for a healthy and vibrant biofield. Each aspect of cleanliness contributes to the overall integrity and strength of the biofield, ensuring that energy flows freely and harmoniously. By maintaining cleanliness, one creates an environment within and around themselves that is conducive to higher states of consciousness, healing, growth and transformation.

The power of cleanliness lies in its ability to remove obstacles and impurities that hinder the natural flow of energy, allowing for the full expression of one's potential. It is a process of continual refinement, aligning the individual with the purest frequencies of life. Through this alignment, one can achieve a state of harmony and balance, which is the essence of 'Biofield Alchemy'.

TYPES OF CLEANLINESS:

1. PHYSICAL

2. MENTAL

3. EMOTIONAL

4. SPIRITUAL

1. 'SAUCHA': THE PHYSICAL CLEANLINESS

In the framework of Ashtanga Yoga, 'Saucha', or purity, is a foundational principle of 'Niyama' that emphasizes physical cleanliness as a pathway to spiritual and energetic purification. When applied to 'Biofield Alchemy', Saucha serves as a critical practice for maintaining the clarity and vibrancy of one's biofield.

Physical cleanliness is not merely about outward hygiene, such as regular bathing and grooming. In 'Biofield Alchemy', it extends to the removal of toxins and impurities from the body that can disrupt the flow of vital energy. Practices like detoxification, the consumption of clean, organic foods, and maintaining a toxin-free environment are essential to sustaining the purity of the biofield.

A clean body fosters a clean mind, which in turn cultivates a pure and balanced biofield. Physical impurities can create blockages within the biofield, leading to energy stagnation or disturbances that may manifest as physical or emotional imbalances. By adhering to 'Saucha', one ensures that the biofield remains clear and receptive to higher energies, facilitating a more profound connection with the self and the universe.

Incorporating 'Saucha' into daily life aligns one's physical state with the principles of 'Biofield Alchemy', allowing for a harmonious flow of energy. This purity enhances the body's natural healing abilities and strengthens the integrity of the biofield, contributing to overall well-being and spiritual growth.

2. 'AHIMSA', 'ASTEYA' & 'APARIGRAHA': THE MENTAL CLEANLINESS

Mental cleanliness refers to the clarity and purity of thought. In 'Biofield Alchemy', the mind is considered a powerful tool that can either enhance or disrupt the flow of energy within the biofield. Mental clutter - such as negative thoughts, stress, and anxiety, can create disturbances in the biofield, leading to a state of imbalance. Mental cleanliness involves cultivating a mindset that is free from negativity and filled with positive, constructive thoughts. Practices like mindfulness, meditation, and mental discipline are vital for maintaining mental cleanliness, helping to clear mental fog and ensuring that the mind remains a conduit for positive energy.

In 'Biofield Alchemy', Ashtanga Yoga's principles of Ahimsa (non-violence), Asteya (non-stealing), and Aparigraha (non-possessiveness) are essential for cultivating a balanced and harmonious biofield. 'Ahimsa' fosters peace and compassion, promoting a flow of positive energy. 'Asteya' encourages integrity, preventing energy theft from oneself and others, while 'Aparigraha' nurtures detachment, freeing the biofield from the burden of material desires. Together, these principles ensure mental cleanliness by aligning thoughts with higher values, fostering a purified mind that enhances the biofield's vibrational harmony and supports spiritual growth.

3. 'SATYA' & 'SANTOSHA': THE EMOTIONAL CLEANLINESS

Emotional cleanliness pertains to the management and purification of emotions. Emotions are powerful energy currents that significantly influence the biofield. Negative emotions such as anger, fear, and jealousy can create energetic blockages, leading to disharmony within the biofield. Emotional cleanliness involves acknowledging and processing emotions healthily rather than suppressing them. Techniques such as emotional release, counseling, and practices like forgiveness are crucial for maintaining emotional cleanliness. By keeping the emotional body clean, one ensures that the biofield remains vibrant and balanced, supporting overall well-being.

In 'Biofield Alchemy', the principles of Santosha (contentment) and Satya (truthfulness) from Ashtanga Yoga are crucial. 'Santosha' cultivates inner peace and gratitude, harmonizing the biofield by reducing negative frequencies, while 'Satya', the adherence to truth, purifies the mind and aligns the biofield with higher vibrations. Together, these principles empower individuals to maintain balance, clarity, and authenticity in their energy fields, fostering spiritual growth and a deeper connection with the universe. Practicing 'Santosha' and 'Satya' - strengthens the biofield, creating a foundation for holistic well-being and transformation.

4. SPIRITUAL CLEANLINESS

Spiritual cleanliness is the purification of the soul or spirit - the core of one's being. In 'Biofield Alchemy', spiritual cleanliness is paramount as it directly influences the highest levels of the biofield. Spiritual impurities, such as unresolved karma, disconnection from one's purpose, or lack of spiritual practices, can lead to a weakened or distorted biofield. Maintaining spiritual cleanliness involves regular spiritual practices, such as prayer, gratitude, meditation, and aligning with higher principles of truth, compassion, and love. It also includes the release of spiritual attachments that no longer serve ones highest good.

In 'Biofield Alchemy', the principles of 'Tapas', 'Ishvara Pranidhana', 'Brahmacharya', and 'Swadhyaya' from 'Ashtanga Yoga' play an extremely crucial role in refining and harmonizing one's biofield. 'Tapas', ignites inner heat, purifying the subtle energies. 'Ishwara Pranidhana', surrender to the divine, aligns the biofield with cosmic frequencies, enhancing spiritual resonance. 'Brahmacharya', the practice of conservation of vital energies strengthens the biofield's integrity. 'Swadhyaya', self-study, deepens self-awareness, facilitating the alignment of the biofield with higher consciousness. Together, these principles cultivate a balanced and resilient biofield, essential for holistic well-being and spiritual evolution.

In conclusion, cleanliness is not just a mundane task but a sacred practice that holds profound significance in the journey of 'Biofield Alchemy'. By embracing cleanliness in all its forms, one paves the way for deeper spiritual awakening and the full realization of the alchemical process within.

PART 3

'BIOFIELD ALCHEMY' & IT'S PRACTICAL APPLICATIONS

- APPLYING THE PHILOSOPHER'S STONE WITH AN ALCHEMIST'S MINDSET

PART 3
CHAPTER 1

CREATIVITY
&
'BIOFIELD ALCHEMY'

- DISTILLING KNOWLEDGE INTO INSIGHT

CREATIVITY & THE ALCHEMY OF "EXPRESSION"

CREATIVITY: BRINGING THE SEED OF 'IDEAS' TO LIFE

In the realm of 'Biofield Alchemy', one of the most fascinating and promising areas of application is its impact on creativity. This chapter delves into how the 'Biofield Alchemy' can enhance creative processes, provides compelling case studies in art and innovation, and offers practical exercises designed to unlock and amplify creative potential.

ENHANCING CREATIVE PROCESSES

Creativity is often seen as a mystical force, an inexplicable spark that drives human ingenuity and artistic expression. However, recent research in the field of biofield science suggests that creativity can be systematically nurtured and enhanced through the manipulation of our biofield. The biofield, an energetic matrix that surrounds and interpenetrates the human body, is believed to play a crucial role in mental clarity, emotional balance, and creative insight.

One way the biofield enhances creativity is by harmonizing the brain's hemispheres. The left hemisphere is typically associated with logical, analytical thinking, while the right hemisphere is linked to intuitive, holistic thought. By using biofield techniques such as energy balancing and chakra alignment, individuals can achieve a state of hemispheric coherence, where both sides of the brain work in tandem.

This state of balance facilitates a more fluid and integrated thought process, allowing creative ideas to flow more freely and effectively

RESEARCH WORK ON CREATIVITY

Albert Einstein's perspective on creativity as the ability to see the world anew resonates deeply with 'Biofield Alchemy', where subtle energies are harnessed to transform reality. By cultivating creative thought, individuals tap into the biofield, innovating, healing, and manifesting desired outcomes. Einstein's emphasis on imagination as a source of knowledge highlights the transformative potential of creative thinking in mastering biofield energies.

Mihaly Csikszentmihalyi's research on 'flow' provides a scientific foundation for understanding peak creative experiences, aligning with 'Biofield Alchemist's' harmonization of energy fields. This state of heightened focus and immersion enhances creative expression and spiritual growth.

Additionally, visionaries like Dr. Jill Bolte Taylor, a neuroscientist who explored the creative potential of the right brain, and Dr. Scott Barry Kaufman, a psychologist who studied the intersection of creativity and spirituality, have contributed to our understanding of 'Biofield Alchemy'. Furthermore, Dr. Amit Goswami, a quantum physicist, has shed light on the role of consciousness in shaping reality, underscoring the creative power of 'Biofield Alchemy'. These pioneers have collectively illuminated the transformative potential of creative thinking and biofield practices in manifesting personal and collective growth.

Furthermore, 'Biofield Alchemy' can help reduce stress and anxiety, which are known inhibitors of creativity. When we are relaxed and free from negative emotions, our minds are more open to new ideas and perspectives. Biofield practices can help individuals enter a state of deep relaxation, fostering an internal environment conducive to creativity.

CASE STUDIES IN ART & INNOVATION

Numerous case studies illustrate the profound impact of biofield practices on creativity across various fields. Here, we explore a few notable examples:

1. THE ARTIST'S TRANSFORMATION

One remarkable case involved a painter struggling with creative block. Despite her technical skills, she found herself unable to produce original work. After engaging in a series of biofield tuning sessions, she reported a dramatic shift. The sessions involved the use of tuning forks to balance her energetic field, particularly focusing on the sacral chakra, which is linked to creativity and emotion. Post-treatment, she experienced a surge of inspiration, producing a series of paintings that she described as her most authentic and expressive work to date.

2. INNOVATION IN TECHNOLOGY

In the technology industry, a team of engineers facing a design deadlock turned to biofield practices to stimulate innovative thinking. They incorporated daily group meditation sessions focused on synchronizing their collective biofields. This practice not only enhanced their individual creativity but also fostered a greater sense of collaboration and idea-sharing. The result was a breakthrough design that won several industry awards.

3. MUSICAL BRILLIANCE

A well-known composer and musician used biofield techniques to overcome performance anxiety and enhance his creative output. By practicing biofield visualization and energy clearing techniques before composing or performing, he was able to tap into a deeper well of inspiration and produce music that resonated more profoundly with his audience.

PRACTICAL EXERCISES

To harness the power of the biofield for your own creative endeavors, consider incorporating the following exercises into your routine:

1. BIOFIELD MEDITATION FOR CREATIVITY:

1. FIND A QUIET SPACE: Sit comfortably and close your eyes.
2. FOCUS ON YOUR BREATH: Take slow, deep breaths, allowing your body to relax.
3. VISUALIZE YOUR BIOFIELD: Imagine a luminous field of energy surrounding your body. See it as vibrant and full of potential.
4. DIRECT ENERGY TO YOUR SACRAL CHAKRA: Located just below your navel, this chakra is the center of creativity. Visualize a warm, orange glow in this area, expanding with each breath.
5. AFFIRM YOUR CREATIVITY: Silently or aloud, repeat affirmations such as, "I am a creative being," or "My creative potential is limitless."

6. END WITH GRATITUDE: Take a moment to feel grateful for the creative energy flowing through you.

2. CHAKRA BALANCING WITH SOUND THERAPY:

1. CHOOSE A SOUND TOOL: This can be a tuning fork, singing bowl, or even a recorded sound frequency that resonates with the sacral chakra (typically around 417 Hz).

2. FIND A COMFORTABLE POSITION: Sit or lie down in a quiet place.

3. PLAY THE SOUND: If using a tuning fork or singing bowl, strike it gently and hold it close to your sacral chakra. If using a recording, play it softly in the background.

4. FOCUS ON THE VIBRATION: Feel the sound waves penetrating your biofield, dissolving any creative blockages and infusing you with vibrant energy.

5. VISUALIZE CREATIVITY: As the sound continues, visualize your creative ideas blossoming and taking shape.

3. BIOFIELD CREATIVE JOURNALING:

1. SET your intention: Before you start, set an intention for your journaling session, such as "I seek creative inspiration" or "I open myself to new ideas."

2. ENTER a relaxed state: Use deep breathing or a short meditation to center yourself.

3. BEGIN free writing: Without overthinking, start writing whatever comes to mind. Let your thoughts flow freely, bypassing any internal censor.

4. FOCUS on sensations: Pay attention to any sensations in your body or shifts in your biofield as you write. Note any areas that feel particularly energized or blocked.

5. REFLECT and integrate: After journaling, read through what you've written and reflect on any patterns or insights. Use these reflections to guide your creative projects.

By integrating these biofield techniques into your creative routine, you can unlock new levels of inspiration and innovation. Whether you are an artist, engineer, musician, or simply someone seeking to enhance your creative potential, the biofield offers a powerful tool for transforming your creative practice.

In conclusion, the connection between the biofield and creativity opens up exciting possibilities for personal and professional growth. By understanding and harnessing the energy within and around us, we can break through creative barriers and achieve new heights of artistic and innovative expression.

PART 3
CHAPTER 2

MANIFESTATION

- THE ALCHEMY OF METAMORPHOSIS

MANIFESTATION: FRUITION OF THE INVISIBLE INNER WORK

LAWS OF ATTRACTION & ENERGY

The concept of manifestation, often associated with the Law of Attraction, is deeply intertwined with the biofield - a complex, dynamic field of energy and information that surrounds and interpenetrates the human body. The biofield, recognized by various cultures and healing traditions, plays a crucial role in the process of manifestation by serving as the conduit through which thoughts, intentions, and emotions influence our physical reality.

The Law of Attraction posits that like attracts like. This principle suggests that our thoughts and emotions, which are energetic vibrations, resonate with similar energies in the universe. Positive thoughts and emotions can attract positive experiences and outcomes, while negative thoughts can attract undesirable circumstances. The biofield is the medium through which these vibrations are transmitted and received, making it a pivotal component in the manifestation process.

The biofield encompasses several layers, including the physical, emotional, mental, and spiritual bodies. Each layer interacts with the others, creating a holistic system that affects and is affected by our intentions and beliefs. When we focus our thoughts and emotions on a particular desire, we are essentially programming our biofield to attract corresponding energies and experiences from the universe.

RESEARCH WORK ON MANIFESTATION

In the realm of 'Biofield Alchemy', manifestation is deeply rooted in scientific insights from visionaries like Gregg Braden, Bruce Lipton, and Dr. Joe Dispenza, who have explored the interplay between thoughts, emotions, and physical reality. Braden emphasizes the heart's electromagnetic field as a key player in manifestation, while Lipton's epigenetic research reveals how beliefs and perceptions shape gene expression. Dr. Dispenza's work on neuroplasticity and mind-body connection further illuminates the role of coherent heart-centered emotions and focused intention in reshaping reality.

Additionally, Dr. David Hawkins, a spiritual teacher and philosopher, has developed a map of consciousness, highlighting the correlation between vibrational frequencies and manifestation. Dr. Rupert Sheldrake, a biologist, has explored the concept of morphic resonance, demonstrating how collective consciousness influences reality. Dr. Nassim Haramein, a physicist, has developed a unified field theory, revealing the interconnectedness of all things and the potential for conscious manifestation. The synthesis of these perspectives offers a scientifically grounded understanding of manifestation in 'Biofield Alchemy', empowering individuals to harness their heart, mind, and intentions to shape their reality.

TECHNIQUES FOR MANIFESTATION

Manifestation techniques leverage the biofield's properties to align our energy with our desires. Here are some simple approaches to harnessing this powerful process:

1. VISUALISATION: Visualization involves creating a vivid mental image of the desired outcome. By consistently focusing on this image, we imprint our biofield with the energy of our goal, thereby attracting it into our reality. To enhance the effectiveness of visualization, incorporate all senses - imagine the sights, sounds, smells, tastes, and feelings associated with your desired outcome. This multisensory approach creates a stronger energetic imprint in the biofield.

2. AFFIRMATION: Affirmations are positive statements that reinforce the belief in our desired outcome. Repeating affirmations daily helps to reprogram the subconscious mind and align the biofield with the energy of success and abundance. Craft personalized affirmations that resonate with your specific goals and repeat them with conviction and emotion.

3. GRATITUDE PRACTICE: Cultivating a sense of gratitude shifts our focus from lack to abundance. By expressing gratitude for what we already have, we raise our vibrational frequency and align our biofield with the energy of receiving more. Maintain a gratitude journal, noting daily the things you are thankful for, and feel genuine appreciation as you do so.

4. MEDITATION: Meditation helps to quiet the mind and tune into the subtle energies of the biofield. Regular meditation practice enhances our ability to focus, reduces stress, and creates a conducive environment for manifestation. Specific meditative practices, such as guided imagery or mantra meditation, can be tailored to reinforce manifestation intentions.

5. ENERGY HEALING: Techniques such as breathwork, meditation, creative visualization, can help to balance and harmonize the biofield, removing blockages that may hinder manifestation. By ensuring the smooth flow of energy, these practices create an optimal energetic state for attracting desired outcomes.

6. VISION BOARDS: Creating a vision board - a collage of images and words that represent your goals - serves as a visual reminder of your intentions. Place the vision board in a prominent location to reinforce your focus and keep your biofield attuned to your desires.

SUCCESS STORIES

The power of manifestation through the biofield is illustrated by numerous real-life success stories, where individuals have transformed their lives by aligning their energy with their desires. Here are a few examples:

1. CAREER TRANSFORMATION: Jhanvi, a marketing executive, felt stuck in her career and desired a more fulfilling role. She began practicing visualization and affirmations, imagining herself in a job that aligned with her passions and values. Within six months, she was offered a position at a company that not only matched her skills but also provided opportunities for growth and creativity. Jhanvi credits her success to her consistent manifestation practices, which reprogrammed her biofield to attract the perfect job.

2. HEALTH RECOVERY: Kartik had been struggling with a chronic illness that conventional treatments couldn't fully address. He decided to incorporate energy healing techniques, such as creative visualization and neuro

linguistic programming into his routine. By focusing on visualizing his body as healthy and vibrant, and practicing gratitude for small improvements, Kartik experienced significant health improvements. His doctors were amazed at his recovery, which Kartik attributes to the positive shifts in his biofield.

3. FINANCIAL ABUNDANCE: Tanya, a single mother, was facing financial difficulties. She started a gratitude journal and created a vision board filled with images representing financial freedom and security. By focusing on these tools daily and maintaining a positive mindset, she gradually began to see opportunities for additional income. Within a year, Tanya had increased her earnings through freelance work and investments, achieving the financial stability she had envisioned.

4. RELATIONSHIP SUCCESS: Pranav desired a loving, supportive relationship but had a history of attracting partners who were not aligned with his values. He began practicing emotional freedom techniques and affirmations focused on self-love and attracting a compatible partner. By clearing old emotional wounds and aligning his biofield with the energy of love and respect, Pranav soon met his current partner, with whom he shares a deep, fulfilling relationship.

CONCLUSION

Manifestation is a profound process that leverages the interplay between our thoughts, emotions, and the biofield. By understanding the laws of attraction and energy, and employing tailored techniques such as visualization, affirmations, gratitude practice, meditation, energy healing, and vision boards, we can effectively align our biofield with our desires. The success stories of individuals who have transformed their careers, health, finances, and relationships through these practices serve as powerful testaments to the potential of manifestation.

As you embark on your own journey of 'Biofield Alchemy', remember that the key to successful manifestation lies in the consistent and intentional alignment of your energy with your goals. By harnessing the power of the biofield, you can create a reality that reflects your deepest desires and highest aspirations.

PART 3
CHAPTER 3

PHYSICAL HEALTH
&
'BIOFIELD ALCHEMY'

ENERGISING THE SACRED
VESSEL OF THE SOUL
- THE HUMAN BODY

ALCHEMY OF HEALING: TURNING WOUNDS INTO WISDOM

PHYSICAL HEALTH & HEALING

In recent years, the concept of the biofield has gained significant attention as a pivotal element in understanding human health and well-being. Biofield, often described as the energy field that surrounds and interpenetrates the human body, is believed to play a crucial role in maintaining physical health. This field, composed of electromagnetic frequencies and subtle energies, interacts dynamically with the physical body, influencing its function and vitality. By exploring the biofield and its impact on physical health, we can unlock new avenues for healing and integrative approaches to wellness.

RESEARCH ON PHYSICAL HEALTH & HEALING

Scientific research increasingly supports the concept that the human biofield-a complex energy field surrounding and permeating the body-can influence physical healing. Dr. Beverly Rubik, a pioneer in biofield science, has shown that the biofield plays a significant role in maintaining health and wellness. Her studies indicate that disturbances in the biofield can precede physical ailments, suggesting that restoring biofield harmony may be essential for healing.

Similarly, Dr. Richard Hammerschlag's research emphasizes the biofield's impact on cellular processes, highlighting its potential in regenerative medicine. Dr. Gary Schwartz's work in energy healing further supports the idea that biofield interactions can influence physical health outcomes.

Additionally, Dr. Konstantin Korotkov has developed methods to visualize the biofield, providing scientific evidence of its existence and changes during healing processes. These scientists collectively contribute to a growing body of evidence that biofield interventions may be a crucial aspect of integrative medicine, offering promising avenues for enhancing health and wellness.

Further research by institutions like the National Institutes of Health (NIH) explores how therapies such as Hypnosis, Silva method, Reiki, EFT, Therapeutic Touch, Yoga, Pranayama and Qigong interact with the biofield to promote healing. These therapies involve the practitioner manipulating or channeling energy to the patient, facilitating a state of balance that is conducive to physical recovery.

Recent studies using advanced imaging technologies, such as bio-photon emission and thermography, have provided visual evidence of biofield interactions during healing practices. The measurable changes in the biofield correlate with improvements in physical health, suggesting a direct link between biofield interventions and the healing process.

This growing body of scientific evidence underscores the potential of 'Biofield Alchemy' as a powerful tool for physical healing, reinforcing the importance of energy-based practices in modern holistic medicine.

ENERGY HEALING FOR SPECIFIC AILMENTS

Energy healing, an ancient practice rooted in various cultural traditions, leverages the biofield to address specific physical ailments. Practitioners of energy healing modalities - work by channeling or manipulating the biofield to promote healing and restore balance. These practices aim to remove blockages, harmonize energy flow, and stimulate the body's innate healing mechanisms.

For instance, in the case of chronic pain, energy healing techniques can help alleviate discomfort by targeting disruptions in the biofield that contribute to the persistence of pain. By applying gentle touch or non-contact methods, practitioners can facilitate the release of stagnant energy, thereby reducing inflammation and promoting relaxation. This approach not only addresses the physical symptoms but also fosters a sense of emotional and mental well-being, which is crucial for holistic healing.

Energy healing has also shown promise in managing conditions such as migraines, arthritis, and fibromyalgia. In migraines, where neurological and vascular factors interplay, energy healing can help in modulating the biofield to reduce the frequency and intensity of headaches. Similarly, for arthritis, where inflammation and joint degeneration are key issues, energy healing can assist in reducing pain and improving joint mobility. By working with the biofield, practitioners can tailor their interventions to meet the specific needs of individuals, providing customized care that addresses the root causes of ailments.

INTEGRATIVE APPROACHES

Integrative approaches to health and wellness recognize the importance of combining conventional medical treatments with complementary therapies that address the biofield. This holistic perspective acknowledges that physical health is influenced by a complex interplay of factors, including energy dynamics, mental state, and environmental influences. By integrating biofield therapies with conventional medicine, healthcare providers can offer more comprehensive and personalized care.

For example, in cancer care, integrative approaches often include energy healing modalities alongside chemotherapy, radiation, and surgery. These complementary therapies can help manage side effects, reduce stress, and enhance the overall quality of life for patients. Studies have shown that practices like Remote Healing, Reiki, Silva Method, Therapeutic Touch can alleviate pain, reduce anxiety, and improve sleep, which are critical components of the healing process. By addressing the biofield, these therapies support the body's resilience and capacity to recover, making them valuable additions to conventional cancer treatment protocols.

Similarly, integrative approaches are beneficial in managing cardiovascular diseases. Stress, a significant risk factor for heart disease, can be effectively mitigated through biofield therapies. Practices like HeartMath, which focuses on heart rate variability and coherence, leverage the biofield to promote emotional balance and physiological harmony. By incorporating these techniques into standard cardiovascular care, patients can achieve better outcomes and improved heart health.

Integrative medicine also emphasizes the importance of lifestyle modifications, such as diet, exercise, and mindfulness, in conjunction with biofield therapies. For instance, yoga and meditation, which are known to influence the biofield, can enhance physical health by reducing stress, improving flexibility, and boosting immune function. By adopting a multifaceted approach that includes biofield practices, individuals can achieve optimal health and well-being.

CASE STUDIES

To illustrate the impact of biofield therapies on physical health, we can explore several case studies that highlight the effectiveness of these approaches.

CASE STUDY 1:

CHRONIC PAIN MANAGEMENT

Babita, a 45-year-old woman suffering from chronic lower back pain, sought relief through conventional treatments, including pain medication and physical therapy, with limited success. She decided to try 'Reiki' sessions to complement her existing treatments. After a series of Reiki sessions, Babita reported a significant reduction in pain intensity and frequency. She also experienced improved sleep and a greater sense of relaxation. This case demonstrates how energy healing can address chronic pain by modulating the biofield, providing a non-invasive and effective adjunct to conventional therapies.

CASE STUDY 2:

CANCER SUPPORT

John, a 60-year-old man diagnosed with prostate cancer, was undergoing chemotherapy and radiation therapy. To manage the side effects and enhance his overall well-being, John incorporated Silva Method techniques into his treatment regimen. Over time, he noticed a reduction in nausea and fatigue, as well as an improvement in his emotional state. The energy healing techniques helped John cope better with the rigors of cancer treatment, highlighting the role of the biofield in supporting holistic healing and improving quality of life.

CASE STUDY 3:

CARDIOVASCULAR HEALTH

Alisa, a 50-year-old woman with a history of hypertension and stress-related heart palpitations, integrated HeartMath techniques into her daily routine. By practicing heart coherence exercises and biofeedback, Alisa was able to regulate her heart rate variability and reduce stress levels. Her blood pressure gradually stabilized, and she felt more emotionally balanced. This case underscores the effectiveness of biofield-based practices in managing cardiovascular health by addressing the underlying energetic and emotional factors.

CASE STUDY 4:

MIGRAINE RELIEF

Dhruv, a 35-year-old man suffering from debilitating migraines, found limited relief from conventional medications. He turned to Qigong, an ancient Chinese practice that balances the biofield through movement and breathwork. After several months of regular practice, Dhruv experienced a significant reduction in the frequency and severity of his migraines. The rhythmic movements and focused breathing helped harmonize his biofield, providing a natural and sustainable solution for migraine management.

CONCLUSION

The exploration of the biofield and its impact on physical health opens new possibilities for healing and wellness. Energy healing practices offer customized and tailored approaches to address specific ailments, complementing conventional medical treatments and enhancing overall health. Integrative approaches that incorporate biofield therapies recognize the interconnectedness of the body, mind, and energy, providing a holistic framework for optimal well-being. Through case studies and practical applications, it is evident that the biofield plays a crucial role in physical health, offering promising avenues for personalized and effective care. By embracing the wisdom of 'Biofield Alchemy', we can unlock the full potential of human health and vitality.

PART 3
CHAPTER 4

WEALTH MANIFESTATION & BIOFIELD ALCHEMY

BIOFIELD: THE ULTIMATE WEALTH MAP - TURNING LEAD INTO GOLD

WEALTH MANIFESTATION: AN ALCHEMICAL POSSIBILTY

'BIOFIELD ALCHEMY':

HARNESSING LIFE ENERGY FOR ABUNDANCE

As discussed in previous chapters, 'Biofield Alchemy' is a relatively new and evolving field, delves into the manipulation and optimization of the human biofield - a complex, dynamic system of energy that surrounds and permeates the body. This biofield, also known as the human energy field or aura interact with our physical, emotional, and mental states, influencing our overall well-being. 'Biofield Alchemist' focuses on using various techniques to balance and enhance this energy field, promoting healing, personal growth, and overall harmony.

RESEARCH WORK ON WEALTH MANIFESTATION

Scientific research on wealth manifestation through 'Biofield Alchemy' has gained traction, with notable contributions from Dr. William A. Tiller, a physicist and former Stanford professor. Tiller's work on the role of human consciousness in altering physical reality is foundational in understanding how biofields can influence material outcomes, including wealth. In his studies, Tiller proposed that human intention, when focused through a coherent biofield, can affect the quantum vacuum, leading to measurable changes in physical systems.

Complementing Tiller's work, Dr. Bruce Lipton, a cell biologist, has explored how beliefs and perceptions influence our biology and external reality. Dr. Konstantin

Korotkov, a physicist, has used bio electrography to visualize how energy fields change with intention. Dr. Dean Radin, a parapsychologist, has examined the role of consciousness in quantum mechanics and its implications for reality shaping. Additionally, Dr. Beverly Rubik, a biophysicist, has conducted extensive research on the human biofield and its impact on health and well-being.

Tiller's experiments, particularly those involving intention-imprinted electronic devices, demonstrated that focused human intention could alter the pH of water, paralleling how 'Biofield Alchemy' might influence wealth manifestation. This approach suggests that wealth manifestation is a process deeply rooted in the interaction between consciousness and the quantum field, offering a scientific basis for ancient practices associated with prosperity.

WEALTH MANIFESTATION THROUGH 'BIOFIELD ALCHEMY'

Wealth manifestation involves attracting abundance and prosperity into one's life through intentional focus and alignment with the universal laws of attraction and energy. By integrating 'Biofield Alchemy' with wealth manifestation practices, individuals can potentially enhance their ability to attract and maintain wealth. This process involves several key principles:

1. ENERGY ALIGNMENT: The first step in using 'Biofield Alchemy' for wealth manifestation is ensuring that your biofield is in harmony with your financial goals. This can be achieved through practices like Neuro Linguistic Programming, meditation, energy healing, visualization and

many other energy healing techniques. By aligning your energy with your intentions, you create a resonance that attracts similar vibrations from the universe.

2. CLEARING BLOCKAGES: Negative beliefs and emotional blockages can hinder the flow of energy in your biofield, preventing you from manifesting wealth. Techniques such as Emotional Freedom Technique, Silva Method, Martial Arts, Pranayama, and Sound Work can help identify and clear these blockages, allowing the energy to flow freely and support your wealth goals.

3. RAISING VIBRATIONS: High-frequency vibrations are associated with positive outcomes, including wealth. Engaging in activities that raise your vibrational frequency - such as practicing gratitude, spending time in nature, and surrounding yourself with positive influences - can amplify your ability to attract wealth.

4. INTENTIONAL FOCUS: Concentrated focus on wealth goals, combined with a clear intention, can significantly impact your biofield. Creating vision boards, affirmations, and setting specific financial goals are practical ways to maintain this focus and align your biofield with your desired outcomes.

WEALTH MINDSET IN 'BIOFIELD ALCHEMY'

A wealth mindset is a crucial component of successful wealth manifestation. It involves adopting beliefs and attitudes that support financial success and abundance. In the context of 'Biofield Alchemy', developing a wealth mindset can be seen as a process of reprogramming the biofield to resonate with abundance. Here are some strategies to cultivate a wealth mindset through 'Biofield Alchemy':

1. BELIEF SYSTEM: Your beliefs about money and abundance significantly influence your biofield. Positive, empowering beliefs can enhance your energy field, while negative, limiting beliefs can create blockages. Practices like affirmations, hypnosis, and cognitive restructuring can help transform limiting beliefs into ones that support wealth.

2. EMOTIONAL RESONANCE: Emotions play a crucial role in shaping your biofield. Cultivating emotions that resonate with abundance - such as joy, gratitude, and confidence - can strengthen your biofield and align it with wealth. Mindfulness Practices, Emotional Freedom Techniques (EFT), and Heart-Centered meditation can help foster these positive emotions.

3. VISUALIZATION & IMAGINATION: The power of visualization in shaping the biofield is profound. Regularly visualizing yourself achieving your wealth goals can create a strong energetic blueprint in your biofield. This blueprint acts as a magnet, drawing opportunities and resources that align with your vision. Incorporating detailed and emotionally charged visualizations into your daily routine can amplify this effect.

4. ENVIRONMENTAL INFLUENCE: Your surroundings can impact your biofield and, consequently, your wealth mindset. Creating an environment that supports your financial goals - such as an organized workspace, inspirational decor, and a supportive social network - can

enhance your biofield's resonance with abundance. Vaastu, Feng Shui and other energy healing practices can optimize your physical space to support wealth manifestation.

PRACTICAL APPLICATIONS FOR WEALTH MANIFESTATION

Integrating 'Biofield Alchemy' into your daily life can take many forms, each tailored to your personal preferences and lifestyle. Here are some practical applications:

1. DAILY ENERGY PRACTICES: Start your day with energy-balancing practices such as Qigong, Yoga, or Tai Chi. These practices not only harmonize your biofield but also set a positive tone for the day, aligning your energy with your wealth goals.

2. MEDITATION & MINDFULNESS: Regular meditation sessions focused on abundance can help clear mental clutter and align your biofield with wealth. Guided meditations, especially those focused on financial success, can be particularly effective.

3. AFFIRMATIONS & MANTRAS: Incorporating affirmations and mantras into your daily routine can reinforce a wealth mindset and positively influence your biofield. Repeating statements like "I am a magnet for abundance" or "Wealth flows to me effortlessly" can help reprogram your energy field.

4. ENERGY HEALING SESSIONS: Periodic sessions with a trained energy healer can help maintain the balance and harmony of your biofield. Techniques like Reiki, acupuncture, and biofield tuning can clear blockages and enhance your energy flow, supporting your wealth manifestation efforts.

5. GRATITUDE PRACTICE: Regularly expressing gratitude for what you already have can raise your vibrational frequency and strengthen your biofield. Keeping a gratitude journal and reflecting on the abundance in your life can help maintain a positive and wealthy mindset.

CONCLUSION

'Biofield Alchemy' offers a unique and powerful approach to wealth manifestation and developing a wealth mindset. By understanding and optimizing your biofield, you can align your energy with your financial goals, clear blockages, and raise your vibrations to attract abundance. Incorporating practices such as meditation, energy healing, and positive affirmations into your daily routine can significantly enhance your ability to manifest wealth. With consistent effort and a deep understanding of your biofield, you can transform your relationship with money and create a life of prosperity and abundance.

PART 3
CHAPTER 5

RELATIONSHIPS
&
BIOFIELD ALCHEMY

ALCHEMICAL RELATIONSHIPS: BREWING THE ELIXIR OF 'PRESENCE'

RELATIONSHIPS: THE ALCHEMY OF HEALING THE FEELINGS

UNDERSTANDING ENERGETIC DYNAMICS IN RELATIONSHIPS

Relationships, whether romantic, familial, or social, are complex networks of interactions and emotions. At the heart of these connections lies an intricate dance of energetic exchanges, often referred to as the biofield. The biofield, an electromagnetic field generated by the body's natural energy, plays a crucial role in how we connect, communicate, and resonate with others.

Every individual possesses a unique biofield that interacts with those around them. This energetic interplay can either create harmony or discord within relationships. Understanding these dynamics is key to fostering healthy and fulfilling connections. When two people interact, their biofields engage in a subtle exchange of energy, emotions, and information. This exchange can significantly influence the quality of their relationship, impacting how they perceive and respond to each other.

In a harmonious relationship, the biofields of the individuals involved resonate at compatible frequencies, leading to a sense of mutual understanding, empathy, and support. Conversely, when biofields are misaligned, it can result in misunderstandings, conflicts, and emotional distance. Recognizing and tuning into these energetic dynamics allows us to address and resolve underlying issues that may not be immediately apparent on a conscious level.

RESEARCH WORK ON RELATIONSHIP DYNAMICS

Attracting loving relationships through 'Biofield Alchemy' involves understanding the subtle energy fields that influence our connections with others. The scientific foundation for this concept can be traced to the work of Dr. Bruce Lipton, a biologist known for his research on the power of belief and the influence of thoughts on our biology. Lipton's studies suggest that our thoughts and emotions can alter our biofield, thereby attracting or repelling relationships.

In addition to Lipton, Dr. Joe Dispenza, has also extensively researched how meditation and focused intention can reprogram our brain and energy fields. His findings suggest that by aligning our biofield with the frequency of love and compassion, we can draw more harmonious relationships into our lives.

The principle of "like attracts like," supported by quantum physics, further underscores this idea. Our biofield, shaped by our thoughts, beliefs, and emotions, acts as a magnet, attracting relationships that resonate with our energy.

'Biofield Alchemy', therefore, involves consciously cultivating a loving, compassionate biofield to attract relationships that reflect those qualities. By engaging in practices that enhance the positive energy of our biofield, we can draw in relationships that are nurturing, fulfilling, and deeply connected.

Attracting loving relationships through 'Biofield Alchemy' can be enriched by insights from renowned relationship experts. Dr. John Gray, author of 'Men Are from Mars, Women Are from Venus', emphasizes the importance of understanding and respecting the differences between genders to foster deeper connections. This understanding aligns with 'Biofield Alchemy' by recognizing the energetic balance required in relationships.

Dr. Gary Chapman, known for 'The 5 Love Languages' highlights the significance of understanding and expressing love in ways that resonate with our partners. In the context of 'Biofield Alchemy', this understanding can help harmonize the energy fields between individuals, ensuring that love is not only expressed but also deeply felt.

Esther Perel, a leading psychotherapist and author of 'Mating in Captivity' explores the complexities of desire and intimacy in long-term relationships. Her work underscores the importance of maintaining a dynamic and evolving connection, which 'Biofield Alchemist' can enhance by keeping the energy within the relationship vibrant and aligned.

By integrating the wisdom of these authors, 'Biofield Alchemy' offers a path to attracting and sustaining loving relationships. By consciously cultivating an energetic field of understanding, respect, and deep connection, individuals can draw in relationships that are both harmonious and fulfilling.

HEALING RELATIONSHIP PATTERNS

Many of us carry deep-seated patterns from past relationships that can influence our current interactions. These patterns, often rooted in childhood experiences or previous emotional traumas, become ingrained in our biofield and can manifest as recurring issues in our relationships. Healing these patterns requires a conscious effort to identify, understand, and transform the underlying energetic imbalances.

One effective approach to healing relationship patterns is through self-awareness and introspection. By examining our past experiences and the emotions attached to them, we can uncover the energetic imprints that shape our current behaviors and reactions. This process involves acknowledging and releasing any unresolved emotions, such as fear, anger, or sadness, that may be stored within our biofield.

Additionally, energy healing techniques, such as Hypnosis, EFT, Holographic Healing, Reiki, Acupressure, Silva Method, and Chakra Balancing accompanied with breathwork and sound work, can be instrumental in clearing and rebalancing the biofield. These practices help to remove energetic blockages and restore the natural flow of energy within the body, promoting emotional healing and overall well-being. By addressing the energetic root causes of our relationship patterns, we can break free from old habits and create healthier, more fulfilling connections.

Another important aspect of healing relationship patterns is cultivating self-love and compassion. Often, our relationships reflect how we feel about ourselves. By nurturing a positive and loving relationship with ourself, we can transform the energy we bring into our interactions with others. This shift in self-perception can lead to more harmonious and authentic connections, as we are no longer seeking validation or approval from external sources.

TECHNIQUES FOR HARMONIOUS RELATIONSHIPS

Creating and maintaining harmonious relationships requires a conscious effort to align our biofield with positive and nurturing energies. Several techniques can help us achieve this alignment, fostering deeper connections and greater harmony in our interactions.

1. MINDFULNESS & MEDITATION

Practicing mindfulness and meditation can help us become more attuned to our own biofield and the energies of those around us. By cultivating a state of present-moment awareness, we can better understand and manage our emotions, thoughts, and reactions. Meditation can help to calm the mind and balance the biofield, promoting inner peace and emotional stability. Regular mindfulness practices can enhance our ability to respond to others with empathy and compassion, rather than reacting out of habit or impulse.

2. ENERGY CLEARING & PROTECTION

In our daily interactions, we are constantly exposed to various energies, some of which may be negative or draining. To maintain a harmonious biofield, it is essential to regularly clear and protect our energy. Techniques such as smudging with herbs, using specific crystals, or practicing visualizations can help to cleanse our biofield of unwanted energies and create a protective barrier. By keeping our energy field clear and balanced, we can interact with others from a place of strength and positivity.

3. HEART - CENTERED COMMUNICATION

Effective communication is fundamental to any healthy relationship. Heart-centered communication involves speaking and listening from a place of love, empathy, and understanding. This technique encourages us to connect with others on a deeper, more authentic level, fostering trust and mutual respect. To practice heart-centered communication, focus on expressing your thoughts and feelings honestly and openly, while also being fully present and attentive to the other person. By engaging in this form of communication, we can create a more harmonious energetic exchange and strengthen our relationships.

4. PRACTICING GRATITUDE & APPRECIATION

Gratitude and appreciation are powerful tools for raising our vibrational frequency and enhancing the quality of our relationships. By regularly acknowledging and expressing gratitude for the positive aspects of our relationships, we can shift our focus from what is lacking to what is abundant and fulfilling. This shift in perspective can help to attract more positive energy into our interactions and create a more harmonious and supportive environment. Simple practices, such as keeping a gratitude journal or expressing appreciation to your loved ones, can have a profound impact on the energetic dynamics of your relationships.

5. EMOTIONAL INTELLIGENCE

Developing emotional intelligence is crucial for understanding and navigating the energetic dynamics of relationships. Emotional intelligence involves the ability to recognize, understand, and manage our own emotions, as well as the emotions of others. By enhancing our emotional intelligence, we can better empathize with others, resolve conflicts, and create more harmonious interactions. Techniques such as active listening, self-reflection, and emotional regulation can help to cultivate emotional intelligence and improve the quality of our relationships.

6. ENERGY ALIGNMENT PRACTICES

Certain practices can help to align our biofield with positive and harmonious energies, promoting balance and well-being in our relationships. Yoga, tai chi, and martial arts are examples of energy alignment practices that combine physical movement, breathwork, and meditation to harmonize the body's energy flow. These practices can help to reduce stress, increase vitality, and enhance our ability to connect with others on an energetic level. By incorporating energy alignment practices into our daily routine, we can maintain a balanced and vibrant biofield, which positively influences our relationships.

7. SETTING HEALTHY BOUNDARIES

Establishing and maintaining healthy boundaries is essential for protecting our biofield and ensuring harmonious interactions. Boundaries help to define our personal space and energy, allowing us to interact with others in a way that is respectful and mutually beneficial. By clearly communicating our needs and limits, we can prevent energetic imbalances and avoid feelings of resentment or depletion. Setting healthy boundaries involves recognizing and honoring our own energy, as well as respecting the energy of others.

In conclusion, understanding and working with the energetic dynamics of the biofield can profoundly enhance the quality of our relationships. By healing relationship patterns, practicing techniques for harmonious interactions, and cultivating a deeper awareness of our own energy, we can create more balanced, fulfilling, and authentic connections with those around us. Embracing the principles of 'Biofield Alchemy' empowers us to transform our relationships and live in greater harmony with ourselves and others.

PART 3
CHAPTER 6

TRAUMA

TRAUMA HEALING -TURNING COALS INTO DIAMONDS

TRAUMA:
THE INNER TREASURE POINT

Healing trauma through biofield practices represents a profound convergence of ancient wisdom and contemporary science, offering individuals a holistic path to recovery and personal transformation. This chapter explores the nuanced understanding of trauma, innovative techniques for release and healing, and ways to support others in their healing journey, all through the lens of 'Biofield Alchemy'.

1. RESEARCH WORK ON TRAUMA HEALING

Scientific research on trauma healing via 'Biofield Alchemy' is gaining attention, with several prominent scientists contributing to the field. The biofield, an energetic matrix surrounding the body, plays a vital role in maintaining physical, emotional, and psychological well-being. Trauma disrupts this biofield, leading to chronic stress and other health issues. Biofield therapies, such as Hypnosis, Therapeutic Touch, and Silva Method, EFT and other energy healing modalities, have shown promise in trauma healing by restoring energetic balance.

Dr. Bessel van der Kolk has made significant contributions by demonstrating how trauma is stored in the body and how body-oriented interventions can promote deep healing and recovery. Additionally, Dr. Peter A. Levine's work on Somatic Experiencing supports the idea that addressing trauma through body awareness can release stored tension and trauma, offering new pathways for healing. Dr. Stephen Porges' Polyvagal Theory further validates the importance of the autonomic nervous system in trauma healing by documenting how regulating the nervous system can lead to profound changes in emotional and physiological responses.

These scientists provide a strong foundation for understanding how 'Biofield Alchemy' - an advanced form of energy medicine - can address the energetic imprints of trauma. By aligning the energetic and physical bodies, 'Biofield Alchemy' offers a scientifically supported approach to healing trauma at its core, promising profound transformation and recovery. As research in this area grows, 'Biofield Alchemy' continues to emerge as a powerful tool in holistic trauma therapy.

2. UNDERSTANDING ENERGETIC IMPRINTS OF TRAUMA

Trauma leaves more than just psychological scars; it imprints itself deeply into the energetic matrix of the individual. This concept, central to biofield healing, posits that every traumatic experience disrupts the harmonious flow of energy within the body's biofield. These energetic imprints can manifest as blockages, stagnation, or distortions within the field, leading to physical, emotional, and spiritual discomfort.

The biofield, an intricate network of electromagnetic energy surrounding and permeating the body, holds the key to understanding how trauma affects us at a fundamental level. According to biofield theory, every thought, emotion, and experience generates a unique vibrational signature. Traumatic experiences, particularly those involving intense fear, pain, or helplessness, create deep and persistent disruptions in this vibrational field.

For example, a person who has experienced a car accident might have an energetic imprint that continuously activates the fight-or-flight response, even in the absence of immediate danger. This ongoing stress response can lead to chronic anxiety, hypervigilance, and other symptoms commonly associated with post-traumatic stress disorder (PTSD). Understanding these energetic imprints is crucial for effective healing, as it allows practitioners to identify and address the root causes of trauma, rather than just alleviating its symptoms.

3. TECHNIQUES FOR ENERGY RELEASE & HEALING

Biofield practices encompass a variety of techniques designed to release these energetic imprints and restore balance and harmony to the individual's energy field. These methods are unique, customized, and tailored to meet the specific needs of each person, ensuring a holistic approach to healing trauma.

a) ENERGY HEALING MODALITIES

Practices such as Hypnosis, EFT, Silva Method, Healing Touch, and Therapeutic Touch and many other energy healing modalities involve channeling healing energy into the biofield to dissolve blockages and restore energetic flow. These modalities often employ gentle, hands-on techniques or even no-touch methods, where the practitioner works within the client's biofield to facilitate healing.

b) SOUND HEALING

Sound healing uses vibrational frequencies from instruments like tuning forks, singing bowls, gongs and even certain mantras and affirmations to resonate with and release energetic blockages. Each instrument emits specific frequencies that correspond to different aspects of the biofield, allowing for precise targeting of traumatic imprints.

For instance, a practitioner might use a tuning fork with a frequency that matches the vibrational disruption caused by a particular traumatic event. When applied to the affected area of the biofield, the tuning fork's resonance helps to dislodge and dissipate the stagnant energy, promoting a return to equilibrium.

c) BIOFIELD TUNING

Biofield tuning utilizes the biofield's natural resonances to identify and correct distortions. By scanning the biofield with tuning forks, practitioners can locate areas of dissonance that correspond to trauma. The application of specific frequencies helps to harmonize these dissonant areas, facilitating the release of trapped emotional energy.

d) EMOTIONAL FREEDOM TECHNIQUE (EFT)

EFT, or tapping, combines acupressure and psychological strategies to address trauma. By tapping on specific meridian points while focusing on traumatic memories or emotions, individuals can release the energetic charge associated with these experiences. This technique integrates principles from Traditional Chinese Medicine with modern psychological practices to provide a powerful tool for trauma healing.

e) MEDITATION & VISUALISATION

Guided meditations and visualizations can help individuals access and release stored trauma within the biofield. Techniques such as inner child healing and trauma-focused mindfulness encourage a deep connection with the body's energy, allowing for the gentle release of traumatic imprints.

For example, a guided meditation might lead an individual to visualize the traumatic event as a dark cloud within their biofield. Through focused intention and visualization, the person can gradually dissolve this cloud, replacing it with light and positive energy.

4. SUPPORTING OTHERS IN THEIR HEALING JOURNEY

Supporting others in their healing journey requires a compassionate, patient, and knowledgeable approach. Practitioners and loved ones can play a crucial role in facilitating healing by creating a safe and supportive environment for individuals to explore and release their trauma.

a) ACTIVE LISTENING & EMPATHY

Active listening and empathy are foundational to supporting someone through their healing journey. Providing a non-judgmental and compassionate presence allows individuals to express their experiences and emotions freely, fostering trust and safety.

b) EDUCATION & EMPOWERMENT

Educating individuals about the nature of trauma and the biofield can empower them to take an active role in their healing. Understanding how trauma affects their energy field and learning self-healing techniques can provide individuals with valuable tools for ongoing recovery.

c) CREATING A SAFE SPACE

Creating a physically and emotionally safe space is essential for trauma healing. This involves not only ensuring a calm and secure environment but also establishing clear boundaries and trust. Practitioners should be mindful of the individual's comfort levels and readiness to engage in healing practices.

d) TAILORED HEALING PLANS

Each person's experience of trauma is unique, necessitating customized and tailored healing plans. Practitioners should consider the individual's specific needs, preferences, and history when designing a healing regimen. This personalized approach ensures that the healing process is both effective and respectful of the individual's journey.

e) ENCOURAGING SELF - CARE & MINDFULNESS

Encouraging self-care practices and mindfulness can support long-term healing. Activities such as journaling, yoga, and regular meditation can help individuals maintain a balanced biofield and continue their healing outside of formal sessions.

CONCLUSION

Healing trauma with biofield practices offers a comprehensive and compassionate approach to personal transformation and growth. By understanding the energetic imprints of trauma, employing tailored techniques for release and healing, and supporting others with empathy and knowledge, we can foster profound recovery and resilience. 'Biofield Alchemy' empowers individuals to reclaim their well-being, transform their lives, and embark on a journey of holistic healing and personal growth.

PART 3
CHAPTER 7

HEALING SELF
&
OTHERS

THE GOLD OF COMPASSION
&
THE ALCHEMY
OF
ENERGY EXCHANGE

HEALING: THE ALCHEMY OF SHARING LIFE ENERGY

HEALING SELF & OTHERS

In the realm of holistic health, 'Biofield Alchemy' stands as a unique practice that merges ancient wisdom with modern understanding to facilitate healing. This energy-based modality focuses on the human biofield - an electromagnetic field that surrounds and permeates the body. Practitioners of 'Biofield Alchemy' believe that by manipulating this field, they can promote physical, emotional, and spiritual well-being. This chapter delves into the nuances of healing others through 'Biofield Alchemy', emphasizing the importance of preparation, session protocols, and ethical considerations.

RESEARCH WORK ON HEALING OTHERS

'Biofield Alchemy', rooted in ancient healing practices, is increasingly supported by scientific research that explores the human biofield - a complex, dynamic energy field surrounding and permeating the body. Prominent scientists like Dr. Herbert Benson, Dr. Fritz-Albert Popp, Dr. Dean Ornish, Dr. Candace Pert, and Dr. Larry Dossey have significantly contributed to understanding the biofield's role in health and healing, providing a scientific foundation for 'Biofield Alchemy'.

Dr. Herbert Benson is a pioneer in mind-body medicine, best known for his research on the relaxation response, demonstrating the impact of meditation and stress reduction techniques on physical and mental health. Dr. Fritz-Albert

Popp's research on biophoton emissions - light particles emitted by living cells - has shown that these emissions are closely linked to the biofield, suggesting a mechanism by which energy healing might occur. Dr. Dean Ornish has conducted groundbreaking research on lifestyle changes, such as diet, exercise, and stress management, showing their effects on reversing heart disease and other chronic conditions, which is integral to understanding the holistic approach in 'Biofield Alchemy'.

Dr. Candace Pert, a neuroscientist and pharmacologist, is recognized for her discovery of the opiate receptor and her research on the biochemical basis of emotions. Her work has had a profound impact on understanding the mind-body connection and its implications for 'Biofield Alchemist'. Dr. Larry Dossey has explored the role of consciousness in healing, particularly through his research on the effects of prayer and intention on health outcomes, aligning closely with the principles of 'Biofield Alchemy'.

Together, these scientists have laid the groundwork for understanding 'Biofield Alchemy' as a scientifically supported approach to healing, demonstrating how conscious intention, lifestyle modifications, and energy manipulation can restore balance and promote well-being.

PRE & POST PREPARATIONS TO WORK WITH CLIENTS

Before engaging in healing sessions, thorough preparation is crucial. This phase involves both personal readiness and client-specific preparations to ensure that each session is tailored to the individual's needs.

1. PERSONAL READINESS

A 'Biofield Alchemist' must be in optimal condition to work effectively with clients. This involves maintaining a high level of personal energy hygiene through regular self-care practices such as meditation, grounding exercises, and energy clearing rituals. Ensuring one's own biofield is balanced and vibrant sets a positive example for clients and enhances the practitioner's ability to channel healing energies.

2. CLIENT ASSESSMENT

Understanding the client's unique biofield configuration is the cornerstone of customized healing. Initial consultations typically include a comprehensive intake process where the practitioner gathers information about the client's physical health, emotional state, lifestyle, and spiritual beliefs. This holistic assessment helps in identifying any imbalances or blockages within the biofield.

3. SETTING INTENTIONS

Setting clear, mutual intentions for the healing session is a collaborative process. Both practitioner and client should agree on the goals and desired outcomes of the session. This shared intention acts as a guiding force throughout the healing process, ensuring that both parties are aligned and focused.

4. SESSION PROTOCOLS

'Biofield Alchemy' sessions are structured yet flexible, allowing for customization based on the client's needs and responses during the session. Here's a general protocol followed by a 'Biofield Alchemist':

A) CREATING A SACRED SPACE

The healing environment should be serene and conducive to relaxation and energy flow. Practitioners often prepare the space by smudging with herbs, essential oils and sound work. The use of soft lighting, calming music, and comfortable furnishings further enhances the ambiance.

B) INITIAL CONNECTION

At the beginning of each session, the practitioner and client engage in a brief meditation or breathing exercise to establish a strong energetic connection. This helps to synchronize their biofields, creating a harmonious starting point for the healing work.

C) SCANNING THE BIOFIELD

Using their hands, pendulums, or other energetic tools, practitioners scan the client's biofield to detect any areas of disturbance or imbalance. This initial scan informs the approach, and techniques used in the session.

D) ENERGY CLEARING & BALANCING

The core of the session involves various techniques to clear, balance, and enhances the biofield. These may include:

a) CHAKRA BALANCING: Focusing on the seven major chakras, the practitioner uses energy techniques to ensure these centers are open and balanced.

b) MERIDIAN TUNING: Working with the body's energy meridians to facilitate the smooth flow of chi or life force energy.

c) AURIC REPAIR: Addressing tears or weak spots in the auric field to protect against negative influences and enhance overall energy integrity.

E) CUSTOMIZED TECHNIQUES

Each session is unique, tailored to the client's current state and specific needs. Practitioners may incorporate sound healing, crystal therapy, specific energy healing and other healing modalities as needed. The practitioner's intuitive guidance plays a significant role in determining the best approach for each client.

F) CLOSING THE SESSION

The session concludes with grounding exercises to help the client integrate the healing work. This may involve guided visualization, breathwork, or gentle physical movements. The practitioner also offers feedback on the session, discussing any significant findings and suggesting follow-up practices for the client to maintain their biofield health.

5. ETHICAL CONSIDERATIONS

Ethics in 'Biofield Alchemy' are paramount, ensuring that the practice remains respectful, safe, and beneficial for all clients. Ethical considerations span several key areas:

A) INFORMED CONSENT

Clients must be fully informed about what 'Biofield Alchemy' entails, including the techniques used and the potential benefits and risks. Practitioners should obtain explicit consent before beginning any session, ensuring that clients feel comfortable and empowered throughout the process.

B) CONFIDENTIALITY

Respecting client confidentiality is a fundamental ethical obligation. All personal information and session details should be kept private unless the client provides explicit permission to share them.

C) PROFESSIONAL BOUNDARIES

Maintaining clear professional boundaries is essential. Practitioners should avoid dual relationships with clients that could impair professional judgment or exploit the client's trust. This includes being mindful of physical boundaries during sessions and ensuring that any touch is appropriate and consensual.

D) NON - JUDGEMENTAL ATTITUDE

Practitioners must approach each client with an open mind and a non-judgmental attitude. Respect for the client's beliefs, experiences, and choices is crucial for fostering a safe and supportive healing environment.

E) CONTINUAL PROFESSIONAL DEVELOPMENT

'Biofield Alchemist' should commit to ongoing learning and professional development. This includes staying updated with the latest research, attending workshops, and engaging in peer supervision. Continuous improvement ensures that practitioners provide the highest quality of care.

F) CULTURAL SENSITIVITY

Practitioners must be aware of and sensitive to cultural differences that may influence a client's experience and perception of healing. This includes being respectful of different spiritual beliefs, practices, and values.

G) TRANSPARENCY & HONESTY

Practitioners should always communicate transparently and honestly with clients. This includes being clear about what they can and cannot offer, managing expectations realistically, and being truthful about their qualifications and experience.

CONCLUSION

'Biofield Alchemy' is a powerful modality for healing others, grounded in the principles of energy medicine and holistic wellness. By preparing thoroughly, adhering to structured yet flexible session protocols, and upholding the highest ethical standards, practitioners can provide deeply customized and effective healing experiences. This approach not only promotes physical health but also nurtures emotional and spiritual well-being, empowering clients to lead balanced and fulfilling lives. As the practice of 'Biofield Alchemy' continues to evolve, its potential to transform lives through personalized and ethical care becomes ever more apparent.

PART 3
CHAPTER 8

SPIRITUAL AWAKENING

'BIOFIELD ALCHEMY'
&
ACTIVATING
THE
PHILOSOPHER'S STONE

SPIRITUAL AWAKENING: REALITY CHECK FOR THE 'ALCHEMIST'

BIOFIELD ALCHEMY & SPIRITUAL GROWTH

In the realm of holistic healing and spiritual development, the concept of the biofield stands as a beacon of transformative power. As discussed in previous chapters, the biofield, which is referred to as the human energy field, encompasses the subtle energies that surround and permeate the human body. It is believed to be intricately connected to our physical, emotional, and spiritual well-being. As we delve into the depths of 'Biofield Alchemy', we uncover the profound relationship between the biofield and spiritual awakening, a process that leads to an elevated state of consciousness and a deeper understanding of our true nature.

RESEARCH WORK ON SPIRITUAL AWAKENING

Pioneering researchers have validated the transformative potential of 'Biofield Alchemy' in catalyzing spiritual awakening. Dr. Richard Davidson, a renowned neuroscientist, has shown that biofield practices can rewire brain activity, inducing states akin to spiritual enlightenment. Similarly, Carl Jung's exploration of the collective unconscious and individuation process highlights the role of biofield practices in integrating the conscious and unconscious mind, leading to spiritual awakening. Additionally, Dr. Rollin McCarty, a prominent researcher on heart intelligence, has explored the biofield's role in heart-centered consciousness, while Abraham Maslow's studies on peak experiences and self-actualization align with the spiritual growth facilitated by biofield practices. Dr. David R. Hawkins' "Map of Consciousness" and Andrew Newberg's work in neurotheology further elucidate how 'Biofield Alchemy' can elevate consciousness and spiritual awareness.

These visionary scientists have bridged the gap between ancient wisdom and modern science, providing a robust foundation for further exploration into 'Biofield Alchemy.' Their work illuminates the vast potential of biofield practices to transform human consciousness, empowering individuals to tap into their deepest essence and unlock their full potential - facilitating profound spiritual growth and self-awareness.

SIGNS OF AWAKENING

Spiritual awakening is a unique and deeply personal experience, often marked by a series of profound changes and realizations. The signs of awakening can vary widely from person to person, reflecting the diverse nature of individual spiritual paths. However, some common indicators can help identify this transformative process:

1. HEIGHTENED AWARENESS

> One of the earliest signs of spiritual awakening is a heightened sense of awareness. Individuals may become more attuned to their surroundings, noticing subtleties in nature, people, and even their own thoughts and emotions.

2. INNER PEACE & CALM

> A growing sense of inner peace and calm often accompanies spiritual awakening. Despite external

chaos, those undergoing awakening may find themselves more centered and less reactive to stress.

3. INCREASED EMPATHY & COMPASSION

Awakening often brings a deepened sense of empathy and compassion for others. There is a recognition of the interconnectedness of all beings, leading to more altruistic behavior and a desire to help others.

4. SHIFT IN PRIORITIES

As spiritual awakening progresses, individuals may experience a shift in their values and priorities. Material possessions and superficial concerns lose their importance, giving way to a focus on personal growth, meaningful relationships, and spiritual fulfillment.

5. SYNCHRONICITIES & INTUITION

An increase in synchronicities, or meaningful coincidences, is another hallmark of awakening. Intuition becomes stronger, guiding individuals toward decisions and paths that align with their higher purpose.

6. PHYSICAL SENSATIONS

Some people report physical sensations during awakening, such as tingling, warmth, or energy moving through their body. These sensations are often linked to the activation of the biofield and the unblocking of energy pathways.

NAVIGATING THE PROCESS

Navigating the process of spiritual awakening can be both exhilarating and challenging. As old patterns and beliefs are dismantled, individuals may experience periods of confusion, emotional upheaval, and even physical discomfort. However, with the right approach and support, this journey can lead to profound growth and transformation.

1. EMBRACE CHANGE: Spiritual awakening often requires letting go of old habits, beliefs, and relationships that no longer serve your higher purpose. Embracing change with an open heart and mind is essential for growth.

2. PRACTICE MINDFULNESS: Mindfulness practices, such as meditation, yoga, and breathwork, can help anchor you in the present moment and provide a sense of stability amidst the turbulence of awakening.

3. SEEK GUIDANCE: Connecting with a mentor, spiritual teacher, or like-minded community can provide valuable support and guidance. Sharing experiences with others who are on a similar path can help alleviate feelings of isolation.

4. JOURNAL YOUR JOURNEY: Keeping a journal can be a powerful tool for self-reflection and tracking your progress. Writing down your thoughts, experiences, and insights can provide clarity and help you understand the deeper meaning behind your awakening.

5. NURTURE YOUR BODY: Physical well-being is closely linked to spiritual health. Eating a balanced diet, getting regular exercise, and ensuring adequate rest are crucial for maintaining the energy needed to navigate the awakening process.

6. SET BOUNDARIES: As you become more sensitive to energies around you, setting healthy boundaries is important. Protecting your energy and avoiding negative influences will help maintain your focus and well-being.

SUPPORTING CONTINUED GROWTH

Spiritual awakening is not a one-time event but an ongoing journey of self-discovery and evolution. Supporting continued growth requires dedication, self-compassion, and a commitment to lifelong learning.

1. CONTINUAL LEARNING: The pursuit of knowledge and understanding is a lifelong endeavor. Reading spiritual texts, attending workshops, and exploring various spiritual practices can deepen your awareness and expand your horizons.

2. REGULAR PRACTICE: Maintaining a regular spiritual practice, whether through meditation, prayer, or other rituals, helps keep you connected to your inner self and the divine. Consistency is key to sustaining the benefits of awakening.

3. SELF - COMPASSION: Spiritual growth is a journey with ups and downs. Practicing self-compassion during challenging times fosters resilience and prevents burnout. Remember that setbacks are part of the process.

4. SERVICE TO OTHERS: Engaging in acts of service and contributing to the well-being of others can accelerate spiritual growth. Helping others fosters a sense of purpose and reinforces the interconnectedness of all life.

5. ENERGY HEALING: Techniques such as hypnosis, acupressure, and sound therapy and emotional freedom

technique can help maintain the balance and flow of your biofield. Regular energy healing sessions can clear blockages and support your continued spiritual evolution.

6. REFLECTION & INTEGRATION: Periodically taking time to reflect on your journey and integrate your experiences is essential. Understanding how far you have come and acknowledging your growth reinforces your commitment to the path.

CONCLUSION

The journey of spiritual awakening through 'Biofield Alchemy' is a profound and transformative process. It is a path that leads to greater self-awareness, inner peace, and a deep connection with the universe. By recognizing the signs of awakening, navigating the process with mindfulness and support, and committing to ongoing growth, individuals can unlock their true potential and live a life of purpose and fulfillment. Each person's journey is unique, but the destination is a shared state of higher consciousness and unity with all that is. As you embark on this path, may you find the courage to embrace change, the wisdom to seek guidance, and the compassion to support both yourself and others on this remarkable journey of awakening.

PART 4

INTEGRATING 'BIOFIELD ALCHEMY' IN REAL LIFE

PART 4
CHAPTER 1

IN EDUCATION

INTEGRATING 'BIOFIELD ALCHEMY' INTO EDUCATION

INTEGRATING BIOFIELD ALCHEMY IN EDUCATION SYSTEM

INTEGRATING 'BIOFIELD ALCHEMY' PRACTICES IN SCHOOLS

In the evolving landscape of education, the integration of holistic approaches such as biofield studies, presents a promising avenue for fostering well-rounded development in students. This chapter delves into the concept of 'Biofield Alchemy', its application in educational settings, and the potential benefits it holds for the future of learning.

'Biofield Alchemy', the practice of understanding and manipulating the human energy field for healing and personal growth, is not just confined to wellness centers and holistic health practitioners. Schools are increasingly recognizing the value of incorporating biofield studies into their curriculum. This integration is seen to enhance students' mental, emotional, and physical well-being.

Biofield studies involve understanding the electromagnetic field that surrounds and penetrates the human body, often referred to as the aura or biofield. By teaching students about their biofield, educators can provide them with tools to manage stress, improve focus, and enhance overall health. This holistic approach can be particularly beneficial in addressing the growing concerns around student's mental health and well-being.

One approach to integrating biofield studies in schools is through dedicated wellness programs that include energy healing practices such as Neuro Linguistic Programming,

Hypnosis, Yoga, Pranayama, Silva Method, EFT, Qigong, and Therapeutic Touch, Acupressure and many other forms of energy healing modalities. These practices can be introduced in a way that is accessible and engaging for students of all ages. For instance, simple mindfulness exercises can be enhanced with biofield awareness techniques, helping students to tune into their own energy fields and recognize imbalances that might be affecting their mood or concentration.

PROGRAMS & CURRICULUM

Developing programs and curriculum that incorporate biofield studies requires a tailored approach. Each school has unique needs and resources, and programs must be customized to fit these specific contexts. Here are some key components that can be included in a biofield-focused educational program:

1. TEACHER TRAINING: Educators must be trained in biofield concepts and practices. This training can be provided through workshops and professional development courses, ensuring that teachers are equipped with the knowledge and skills to integrate these practices into their classrooms effectively.

2. CLASSROOM INTEGRATION: Biofield studies can be woven into various subjects. For example, science classes can explore the physics of the human energy field, while physical education can incorporate energy balancing exercises. Art classes might use creative visualization techniques that align with biofield principles, and health classes can cover the basics of energy hygiene.

3. EXTRACURRICULAR ACTIVITIES: Schools can offer clubs and after-school programs focused on biofield practices. These might include yoga, meditation, and energy healing workshops. Such activities provide students with additional opportunities to engage with biofield concepts outside the traditional classroom setting.

4. PARENT & COMMUNITY INVOLVEMENT: Engaging parents and the broader community is crucial for the success of these programs. Schools can hold informational sessions, workshops, and open houses to educate parents about the benefits of biofield studies and how they can support their children's learning at home.

CASE STUDIES

Several pioneering schools and programs have already begun integrating biofield studies with remarkable results. These case studies illustrate the potential impact of 'Biofield Alchemy' in education.

CASE STUDY 1:

THE WALDORF SCHOOL MODEL

Waldorf schools, known for their holistic approach to education, have been incorporating biofield concepts for years. At Waldorf schools, students practice Eurythmy, a form of expressive movement that balances energy and fosters a connection between the mind and body. Teachers also use storytelling and imaginative play, which are believed to harmonize the students' biofields. Studies have shown that Waldorf students often exhibit higher levels of creativity, emotional intelligence, and academic achievement.

CASE STUDY 2:

THE LOS ANGELES UNIFIED SCHOOL DISTRICT (LAUSD)

The LAUSD has piloted a program integrating mindfulness and energy healing techniques into their curriculum. In partnership with local holistic health practitioners, the district implemented a program where students participate in guided meditation sessions and learn about biofield health. Preliminary results indicate improvements in student behavior, reduced anxiety levels, and enhanced focus during academic tasks.

CASE STUDY 3:

THE HOLISTIC EDUCATION CHARTER SCHOOL

A charter school in Colorado has designed its curriculum around holistic education principles, including biofield studies. Students start their day with a "morning energy tune-up," which involves grounding exercises, energy balancing activities, and setting positive intentions. The school reports that students are more centered, exhibit fewer behavioral problems, and show increased academic engagement.

CASE STUDY 4:

THE INTEGRATIVE MEDICINE PROGRAM AT DUKE UNIVERSITY

At the collegiate level, Duke University's Integrative Medicine Program offers courses that explore the scientific and experiential aspects of biofield therapies. Students from various disciplines, including pre-med, nursing, and psychology, learn about the biofield's role in health and healing. Graduates of this program often pursue careers that incorporate biofield principles, contributing to a broader acceptance and application of these practices in healthcare.

CONCLUSION

Integrating biofield studies into educational systems offers a unique, customized, and tailored approach to fostering holistic development in students. By understanding and harnessing the power of the biofield, educators can provide students with tools to enhance their physical, mental, and emotional well-being. Programs and curricula designed with biofield principles in mind can create a more balanced and supportive learning environment, ultimately contributing to the overall success and happiness of students.

The case studies highlighted in this chapter demonstrate the transformative potential of 'Biofield Alchemy' in education. As more schools recognize and adopt these practices, the future of education may increasingly embrace a holistic approach that nurtures not just the mind, but the body and spirit as well. This integration marks a significant step towards a more inclusive, comprehensive, and effective educational system that prepares students for the complexities of the modern world while maintaining their inner harmony and well-being.

PART 4
CHAPTER 2

IN HEALTHCARE

INTEGRATING BIOFIELD ALCHEMY IN HEALTH CARE

'BIOFIELD ALCHEMY' PRACTICES IN HEALTH CARE SYSTEM

Biofield practices, rooted in ancient healing traditions, focus on the concept of a vital energy field that surrounds and penetrates the human body. These practices aim to restore balance and harmony within this field to promote health and well-being. Integrating biofield practices into modern healthcare represents a unique, customized, and tailored approach to patient care. This integration has gained attention for its potential to enhance healing outcomes, reduce stress, and improve overall quality of life. In this chapter, we will explore the integration of biofield practices into healthcare through case studies and examples, collaboration with healthcare professionals, and evidence-based approaches.

CASE STUDIES & EXAMPLES

CASE STUDY 1:

HEALING TOUCH IN ONCOLOGY CARE

Healing Touch (HT) is a biofield therapy that involves gentle hand movements to balance and align the energy field. A notable example of HT integration is in oncology care. At a leading cancer center, HT was offered to patients undergoing chemotherapy. Patients reported reduced anxiety, pain, and nausea. One patient, Sarah, who was initially skeptical, experienced significant relief from chemotherapy-induced neuropathy after HT sessions. This case underscores the potential of biofield practices to complement conventional treatments and improve patient outcomes.

CASE STUDY 2:

REIKI IN POST - SURGICAL RECOVERY

Reiki, another popular biofield practice, involves channeling energy through the practitioner's hands to the patient. At a major hospital, Reiki was introduced in the post-surgical unit. John, a patient recovering from heart surgery, received Reiki sessions to alleviate pain and speed up recovery. John noted a marked decrease in pain levels and a quicker return to normal activities compared to his previous surgery. This example highlights how integrating biofield practices can accelerate healing and enhance patient comfort.

CASE STUDY 3:

QIGONG FOR CHRONIC PAIN MANAGEMENT

Qigong, a practice combining movement, meditation, and breath regulation, has shown promise in managing chronic pain. In a pain management clinic, Qigong classes were offered to patients with chronic lower back pain. Maria, a long-term sufferer, found that regular Qigong practice not only reduced her pain but also improved her emotional well-being. The integration of Qigong into her treatment plan provided a holistic approach to managing chronic pain, demonstrating the versatility of biofield practices in addressing various health conditions.

COLLABORATING WITH HEALTHCARE PROFESSIONALS

Integrating biofield practices into healthcare requires collaboration between biofield practitioners and conventional healthcare professionals. This collaboration ensures that biofield therapies are used safely and effectively, complementing traditional medical treatments.

1. BUILDING TRUST & UNDERSTANDING

The first step in collaboration is building trust and understanding between biofield practitioners and healthcare providers. Biofield practitioners must communicate the principles and benefits of their practices clearly. Likewise, healthcare professionals should be open to exploring these complementary therapies. Regular interdisciplinary meetings, workshops, and seminars can facilitate mutual understanding and foster collaborative relationships.

2. DEVELOPING INTEGRATIVE TREATMENT PLANS

Integrative treatment plans involve combining conventional medical treatments with biofield practices to create a comprehensive care strategy tailored to the patient's needs. For instance, a patient undergoing surgery might receive pre-operative Reiki to reduce anxiety, followed by post-operative Healing Touch to promote faster recovery. Developing such plans requires ongoing communication and coordination between all healthcare providers involved in the patient's care.

3. TRAINING & CERTIFICATION

To ensure the safe and effective integration of biofield practices, healthcare professionals should receive proper training and certification. Many institutions offer certification programs for biofield therapies like Reiki, Healing Touch, and Qigong. By obtaining certification, healthcare professionals can confidently incorporate these practices into their patient care routines, ensuring high standards of practice.

EVIDENCE - BASED APPROACHES

1. RESEARCH & CLINICAL TRIALS

The integration of biofield practices into healthcare must be supported by rigorous research and clinical trials. Several studies have demonstrated the effectiveness of biofield therapies in various health conditions. For example, a randomized controlled trial published in the "Journal of Pain and Symptom Management" found that Healing Touch significantly reduced pain and fatigue in cancer patients. Similarly, research published in "The Journal of Alternative and Complementary Medicine" showed that Reiki reduced stress and improved quality of life in patients with chronic illnesses.

2. MECHANISMS OF ACTION

Understanding the mechanisms of action behind biofield practices is crucial for their acceptance in mainstream healthcare. While the exact mechanisms remain a subject of ongoing research, several hypotheses exist. One theory suggests that biofield practices influence the autonomic nervous system, promoting relaxation and reducing stress. Another hypothesis posits that these practices enhance the body's natural healing processes by optimizing energy flow. Continued research into these mechanisms will provide a stronger scientific foundation for biofield practices.

3. INTEGRATIVE HEALTH MODELS

Integrative health models that include biofield practices are becoming more common in healthcare settings. For instance, integrative health clinics often combine conventional medicine with complementary therapies such as acupuncture, biofield practices, and nutritional counseling. These models emphasize treating the whole person - body, mind, and spirit - rather than just the symptoms of disease. Evidence from these integrative models indicates improved patient outcomes, higher patient satisfaction, and reduced healthcare costs.

4. PATIENT - CENTERED CARE

Biofield practices align well with the principles of patient-centered care, which emphasizes the importance of respecting patients' preferences, needs, and values. By offering biofield therapies, healthcare providers can address the holistic needs of patients, enhancing their overall experience and satisfaction with care. For example, a patient with terminal illness may find comfort and spiritual support through biofield practices, improving their quality of life in their final days.

CONCLUSION

Integrating biofield practices into healthcare offers a unique, customized, and tailored approach to patient care. Through case studies, we have seen the potential benefits of biofield therapies in various clinical settings. Collaboration with healthcare professionals is essential for successful integration, ensuring that biofield practices complement traditional treatments and meet high standards of care. Evidence-based approaches, supported by research and clinical trials, provide a scientific foundation for these practices, enhancing their credibility and acceptance in mainstream healthcare. As we continue to explore and understand the mechanisms behind biofield practices, their role in holistic, patient-centered care will undoubtedly expand, offering new avenues for healing and wellness.

PART 4
CHAPTER 3

IN DIAGNOSTICS

'BIOFIELD ALCHEMY' & DIAGNOSTICS

- The Science of Biofield Measurement & Instrumentation

'BIOFIELD ALCHEMY' IN DIAGNOSTICS

TECHNIQUES FOR ASSESSING THE BIOFIELD

Biofield diagnostics represent the cutting-edge intersection of ancient healing wisdom and modern scientific inquiry. Assessing the biofield - a dynamic field of energy and information that surrounds and interpenetrates the human body - is fundamental to understanding an individual's health and well-being at a more subtle level. Here, we explore various techniques that have been developed to evaluate this vital aspect of our existence.

One of the primary techniques used in biofield diagnostics is Energy Field Imaging. This method involves capturing visual representations of the biofield using specialized cameras and software. Kirlian photography, for instance, has been used for decades to visualize the electromagnetic fields emitted by living organisms. More recently, advancements in GDV (Gas Discharge Visualization) technology have allowed for more detailed and nuanced images of the biofield, providing insights into the overall energy distribution and potential areas of imbalance.

Another key technique is Biofield Mapping. This involves the use of sensitive instruments to detect variations in the biofield across different parts of the body. Practitioners may employ tools such as dowsing rods or pendulums, which respond to subtle energy fluctuations, to map the biofield. This technique can reveal areas where the biofield is either overactive or deficient, which can correspond to physical, emotional, or spiritual issues.

"Thermal Imaging" is also used in biofield diagnostics. Infrared cameras detect heat patterns emitted by the body, which can reflect underlying biofield disturbances. Variations in thermal patterns can indicate areas where energy flow is blocked or excessive, often correlating with inflammation, stress, or other health concerns.

TOOLS & TECHNOLOGY

The evolution of technology has significantly enhanced our ability to diagnose and understand the biofield. Several advanced tools are now available to practitioners, each offering unique insights into the biofield's complexities.

"Electrodermal Screening Devices (ESD)" measure the electrical conductance of the skin at specific acupuncture points. These devices can detect imbalances in the biofield by identifying areas where energy flow is either excessive or deficient. ESD provides a quantitative measure that can be used to track changes over time and evaluate the effectiveness of interventions.

"Biofield Analyzers" are sophisticated instruments that use a combination of electromagnetic sensors and computer algorithms to analyze the biofield. These devices can provide a detailed assessment of energy patterns, including frequency, amplitude, and coherence. The data collected can be used to create personalized treatment plans that address specific imbalances.

"Bio-Well" is a modern tool that uses GDV technology to assess the biofield. By placing fingertips on a glass surface, the Bio-Well captures and analyzes the energy emissions, providing a comprehensive overview of the biofield. The resulting data can be used to identify stress levels, organ function, and overall energy balance.

INTERPRETING BIOFIELD IMBALANCES

Understanding and interpreting biofield imbalances is crucial for effective diagnosis and treatment. Imbalances in the biofield can manifest in various ways, reflecting physical, emotional, mental, or spiritual disturbances.

"Energy Deficiencies" are often indicated by weak or fragmented biofield emissions. These deficiencies can correspond to chronic fatigue, depression, or weakened immune function. Identifying and addressing these deficiencies involves techniques such as energy healing, and lifestyle changes to restore balance.

Conversely, "Energy Excesses" are characterized by overly strong or chaotic biofield emissions. These can be associated with conditions such as inflammation, anxiety, or hyperactivity. Balancing these excesses requires calming and grounding practices, such as meditation, deep breathing exercises, and grounding techniques.

"Blockages" in the biofield are areas where energy flow is restricted or stagnant. These blockages can manifest as physical pain, emotional trauma, or mental stress. Techniques such light therapy and sound therapy can help to release these blockages, allowing for the free flow of energy.

"Distortions" in the biofield are irregular patterns that disrupt the harmonious flow of energy. These distortions can be caused by external factors such as electromagnetic pollution, or internal factors such as unresolved emotional conflicts. Addressing these distortions involves both environmental adjustments and inner work to clear the energy field.

In conclusion, biofield diagnostics offer a unique and comprehensive approach to understanding health and well-being. By assessing and interpreting the biofield using a variety of techniques and tools, practitioners can identify imbalances that may not be evident through conventional diagnostics. This holistic approach allows for personalized and tailored interventions, promoting optimal health and harmony in the individual. As we continue to explore and refine these methods, the potential for biofield diagnostics to transform healthcare becomes increasingly apparent, heralding a new era of integrative medicine.

PART 4
CHAPTER 4

IN MODERN SCIENCE

'BIOFIELD ALCHEMY' - A MODERN SCIENCE EXPLORATION

'BIOFIELD ALCHEMY' & MODERN SCIENCE

RESEARCH STUDIES AND FINDINGS

The concept of the biofield, though ancient in origin, has found a significant place in modern scientific inquiry. The biofield is understood as a complex, dynamic field of energy and information that surrounds and permeates living organisms. This idea aligns with traditional notions of life force energy, such as 'qi' in Chinese Medicine, 'prana' in Ayurveda, and the 'human aura' in Western Esoteric Traditions. Recent scientific studies have begun to investigate these fields with increasing rigor.

One of the key areas of research has been the measurement and analysis of the biofield. Technologies such as electroencephalography (EEG), magnetoencephalography (MEG), and bio-photon emission measurements have provided insights into the electromagnetic aspects of the human biofield. For instance, studies have demonstrated that practitioners of energy healing modalities, exhibit unique biofield patterns compared to non-practitioners. These patterns often correlate with heightened states of mental focus and physical relaxation.

Furthermore, biofield therapies have shown promising results in clinical settings. Research conducted at major medical institutions has documented the effectiveness of these therapies in reducing pain, anxiety, and stress. For example, a study at the University of California, San Diego, found that patients receiving biofield therapy experienced significant reductions in pain and fatigue compared to those receiving standard care. Similar results have been observed in studies on cancer patients, where biofield therapies have been associated with improved quality of life and reduced side effects from conventional treatments.

THE FUTURE OF BIOFIELD SCIENCE

The future of biofield science looks promising as interdisciplinary collaborations between physicists, biologists, and medical researchers continue to grow. Advances in quantum biology and biophysics are particularly relevant, as they offer frameworks to understand how biofields interact with cellular processes. Quantum coherence and entanglement, for instance, might explain how biofield interactions could occur over seemingly long distances, a phenomenon often reported in distance healing practices.

Moreover, the integration of biofield science with cutting-edge technologies such as artificial intelligence (AI) and machine learning could revolutionize healthcare. AI algorithms can analyze vast amounts of biofield data to detect subtle changes that precede physical symptoms, potentially leading to early diagnosis and personalized treatment plans. Wearable devices that monitor biofield parameters in real-time are also on the horizon, offering individuals continuous feedback on their energetic health.

BRIDGING THE GAP BETWEEN SCIENCE & SPIRITUALITY

One of the most compelling aspects of biofield science is its potential to bridge the gap between science and spirituality. Historically, the scientific method has often been at odds with spiritual and metaphysical concepts. However, the study of the biofield encourages a holistic view of health and well-being that encompasses both physical and non-physical dimensions of existence.

The biofield concept resonates with spiritual traditions that view humans as interconnected beings of energy. Practices like meditation, prayer, and energy healing, which have been used for millennia to foster spiritual well-being, are now being studied for their biofield effects. This convergence of science and spirituality suggests that these practices might work through biofield mechanisms, harmonizing the body's energy systems and promoting healing.

For instance, heart rate variability (HRV) and other physiological markers have been shown to improve during meditative states, indicating a balanced autonomic nervous system. This physiological coherence might be one manifestation of an optimized biofield. Similarly, group meditations and prayers, which have been shown to influence outcomes such as crime rates and hospital admissions, could be explained by collective biofield interactions.

In this context, the biofield serves as a scientific bridge to spiritual experiences, validating ancient wisdom through modern research. This holistic understanding encourages a new paradigm in healthcare - one that values the interplay between mind, body, and spirit.

PERSONALIZED BIOFIELD PRACTICES

Unique, Customized, and Tailored Approaches in 'Biofield Alchemy'- Given the individual nature of biofields, a one-size-fits-all approach is insufficient. 'Biofield Alchemy' emphasizes unique, customized, and tailored practices that resonate with each person's specific energetic makeup. This personalized approach can significantly enhance the efficacy of biofield therapies and self-care practices.

Biofield practitioners often conduct comprehensive assessments to understand a client's specific energetic needs. These assessments might include intuitive readings, analysis of biofield images, and consideration of the client's physical, emotional, and spiritual history. Based on this information, practitioners design customized interventions, which may include energy healing sessions, personalized meditation techniques, sound therapy, or the use of specific crystals and herbs known to influence biofield dynamics.

CASE STUDIES & PERSONAL TRANSFORMATIONS

The impact of personalized biofield practices is well-documented in numerous case studies. For example, a client suffering from chronic fatigue might receive a tailored regimen combining Hypnosis sessions, specific dietary recommendations to support energetic balance, and guided visualizations aimed at enhancing energy flow. Over time, these interventions can lead to significant improvements in energy levels, mood, and overall well-being.

Another case might involve an individual dealing with emotional trauma. Customized biofield practices could include sound healing sessions using frequencies known to release emotional blockages, combined with daily practices of heart coherence meditation. This holistic approach addresses both the energetic and emotional dimensions of trauma, facilitating deep healing and transformation.

INTEGRATING 'BIOFIELD ALCHEMY' INTO DAILY LIFE

Integrating biofield practices into daily life can yield profound benefits. Simple techniques such as grounding, where individuals connect with the Earth's energy by walking barefoot on natural surfaces, can help stabilize and strengthen the biofield. Regular practices like tai chi, qigong, or yoga, which combine movement, breath, and intention, can harmonize and balance the biofield, enhancing physical and mental health.

Moreover, the environment plays a crucial role in biofield health. Creating spaces that support energetic well-being using natural materials, living plants, and mindful arrangement of furniture can positively influence the biofield. Similarly, reducing exposure to electromagnetic pollution from devices and maintaining a mindful relationship with technology can help preserve biofield integrity.

ROLE OF COMMUNITY & CONNECTION

Human connection is a vital component of 'Biofield Alchemy'. Engaging in group activities such as collective meditations, healing circles, or community rituals can amplify biofield effects. These shared experiences create a collective biofield, fostering a sense of unity and mutual support that enhances individual and group well-being.

Community also provides a platform for sharing knowledge and experiences, which is essential for the growth of biofield practices. Learning from others, whether through formal education or informal exchanges, can inspire new insights and techniques, contributing to the evolving field of biofield science.

CONCLUSION

'Biofield Alchemy' represents a unique, customized, and tailored approach to understanding and enhancing human health and well-being. By integrating modern scientific research with ancient spiritual wisdom, it offers a comprehensive framework for exploring the complex interplay of energy and information that defines life. As we continue to investigate the biofield with ever more sophisticated tools and open minds, the potential for profound personal and collective transformation becomes increasingly apparent. This holistic approach not only bridges the gap between science and spirituality but also fosters a deeper connection to us, each other, and the universe at large.

PART 4
CHAPTER 5

IN TECHNOLOGY

INTERSECTION OF 'BIOFIELD ALCHEMY' & MODERN TECHNOLOGY

'BIOFIELD ALCHEMY' & BIOFIELD TECHNOLOGIES

The intersection of biofield practices and modern technology is a growing area of interest in both scientific and holistic healing communities. The biofield, often referred to as the energy field or aura, is considered by many to be a subtle but vital aspect of human health and well-being. This field is said to interact with the body's physical, emotional, and spiritual components, influencing and reflecting our overall state of health. Traditional biofield practices, such as Reiki, Acupuncture, and Qi gong, have long aimed to balance and harmonize this energy. Today, modern technology is beginning to play a pivotal role in enhancing and expanding these ancient practices.

One of the most significant advancements at this intersection is the use of biofeedback devices. These devices measure physiological functions - such as heart rate, skin conductivity, and brainwave patterns - to provide real-time data that can be used to understand and influence the biofield. For example, heart rate variability (HRV) monitors help practitioners gauge stress levels and overall heart health, allowing for tailored interventions aimed at improving biofield coherence.

Similarly, advancements in imaging technology, like Kirlian photography and Gas Discharge Visualization (GDV), provide visual representations of the biofield. These technologies capture the energy emanations from the body, offering insights that can guide personalized healing strategies. By visualizing disturbances or imbalances in the biofield, practitioners can more accurately target their interventions, making treatments more effective.

DIGITAL TOOLS FOR BIOFIELD WORK

The digital revolution has ushered in a plethora of tools designed to support and enhance biofield work. Mobile applications and wearable devices are at the forefront, offering convenient and accessible ways for individuals to monitor and influence their energy fields.

One prominent example is the emergence of biofield tuning apps. These applications utilize sound frequencies to help balance the biofield. Users can choose specific frequencies that correspond to different aspects of their energy field, listening to them through headphones or external speakers. This method leverages the principle of resonance, where certain frequencies can bring the biofield into greater harmony.

Wearable technology also plays a crucial role in modern biofield practices. Devices such as the HeartMath Inner Balance sensor connect to smartphones and provide feedback on heart rate variability, offering guided breathing exercises and other techniques to promote emotional and physiological coherence. By providing real-time feedback, these tools help users develop a deeper awareness of their biofield and how it fluctuates with their emotional and mental states.

Another innovative tool is virtual reality (VR). VR environments can simulate therapeutic experiences that influence the biofield. For instance, VR meditation programs immerse users in calming, visually rich environments that promote relaxation and biofield harmony. These experiences can be tailored to individual needs, providing a highly customized approach to biofield therapy.

Additionally, online platforms and communities have become invaluable resources for those interested in biofield work. Virtual workshops, webinars, and forums allow practitioners and enthusiasts to share knowledge, techniques, and experiences. This digital connectivity fosters a global community, enriching the field through shared insights and collective exploration.

FUTURE POSSIBILITIES

The future of biofield practices, augmented by technology, is teeming with exciting possibilities. As scientific understanding of the biofield deepens and technological innovations continue to advance, we can anticipate even more sophisticated and effective tools for biofield work.

One promising area is the integration of artificial intelligence (AI) in biofield practices. AI algorithms could analyze vast amounts of biofield data, identifying patterns and correlations that might elude human observation. This analysis could lead to highly personalized biofield interventions, optimizing health outcomes for individuals based on their unique energy profiles.

Nanotechnology also holds potential for biofield enhancement. Future developments might include nanoscale devices that interact directly with the biofield, providing targeted energy adjustments at the cellular level. These devices could be designed to detect and correct biofield imbalances before they manifest as physical symptoms, offering a proactive approach to health and well-being.

Moreover, advancements in quantum computing could revolutionize our understanding of the biofield. Quantum computers can process information at unprecedented speeds, potentially unraveling the complexities of the biofield and its interactions with the body. This deeper understanding could lead to groundbreaking techniques for biofield manipulation and healing.

Telemedicine and remote healing are also likely to evolve with technological advancements. Enhanced video conferencing tools, coupled with sophisticated biofield monitoring devices, could allow practitioners to conduct remote biofield assessments and treatments with greater accuracy and effectiveness. This would make biofield therapies more accessible to people regardless of their geographical location.

Furthermore, the development of personalized biofield therapies will continue to grow. By combining genetic information, lifestyle data, and biofield measurements, practitioners could create customized healing plans that cater to the specific needs of everyone. This tailored approach would maximize the effectiveness of biofield interventions, promoting optimal health and well-being.

The convergence of biofield practices and technology is a dynamic and rapidly evolving field, poised to transform our understanding and approach to health and healing. As we continue to explore and integrate these technologies, the potential to enhance human well-being through the biofield will only expand, offering new pathways to balance, harmony, and holistic health.

In conclusion, the intersection of biofield practices and modern technology represents a fascinating and promising frontier. Using biofeedback devices, imaging technologies, mobile applications, wearable devices, and virtual reality, we are beginning to unlock new dimensions of understanding and influencing the biofield. Looking ahead, advancements in AI, nanotechnology, quantum computing, telemedicine, and personalized therapies will further revolutionize this field. As these innovations unfold, they hold the potential to significantly enhance our ability to promote health, balance, and well-being through the biofield.

PART 4
CHAPTER 6

BIOFIELD TECHNOLOGIES

'BIOFIELD ALCHEMY'
&
EMERGING BIOFIELD TECHNOLOGIES

EMERGING BIOFIELD TECHNOLOGIES IN 'BIOFIELD ALCHEMY'

BIOFIELD TECHNOLOGIES

As we stand on the cusp of a new era in holistic health, biofield technologies are set to revolutionize the way we understand and interact with the energetic dimensions of human health. This chapter explores the emerging tools and devices, innovations in biofield science, and future trends that are poised to shape the next frontier of 'Biofield Alchemy'.

EMERGING TOOLS & DEVICES

The rapid advancements in technology have paved the way for sophisticated tools and devices designed to measure, manipulate, and enhance the biofield. These technologies aim to provide a deeper understanding of the subtle energy fields that surround and permeate the human body, facilitating more precise and effective therapeutic interventions.

1. BIOFIELD IMAGING SYSTEMS: Advanced imaging systems, such as Gas Discharge Visualization (GDV) and Kirlian photography, have been developed to visualize the biofield. These systems capture the electromagnetic energy emitted by the body, providing visual representations of the biofield's state and allowing practitioners to identify imbalances or disruptions.

2. BIOFIELD MEASUREMENT DEVICES: Devices like Electro-Photonic Imaging (EPI) and Bio-Well are being used to measure the biofield's strength and coherence. These tools offer quantitative data on the biofield, enabling practitioners to track changes over time and tailor interventions accordingly.

3. RESONANCE TECHNOLOGIES: Emerging resonance technologies, such as the Quantum Resonance Spectrometer (QRS), utilize quantum principles to assess the biofield. These devices can detect subtle energy imbalances and provide targeted frequencies to restore harmony within the biofield.

4. WEARABLE BIOFIELD ENHANCERS: Innovations in wearable technology have led to the creation of devices that can be worn on the body to enhance the biofield. These wearables, embedded with crystals or utilizing frequency-emitting technologies, aim to support the body's natural energy flow and promote overall well-being.

5. ENERGY MODULATION DEVICES: Tools like PEMF (Pulsed Electromagnetic Field) therapy devices and Rife machines are designed to modulate the biofield through specific frequencies. These devices can help address various health conditions by resonating with the body's natural frequencies and promoting cellular repair and regeneration.

INNOVATIONS IN BIOFIELD SCIENCE

The field of biofield science is witnessing groundbreaking innovations that are expanding our understanding of the biofield and its role in health and healing. Researchers are exploring new paradigms and methodologies to elucidate the mechanisms underlying biofield interactions and their therapeutic potential.

1. QUANTUM BIOLOGY: The integration of quantum physics with biology has led to the emergence of quantum biology, a field that investigates the quantum phenomena underlying biological processes. This interdisciplinary approach is providing new insights into how biofields operate at the quantum level and how they influence cellular functions.

2. EPIGENETICS & THE BIOFIELD: Epigenetics, the study of how environmental factors influence gene expression, reveals the profound impact of the biofield on genetic regulation. Research is uncovering how biofield therapies can modulate epigenetic markers, offering new avenues for personalized medicine and holistic health.

3. BIOFIELD MAPPING: Advances in computational modeling and bioinformatics are enabling the creation of detailed biofield maps. These maps provide a comprehensive view of the biofield's structure and dynamics, facilitating more accurate diagnoses and targeted interventions.

4. INTEGRATIVE APPROACHES: Integrative approaches that combine biofield therapies with

conventional medical treatments are gaining traction. These multidisciplinary strategies are being studied for their synergistic effects, offering new hope for managing chronic diseases and enhancing overall health outcomes.

5. BIOFIELD RESEARCH NETWORKS: Collaborative research networks and consortia are being established to advance biofield science. These networks bring together scientists, practitioners, and institutions to conduct rigorous research, share knowledge, and promote evidence-based practices in the field of biofield therapy.

FUTURE TRENDS

The future of biofield technologies and science holds immense promise, with several trends poised to drive the next wave of innovation and application in this burgeoning field.

1. PERSONALIZED BIOFIELD THERAPIES: The trend towards personalized medicine is extending into the realm of biofield therapies. Advances in biofield measurement and analysis are enabling the customization of therapeutic interventions based on an individual's unique biofield characteristics, leading to more effective and tailored treatments.

2. INTEGRATION WITH DIGITAL HEALTH: The convergence of biofield technologies with digital health platforms is creating new possibilities for remote monitoring and intervention. Mobile apps and telemedicine platforms are being developed to

track biofield metrics, deliver remote biofield therapies, and provide real-time feedback to users and practitioners.

3. AI & MACHINE LEARNING: Artificial intelligence (AI) and machine learning are being harnessed to analyze complex biofield data and predict health outcomes. These technologies can identify patterns and correlations within biofield metrics, offering predictive insights and enhancing the precision of biofield interventions.

4. REGULATORY & STANDARDIZATION EFFORTS: As the field of biofield science matures, efforts are being made to establish regulatory frameworks and standards for biofield technologies. These initiatives aim to ensure the safety, efficacy, and reliability of biofield devices and therapies, fostering greater acceptance and integration within mainstream healthcare.

5. EDUCATIONAL & TRAINING PROGRAMS: The growing interest in biofield therapies is driving the development of specialized educational and training programs. These programs are designed to equip practitioners with the knowledge and skills needed to effectively utilize biofield technologies and integrate them into their practice.

6. GLOBAL COLLABORATION: The globalization of biofield research and practice is fostering international collaboration and knowledge exchange. Researchers and practitioners from diverse cultural backgrounds are coming together to share insights, explore new methodologies, and

promote the holistic health benefits of biofield therapies.

7. PUBLIC AWARENESS & ACCEPTANCE: Increasing public awareness and acceptance of biofield therapies are paving the way for broader adoption. Educational campaigns, media coverage, and endorsements from influential figures are helping to demystify biofield science and highlight its potential benefits for health and wellness.

In conclusion, the future of biofield technologies is bright, with numerous innovations and trends set to transform the field. As emerging tools and devices continue to evolve, and as our understanding of the biofield deepens, we can anticipate a new era of personalized, integrative, and holistic health care. By staying at the forefront of these developments, practitioners and researchers can harness the full potential of 'Biofield Alchemy' to promote healing, well-being, and a deeper connection to the energetic dimensions of life.

PART 4
CHAPTER 7

GLOBAL HEALING

BIOFIELD ALCHEMY
&
THE POWER
OF
GLOBAL HEALING

'BIOFIELD ALCHEMY' & GLOBAL HEALING

'BIOFIELD ALCHEMY': UNVEILING THE POWER OF GLOBAL HEALING

In an age where the convergence of science and spirituality is becoming increasingly relevant, the concept of the biofield has emerged as a powerful paradigm for understanding health and healing. Biofield, an intricate network of energy fields and information, surrounds and interpenetrates the human body, influencing physical, mental, emotional, and spiritual well-being. This dynamic and fluid field is a bridge between the physical world and the subtle realms of consciousness. In this chapter, we explore the profound impact of the biofield on global healing, examining the collective biofield, techniques for fostering global healing, and stories of personal and collective transformation.

COLLECTIVE BIOFIELD & CONSCIOUSNESS

The collective biofield represents the interconnected web of energy that links all living beings. It is a testament to the fundamental unity of life, transcending geographical boundaries and cultural differences. This shared energy field is a repository of collective consciousness, where individual intentions and emotions contribute to the overall health and harmony of the planet.

UNDERSTANDING THE COLLECTIVE BIOFIELD

The collective biofield can be likened to a vast ocean, where everyone's biofield is a drop of water. Every thought, emotion, and action can create ripples that influence the entire ocean. This interconnectedness implies that individual well-being is intrinsically linked to the well-being of the whole. When we heal ourselves, we contribute to the healing of the collective biofield.

Quantum physics supports this concept through the principle of non-locality, which suggests that particles separated by vast distances can instantaneously affect each other's states. Similarly, the collective biofield operates beyond the constraints of time and space, allowing for instantaneous communication and influence among individuals.

CONSCIOUSNESS & GLOBAL IMPACT

Consciousness is the driving force behind the collective biofield. It is awareness that shapes our perceptions, beliefs, and interactions with the world. When individuals elevate their consciousness, they contribute positively to the collective biofield, fostering global healing and transformation.

Practices such as meditation, breathwork, mindfulness, and prayer are powerful tools for elevating consciousness. These practices help individuals cultivate inner peace, compassion, and empathy, which resonate outwardly and uplift the collective energy. By aligning personal intentions with the greater good, individuals can initiate a ripple effect that promotes global harmony and healing.

TECHNIQUES FOR GLOBAL HEALING

Healing the collective biofield requires a multifaceted approach that combines individual practices with collective efforts. The following techniques are tailored to foster global healing by addressing the physical, emotional, and spiritual dimensions of the biofield.

1. MEDITATION & MINDFULNESS

Meditation and mindfulness are cornerstone practices for cultivating a coherent and harmonious biofield. These practices enable individuals to connect with their inner selves, fostering a sense of peace and clarity. When practiced collectively, meditation can create a powerful field of positive energy that influences the global biofield.

Group meditation events, such as synchronized global meditations, have demonstrated the potential to reduce violence, promote peace, and enhance overall well-being in communities. These events harness the power of collective intention, amplifying the impact of individual efforts.

2. ENERGY HEALING MODALITIES

Energy healing modalities, such as EFT, Hypnosis, Silva Method, Qi gong, and Healing Touch, work directly with the biofield to restore balance and harmony. Practitioners channel healing energy to individuals, promoting physical, emotional, and spiritual well-being. When applied on a global scale, these modalities can contribute to the healing of the collective biofield.

Healing circles and group healing sessions are effective ways to extend the benefits of energy healing to larger populations. By coming together with a shared intention for healing, participants create a synergistic effect that magnifies the healing potential.

3. SOUND & VIBRATION THERAPY

Sound and vibration therapy utilize the healing frequencies of sound to balance the biofield. Mantras and affirmations have spectacular power to empower the biofield. Instruments such as singing bowls, tuning forks, and gongs generate vibrations that resonate with the body's energy centers, promoting healing and relaxation. When used collectively, sound therapy can harmonize the collective biofield, fostering a sense of unity and peace.

Global sound healing events, where individuals and groups participate in synchronized sound therapy sessions, have the potential to create profound shifts in the collective consciousness. These events tap into the universal language of sound, transcending cultural and linguistic barriers.

4. HEART COHERENCE PRACTICES

Heart coherence practices, such as those developed by the HeartMath Institute, focus on aligning the heart and mind to create a state of optimal well-being. Techniques such as heart-focused breathing and gratitude exercises promote a coherent heart rhythm, which positively influences the biofield.

When practiced collectively, heart coherence techniques can create a powerful field of electromagnetic energy that impacts the collective biofield. Research has shown that groups practicing heart coherence can generate a measurable effect on the surrounding environment, promoting harmony and reducing stress.

STORIES OF IMPACT

The transformative power of the biofield is best illustrated through stories of individuals and communities who have experienced profound healing and change. These stories serve as beacons of hope, demonstrating the potential of 'Biofield Alchemy' to foster global healing.

1. A COMMUNITY TRANSFORMED BY MEDITATION

In a small town plagued by high crime rates and social unrest, a group of dedicated individuals decided to implement a community-wide meditation program. They organized daily meditation sessions in public spaces, inviting residents to participate. Over time, the collective energy of the town began to shift. Crime rates dropped, community relationships improved, and a sense of peace and harmony permeated the town. This transformation was attributed to the cumulative effect of the collective biofield being elevated through consistent meditation practice.

2. HEALING THROUGH SOUND IN A WAR

In a region ravaged by conflict, a group of sound healers traveled to provide relief to affected communities. They conducted sound healing sessions using instruments such as crystal bowls and gongs, creating a sanctuary of healing frequencies. Participants reported profound experiences of relaxation, emotional release, and a renewed sense of hope. The collective energy of the region began to shift as the vibrations of sound penetrated the collective biofield, promoting healing and reconciliation.

3. HEART COHERENCE IN SCHOOLS

A school district facing challenges such as bullying and academic underperformance implemented heart coherence practices for students and staff. Daily heart-focused breathing exercises and gratitude practices were introduced into the curriculum. As the school community embraced these practices, a noticeable shift occurred. Instances of bullying decreased, academic performance improved, and the overall atmosphere of the schools became more positive and supportive. The collective biofield of the school community had been transformed through the practice of heart coherence.

CONCLUSION

The concept of the biofield offers a profound understanding of the interconnectedness of all life. By recognizing and harnessing the power of the collective biofield, individuals and communities can contribute to global healing and transformation. Techniques such as meditation, visualization, energy healing, sound therapy, and heart coherence practices provide practical tools for elevating consciousness and harmonizing collective energy. The stories of impact presented here illustrate the tangible benefits of 'Biofield Alchemy', offering hope and inspiration for a world in need of healing.

As we continue to explore and expand our understanding of the biofield, we are reminded of our inherent connection to one another and the planet. Through conscious effort and collective intention, we have the power to create a harmonious and thriving world, one that reflects the true potential of the human spirit.

FINAL CONCLUSION

- THE FINAL TRANSMUTATION

- BECOMING THE 'PHILOSOPHER'S STONE'

FINAL CONCLUSION: CRAFTING A NEW CHAPTER OF LIFE

'BIOFIELD ALCHEMY' & THE FINAL CONCLUSION

The journey through 'Biofield Alchemy' has been an exploration of the intricate and powerful energies that influence our physical, emotional, and spiritual well-being. This concluding chapter aims to distill the essence of what we have uncovered, offering key takeaways, final reflections, and actionable steps for readers who wish to further their journey into the realms of 'Biofield Alchemy.'

SUMMARIZING THE JOURNEY

Our exploration began with an understanding of the biofield, an essential concept that bridges ancient healing traditions with modern science. We delved into the historical context, tracing the origins of biofield concepts from various cultures and philosophies, and their resurgence in contemporary alternative medicine. This journey highlighted how the biofield, a field of energy and information that surrounds and interpenetrates the human body, serves as a crucial aspect of our health and vitality.

Key topics covered included the scientific foundations of the biofield, with insights into quantum biology, biophotonics, and the role of consciousness in shaping our energetic states. We discussed the various techniques used to assess and interact with the biofield, from traditional methods like hypnosis and acupuncture to modern technologies like biofield imaging and biofeedback.

A significant portion of our exploration focused on the practical applications of 'Biofield Alchemy'. Readers were introduced to various approaches for utilizing biofield techniques to enhance personal health, address specific ailments, and promote overall well-being. These methods ranged from daily practices like meditation and grounding to more advanced techniques such as energy healing sessions and biofield tuning.

KEY TAKEAWAYS:

1. HOLISTIC PERSPECTIVE: The biofield offers a comprehensive understanding of health that encompasses physical, emotional, mental, and spiritual dimensions. This holistic view is essential for achieving true well-being.

2. INTERCONNECTEDNESS: Our biofields are interconnected with the environment, other living beings, and the broader cosmos. This interconnectedness suggests that our health and healing are not isolated phenomena but part of a larger, dynamic system.

3. PERSONAL EMPOWERMENT: By learning to sense, interpret, and influence our biofield, we gain tools for personal empowerment. These tools enable us to take an active role in our health and healing processes.

4. SCIENTIFIC VALIDATION: Emerging scientific research is increasingly validating the principles underlying biofield therapies. This growing body of evidence supports the efficacy of biofield practices in promoting health and healing.

5. CUSTOMIZATION & TAILORING: Effective biofield work is highly individualized. Tailoring approaches to fit one's unique energetic constitution, health status, and personal goals is crucial for achieving optimal outcomes.

FINAL REFLECTIONS

Reflecting on this journey, 'Biofield Alchemy' is both an 'Art' and a 'Science'. It requires an open mind, a willingness to explore beyond conventional boundaries, and a commitment to personal growth and healing. The fusion of ancient wisdom with modern scientific insights has the potential to revolutionize our understanding of health and well-being.

One of the most profound aspects of 'Biofield Alchemy' is its ability to foster a deep sense of connection - to oneself, to others, and to the universe. This connection nurtures compassion, empathy, and a sense of belonging, which are fundamental to our collective healing.

Moreover, the practice of 'Biofield Alchemy' encourages mindfulness and presence. By tuning into our energetic states, we become more aware of our thoughts, emotions, and behaviors. This heightened awareness facilitates personal transformation and empowers us to make conscious choices that support our well-being.

NEXT STEPS FOR THE READERS

For readers inspired to continue their journey into 'Biofield Alchemy', here are some practical steps to consider:

1. DEEPEN YOUR KNOWLEDGE: Continue to educate yourself about the biofield and its various

aspects. Seek out books, articles, workshops, and courses that expand your understanding and skills.

2. CULTIVATE DAILY PRACTICES: Integrate biofield practices into your daily routine. Simple activities like meditation, grounding exercises, and energy clearing techniques can have a profound impact on your well-being.

3. SEEK PROFESSIONAL GUIDANCE: Consider working with a qualified biofield practitioner for personalized sessions. Professional guidance can help you navigate your unique energetic landscape and address specific health concerns.

4. JOIN A COMMUNITY: Connect with like-minded individuals who share an interest in 'Biofield Alchemy'. Joining a community can provide support, encouragement, and opportunities for collaborative learning.

5. EXPERIMENT & REFLECT: 'Biofield Alchemy' is a personal journey. Experiment with different techniques, observe their effects, and reflect on your experiences. This process of experimentation and reflection will help you discover what works best for you.

6. EMBRACE A HOLISTIC LIFESTYLE: Recognize that 'Biofield Alchemy' is part of a broader holistic lifestyle. Pay attention to your diet, exercise, sleep, and emotional health. These factors are interconnected and collectively influence your biofield.

7. STAY OPEN & CURIOUS: The field of 'Biofield Alchemy' is continually evolving. Stay open to new ideas, research, and practices. Cultivate a sense of curiosity and wonder as you explore this fascinating domain.

In conclusion, the journey through 'Biofield Alchemy' is a transformative one, offering profound insights into the nature of health, healing, and human potential. By embracing the principles and practices of 'Biofield Alchemy', you embark on a path of self-discovery, empowerment, and holistic well-being. This journey is unique to everyone, yet it connects us all to the universal energy that sustains and nurtures life. As you continue your exploration, may you find joy, healing, and a deeper connection to the vibrant energy that surrounds and permeates all existence.

'ENDINGS' ...
ARE
THE
'NEW BEGINNINGS'...

'ENDING' & THE ALCHEMY OF A 'NEW BEGINNING' …

A Journey Beyond the Pages: The Beginning of a Lifelong Exploration in 'Biofield Alchemy'

As we conclude this first book in the 'Biofield Alchemy' Series, it is essential to understand that this is not the end but a new beginning. The journey you have embarked upon will unfold over time, revealing layers of knowledge, experience, and practice that go far beyond the confines of this initial volume. 'Biofield Alchemy' is not a concept that can be fully grasped in a single reading or even a single book. It is a profound and complex field of study that requires ongoing dedication, practice, and openness to new ideas and experiences.

This book is designed as an introduction to the core principles and foundational practices of 'Biofield Alchemy'. It is a starting point - a guide to help you begin to understand the vast potential that lies within your own biofield and the energy that surrounds and permeates all living things. The concepts and practices outlined in these pages are just the beginning. They are the seeds that, with time and care, will grow into a deep and rich understanding of 'Biofield Alchemy'.

THE 'CONTINUATION' OF THE JOURNEY

The 'Biofield Alchemy' Series is a long-term commitment to exploring the depths of this ancient and evolving field. This first book has introduced you to the basics - the fundamental ideas and practices that form the foundation of

'Biofield Alchemy'. But there is so much more to discover. Each subsequent book in this series will build upon the knowledge and practices you have learned here, guiding you deeper into the mysteries of the biofield and its transformative power.

The second book in the 'series' is already in the works and will be available soon. This next installment will delve into more advanced concepts and practices, offering you the opportunity to expand your understanding and deepen your experience of 'Biofield Alchemy'. As you continue on this journey, you will find that each book brings new insights, new techniques, and new ways to connect with the energy that flows within and around you.

But before you move on to the next book, it is crucial to take the time to fully integrate the knowledge and practices you have learned in this one. 'Biofield Alchemy' is not just an intellectual exercise; it is an experiential process. It requires you to practice, to experiment, and to allow the concepts to sink deeply into your psyche. The more you practice, the more these ideas will become a natural part of your understanding and your life.

A 'SERIES' OF EXPERIENTIAL LEARNING

The 'Biofield Alchemy' Series is designed to be more than just a collection of books; it is a series of experiential learning opportunities. Each book is a step along a path that will lead you to a deeper understanding of yourself and the world around you. But this understanding does not come from reading alone. It comes from practice, from experience, and from a willingness to explore the unknown.

The practices outlined in this book are just the beginning. They are the tools that will help you to begin to connect with your biofield and the energy that flows through it. But to truly understand and master 'Biofield Alchemy', you must go beyond these basics. You must be willing to experiment, to push the boundaries of your understanding, and to explore the deeper levels of your own consciousness.

As you continue on this journey, you will find that the concepts and practices of 'Biofield Alchemy' begin to resonate more deeply within you. They will become a part of your daily life, influencing the way you think, feel, and interact with the world. This is the true power of 'Biofield Alchemy' - the ability to transform your life from the inside out.

THE IMPORTANCE OF 'PRACTICE'

One of the most important aspects of 'Biofield Alchemy' is practice. The concepts and techniques you have learned in this book are not just theoretical; they are practical tools that you can use to enhance your life and your understanding of the world. But like any skill, they require practice to master.

The more you practice, the more you will begin to see the effects of 'Biofield Alchemy' in your life. You will notice changes in your energy, your emotions, and your overall sense of well-being. You will begin to see the connections between your thoughts, your energy, and the world around you. And as you continue to practice, you will develop a deeper and more intuitive understanding of the biofield and its role in your life.

It is important to approach this practice with patience and an open mind. 'Biofield Alchemy' is not a quick fix or a one-size-fits-all solution. It is a journey of discovery, and it requires time and dedication to fully understand and experience its benefits. But with practice, you will find that the concepts and techniques you have learned in this book become second nature, and you will be ready to move on to the more advanced practices in the next book.

DOWNLOADING THE CONCEPTS INTO THE 'PSYCHE'

As you continue to practice and explore the concepts of 'Biofield Alchemy', it is important to allow these ideas to sink deeply into your psyche. The knowledge you have gained from this book is not just for your mind; it is for your entire being. The more you practice, the more these concepts will become a part of your subconscious mind, influencing the way you think, feel, and experience the world.

This process of downloading the concepts of 'Biofield Alchemy' into your psyche is a crucial part of the learning process. It is not enough to simply understand these ideas intellectually; you must also embody them. This means allowing them to become a natural part of your thought processes, your emotions, and your energy.

As you continue to practice, you will find that these concepts begin to resonate more deeply within you. They will become a part of your inner landscape, influencing the way you perceive and interact with the world. This is the true power of 'Biofield Alchemy' - the ability to transform your inner world and, in turn, your outer world.

A NEW BEGINNING ...

As we come to the end of this first book in the 'Biofield Alchemy' Series, it is important to remember that this is not the end of the journey - it is just the beginning. The knowledge and practices you have learned here are the foundation for a much deeper and more expansive exploration of 'Biofield Alchemy'. The next book in the "Biofield Series" will build upon this foundation, guiding you further into the mysteries of the biofield and its transformative power.

But before you move on to the next book, take the time to fully integrate the knowledge and practices you have learned here. Practice the basics, experiment with the techniques, and allow these concepts to sink deeply into your psyche. The more you practice, the more you will be ready to move on to the advanced concepts and practices that await you in the next book.

So, stay tuned, continue your practice, and prepare yourself for the next stage of your journey in 'Biofield Alchemy'. This is just the beginning, and there is so much more to discover. The 'Biofield Alchemy' Series is a lifelong journey of exploration, learning, and transformation, and I am honored to be your 'Guide' on this path.

AUTHOR'S NOTE

The study of 'Biofield Alchemy' is, at its core, a journey toward understanding and harnessing this universal energy for the betterment of self and humanity. I am humbled and honored to be part of this exploration, and I am grateful for the opportunity to share this knowledge with others.

'Biofield Alchemy', for me, is far more than a study; it is a sacred pilgrimage, a soul-stirring quest to comprehend and channel this divine energy for the upliftment of both self and humanity. I stand in awe and reverence, deeply humbled by the honor of walking this path. My heart brims with gratitude for the divine privilege of sharing this profound wisdom with the world.

'Biofield Alchemy' is not just a field of study for me; it is a sacred pilgrimage that transcends the boundaries of ordinary knowledge. It is a soul-stirring quest, a journey into the very essence of existence, where the mysteries of life are not merely unraveled but embraced with profound reverence. This path, illuminated by the light of divine wisdom, calls me to go beyond the confines of intellect and step into a realm where science meets mysticism, where the tangible and intangible weave together in a dance of cosmic harmony.

Walking this path of 'Biofield Alchemy', I find myself in constant awe and wonder. Each day, as I delve deeper into this ancient art, I am reminded of the immense responsibility that comes with it. The understanding and channeling of 'biofield energy' are not tasks to be taken lightly; they demand a heart that is pure, intentions that are noble, and a mind that is open to the infinite possibilities that the universe offers. It is a journey that requires one to be both a student and a teacher, constantly learning from the energies that flow through the cosmos while also sharing this knowledge with those who seek it.

This journey is not one of ego or self-magnification but one of humility. I stand humbled before the vastness of the universe, recognizing that the energy I seek to understand and harness is but a small fragment of the divine. Yet, in this small fragment lies the power to transform lives, heal wounds, to elevate consciousness, and bring about a profound shift in the way we perceive ourselves and the world around us.

My heart brims with gratitude for the privilege of walking this sacred path. It is a divine honor, bestowed upon me by forces greater than myself, to be a conduit for this profound wisdom. Every day, I am reminded of the trust that has been placed in me by the universe, a trust that I must honor with every thought, word, and action. This is not a journey that I undertake alone; it is one that I share with all of humanity, for the energy that flows through me is not mine to keep but to share.

In 'Biofield Alchemy', I see the potential for a new world, one where the lines between science and spirituality blur, where the energy fields that surround and permeate all living beings are recognized as the fundamental building blocks of reality. This is not a distant dream but a reality that is within our grasp, if only we have the courage to step into the unknown, to embrace the mysteries of the universe with an open heart and mind.

I am deeply humbled by the opportunity to share this wisdom with the world. It is a task that I approach with the utmost seriousness, knowing that the knowledge I impart has the power to change lives. But this power is not mine; it is the power of the divine, channeled through me as a vessel. I am merely the container, carrying forth the ancient wisdom that has been passed down through the ages, now ready to be shared with those who are ready to receive it.

This journey of 'Biofield Alchemy' is not one that I undertake lightly. It is a path that requires dedication, discipline, and an unwavering commitment to the truth. It is a path that demands that I remain grounded in reality while also reaching for the stars, constantly striving to balance the material and the spiritual, the seen and the unseen.

But it is also a path of immense joy and fulfillment. There is no greater satisfaction than knowing that the work I do has the potential to bring about positive change, to heal, to uplift, and to inspire. Every time I see the light of understanding dawn in someone's eyes, every time I witness the healing power of biofield energy in action, I am reminded of why I embarked on this journey in the first place.

It is a journey that I will continue for as long as I am able, for the pursuit of 'Biofield Alchemy' is not one that has a definitive endpoint. There is always more to learn, more to discover, more to share. And with each step I take, I do so with a heart full of gratitude, knowing that I am part of something much larger than myself, a divine mission to bring light and healing to the world.

'Biofield Alchemy' is, at its core, a journey of the soul. It is a quest to understand the unseen forces that shape our reality, to harness those forces for the greater good, and to share that understanding with the world. It is a path that requires courage, humility, and a deep sense of responsibility. But it is also a path of profound beauty, a path that leads to the realization that we are all connected, all part of the same divine energy that flows through the universe.

As I continue on this sacred pilgrimage, I do so with a heart full of gratitude, knowing that I have been given a great gift - the gift of understanding, of healing, of transformation. And it is a gift that I am honored to share with the world, in the hope that it will bring about a greater understanding of who we are, why we are here, and what we are capable of achieving when we align ourselves with the divine energy that flows through all things.

In conclusion, 'Biofield Alchemy' is more than just a study; it is a sacred pilgrimage, a soul stirring quest to comprehend and channel divine energy for the upliftment of both self and humanity. It is a journey of humility, responsibility, and profound gratitude, a journey that I am honored to undertake and to share with the world. Through this journey, I hope to bring about a greater understanding of the mysteries of the universe and to help others realize their own potential to connect with and harness the divine energy that surrounds us all.

LIFE OF A 'BIOFIELD ALCHEMIST'

- THE HERMETIC PATH OF AN UNDERCOVER YOGI

LIFE OF A 'BIOFIELD ALCHEMIST'

DR. NAMITA AGGARWAL'S LIFE & LIFESTYLE

In a world that often seems to move at the speed of light, where materialism and superficial success are frequently placed above inner peace and spiritual fulfillment, Dr. Namita Aggarwal has chosen a path less traveled - a path of deep introspection, simplicity, and spiritual devotion. This journey is not merely a lifestyle choice but a form of virtual "Sanyas" - a vow of renunciation that aligns with the life of a hermit or a monk.

Dr. Namita's spiritual journey began at a very young age, influenced by profound Vedic teachings that shaped her perception of life and existence. These teachings were not just lessons from sacred texts but were deeply rooted in her lived experiences, guided by 'Masters' who embodied the wisdom of the ancient Vedic tradition. The seeds of spirituality were sown in her being when she was just a small child of 4-5 years, and over the years, these seeds have blossomed into a life devoted to the principles of 'Biofield Alchemy.'

Dr. Namita Aggarwal's life is a living testament to the principles of 'Biofield Alchemy', rooted deeply in ancient Vedic traditions. For over 25 years, she has dedicated herself to a lifestyle that transcends mere knowledge and practice, embodying the very essence of the wisdom she imparts. Her life is a profound reflection of the age-old principle of "simple living and high thinking," where every action and choice is meticulously aligned with her spiritual path.

DR. NAMITA AGGARWAL'S "VIRTUAL SANYAS"

In the ancient Vedic tradition, "Sanyas" represented the final stage of a person's life, a renunciation of worldly ties to pursue spiritual liberation. This concept of complete detachment was often associated with physical withdrawal from society, material possessions, and even one's identity. However, in a modern context, and especially within the realm of 'Biofield Alchemy', "Sanyas" can take on a new form - one that aligns with our contemporary existence while still honoring the spirit of deep spiritual practice. This evolution in understanding has manifested in what Dr. Namita calls "Virtual Sanyas."

According to Dr. Namita, "Virtual Sanyas" is a deliberate and conscious practice of withdrawing from the temptations and distractions of the external world, not by retreating to a cave or forest, but by creating an inner sanctum of peace and bliss within the framework of our daily lives. In this form of "Sanyas," the physical world is not shunned but rather recontextualized, allowing us to engage with it in a way that supports and nurtures our spiritual evolution. It is a state of being that prioritizes the cultivation of the inner self, harnessing the power of the biofield to elevate consciousness and align with the cosmic energy.

In Dr. Namita's practice, "Virtual Sanyas" has been the cornerstone of her work in 'Biofield Alchemy'. For over two decades, she has lived a life akin to that of a monk, adhering to Vedic traditions with a focus on fasting, a plant-based diet, minimalistic living, the practice of brahmacharya and following the path of dharma. These practices are not merely lifestyle choices but are deliberate methods to purify the biofield, removing energetic blockages that hinder spiritual growth. By reducing the distractions of the physical world, the biofield becomes a clear conduit for cosmic energy, allowing for profound transformations at the deepest levels of consciousness.

In the context of 'Biofield Alchemy', "Virtual Sanyas" can be seen as a form of energetic purification, a process of distilling the essence of our being by removing the impurities that cloud our consciousness Just as an alchemist seeks to transform base metals into gold, the practice of "Virtual Sanyas" transforms the ordinary human experience into one of divine realization. By withdrawing from the temptations and distractions of the external world, we allow the biofield to become a vessel for the purest form of energy, the "prana" that sustains all life.

According to Dr. Namita, the journey of "Virtual Sanyas" is deeply personal. It begins with the conscious decision to step away from the ego-driven motivations that often dominate our lives - whether they be material success, social validation, or sensory pleasures. This withdrawal is not an abandonment of life but a shift in how we engage with it. By turning inward, we access the vast, untapped potential of the biofield, the energetic blueprint that governs our physical, mental, emotional and spiritual well-being.

THE PATH OF DHARMA & TRUTHFULNESS

The path of dharma and truthfulness is a commitment to living a life of purpose, guided by higher cosmic principles, and dedicated to the service of humanity. It is a path that demands courage, patience, resilience, and a deep sense of responsibility - qualities that Dr. Namita embodies in every aspect of her life.

Following the path of dharma - righteousness and duty - has been a guiding principle in Dr. Namita's life. Even in the face of the toughest situations, she has remained steadfast in her commitment to truthfulness and ethical living. The power of following dharma is not just in adhering to moral codes; it is about living in accordance with the universal laws that govern existence. For Dr. Namita, this means making choices that are aligned with her higher self and the greater good, even when those choices are difficult.

The path of dharma is a journey of living in harmony with one's true nature and the cosmic order. It involves recognizing the interconnectedness of all life and acting with integrity, compassion, and wisdom. For Dr. Namita, dharma is not just a set of rules but a way of being that reflects the deepest understanding of who we are and our purpose in the world.

Truthfulness, as a core component of dharma, requires unwavering honesty with oneself and others. It is the foundation of trust and the cornerstone of spiritual growth. Dr. Namita believes that living truthfully means being authentic, transparent, and fearless in the face of challenges. By embracing truth, she aligns her actions with the divine will, fostering inner peace and contributing to the well-being of all.

ANTI - LUSTING: SENSORY CONTROL

In 'Biofield Alchemy', Dr. Namita Aggarwal explores the transformative power of sensory control and anti-lusting as fundamental practices in her alchemical journey. For over two decades, she has meticulously honed her ability to master the senses, seeing this discipline as essential for purifying both mind and body. To her, controlling the senses is not merely an act of restraint but a powerful tool to elevate one's consciousness. She emphasizes that sensory indulgence leads to spiritual stagnation, while mastery over these impulses allows for the conservation and redirection of vital energy toward higher states of being.

DR. NAMITA'S 'NO GRAIN BRAIN'

One of the most striking aspects of Dr. Namita's lifestyle is her dedication to strict fasting. This practice is not merely a physical discipline but is deeply rooted in the Vedic understanding of purification, both of the body and the mind, to make them suitable vessels for spiritual energies

Dietary discipline is a fundamental aspect of Dr. Namita Aggarwal's practice of 'Biofield Alchemy'. For the past 20 to 25 years, she has committed herself to a highly disciplined fasting regimen, consuming only one meal a day. Her diet is extremely pure and simple, consisting only of plant-based vegetables, fruit and nuts.

Dr. Namita maintains her "No Grain Brain" (for 20-25 years) by completely abstaining from all kinds of grains and pulses, all forms of sugar, all kinds of dairy and dairy products, all kinds of animal products, and all types of processed foods, aligning her dietary choices with the Vedic principle of 'ahimsa' or non-violence, which is central to her spiritual practice. This strict plant-based approach is not just about physical health; it is a deliberate effort to purify her biofield.

In Vedic tradition, the food one consumes has a profound impact on the mind and soul. Dr. Namita follows a "sattvic" diet, which is considered pure, balanced, and rich in "prana" - the vital 'life force energy'. By consuming foods that are fresh, natural, and filled with life force energy, she nourishes her body while maintaining mental clarity and spiritual alignment. This approach ensures that her physical form remains a vessel of harmony, resonating with the higher frequencies needed for deep spiritual practice. This harmony is essential for her continued journey toward spiritual enlightenment and service to humanity.

PRACTICE OF 'BRAHMACHARYA'

Dr. Namita's commitment to the practice of Brahmacharya, a Vedic principle of celibacy and energy conservation. For her, Brahmacharya is far more than abstinence; it is a conscious effort to transform primal urges into spiritual vitality. This practice has been a cornerstone of her life, as she has deliberately avoided all forms of social distraction, including parties and holidays, for the last 20 to 25 years. Each moment of her life is meticulously devoted to the evolution of the soul, demonstrating her belief that true spiritual growth is achieved through the disciplined redirection of energy. In 'Biofield Alchemy', Dr. Namita reveals how these practices can serve as powerful tools for anyone seeking to transcend the limitations of the physical world and achieve higher consciousness.

DR. NAMITA'S 'MIND POWER'

In the practice of 'Biofield Alchemy', the mind is a potent force capable of shaping reality. Dr. Namita Aggarwal, through years of disciplined spiritual practice, has discovered that the mind is both the architect of our inner world, and the battlefield warrior of our life - where our deepest struggles unfold. By mastering her thoughts and emotions, she has learned to channel the mind's energy into creating a life aligned with her highest spiritual ideals. This mental alchemy transforms challenges into opportunities for growth, revealing the mind's true potential as a tool for spiritual evolution and self-realization.

In 'Biofield Alchemy', the mind is recognized as a powerful tool that shapes not only our perceptions but also the reality we experience. By mastering her thoughts, emotions, and reactions, Dr. Namita has learned to harness the mind's energy, transforming it into a source of spiritual strength and clarity. This mental discipline goes beyond mere self-control; it is about consciously directing the mind to align with one's highest spiritual goals. In doing so, she has unlocked the mind's potential to transcend ordinary limitations and manifest a reality that reflects her deepest spiritual aspirations. This alchemical process of mind mastery is central to 'Biofield Alchemy', offering a path to profound personal and spiritual transformation.

PRACTICE OF 'SILENCE' & 'SOLITUDE'

Furthermore, Dr. Namita explains that the key element in her alchemist journey is the practice of solitude and silence. "In the stillness, we can listen to the subtle vibrations of the biofield, attuning ourselves to the higher frequencies that guide us towards enlightenment. This solitude is not about being alone but about being fully present with oneself, free from the influence of external energies that can disrupt our inner harmony. Through this practice, the biofield becomes more refined, more attuned to the divine energies" - she says.

Integral to this alchemical journey is the practice of silence. which for Dr. Namita is more than just a quiet moment. it is a gateway to deeper understanding, inner peace, and a connection with the divine, catalyzing profound spiritual alchemy. It is during these moments of quiet reflection that she connects with the deeper truths of existence, gaining insights that cannot be found in books or through intellectual study.

PRACTICE OF 'MINDFUL LIVING' & 'CONSCIOUS SPEAKING'

Dr. Namita's life is a testament to the power of conscious and mindful living. Every action she takes and every word she speaks is infused with awareness and intention. She understands that thoughts and words carry energy, and thus, they must be wielded with care and wisdom. By practicing mindful thinking and speaking, she ensures that her actions and communications are in harmony with the principles of truthfulness and compassion, which are central to the path of dharma.

LIVING A LIFE OF 'DISCIPLINE' & 'DEVOTION'

Central to Dr. Namita Aggarwal's life is an unwavering commitment to a disciplined daily routine that integrates ancient Vedic practices. For over two decades, she has lived a life deeply rooted in the principles of 'Biofield Alchemy', a path that emphasizes the purification and alignment of one's biofield.

Dr. Namita's daily routine is a remarkable example of Vedic discipline, a life where every moment is intentionally dedicated to aligning her body, mind, and spirit with the universal energies. Her commitment to a disciplined and minimalistic lifestyle is evident in her adherence to practices designed to purify both mind and body, fostering a deep connection with the self and the cosmos.

PRACTICE OF 'MANTRAS' & 'RITUALS'

Mantras and traditional rituals are at the soul of Dr. Namita's daily practice. From a young age, she embraced the power of mantras - sacred sounds imbued with spiritual significance. These mantras, chanted with devotion and precision, serve as powerful tools for connecting with the divine, purifying her biofield, and harmonizing her energy with the greater cosmic forces. Each syllable, each vibration, is an offering, a means of spiritual attunement that enhances her well-being and spiritual growth.

Traditional rituals, too, play a crucial role in her disciplined lifestyle. These rituals are not mere routines but sacred acts of devotion, carefully designed to maintain the sanctity of her spiritual practice and biofield. Regular visits to temples and other energetically potent places form a significant part of her spiritual regimen. These visits are more than pilgrimages; they are opportunities to recharge, cleanse, and align her energy with the powerful forces that reside in these sacred spaces.

Dr. Namita's life of discipline and devotion is a testament to the transformative power of 'Biofield Alchemy', a journey of spiritual refinement and alignment with the divine.

DR. NAMITA'S POWER OF 'SIMPLICITY'

Dr. Namita's life is a powerful example of how simplicity can be a source of immense strength and power. She practices minimalism not just as a concept but as a way of life, embodying the belief that true wealth lies not in possessions but in spiritual richness. Her possessions are few, and her needs are minimal, reflecting a life lived in harmony with the natural world.

This simplicity extends to every aspect of her life, including her sleeping arrangements. Dr. Namita sleeps on the floor, a practice that keeps her grounded and connected to Mother Earth. This practice is not merely physical but serves as a way of aligning herself with the natural rhythms of the universe, maintaining a constant connection with the elemental forces that govern all life.

A LIFE OF 'SERVICE' & 'HUMILITY'

Dr. Namita's life is also a powerful example of service and humility. Despite her vast knowledge and high accomplishments, she remains humble and grounded. Her life is dedicated to serving others, not out of a sense of duty but from a deep understanding of the interconnectedness of all life.

Her commitment to simplicity is also evident in her approach to material wealth. Dr. Namita dedicates 25 to 50 percent of her resources (which include her time, money, food, clothes, knowledge and other resources) to selfless service, a practice that exemplifies the Vedic principle of 'seva' or selfless service. This is not just an act of charity but a profound spiritual practice that fosters humility, detachment, and a deep sense of interconnectedness with all beings. She shares 25 to 50 percent of her resources freely and unconditionally, without expecting anything in return. This selflessness is a key aspect of her practice and is a reflection of her deep commitment to spiritual evolution and self-alchemy.

Her approach to life is one of detachment and surrender, where she lives in the world but is not of the world. This is the essence of Vedic wisdom, where one engages in the world's activities without getting entangled in them. Dr. Namita's life is a powerful reminder that true spirituality is not about renouncing the world but about living in it with a sense of purpose, service, and detachment.

SHARING 'KNOWLEDGE' & SERVING 'HUMANITY'

Throughout her life, Dr. Namita has recognized the importance of sharing knowledge and serving humanity. She believes that wisdom is not something to be hoarded but something to be shared generously with others. Her commitment to selfless service is reflected in her dedication to teaching and mentoring others on the path of spiritual growth and 'Biofield Alchemy'.

For Dr. Namita, true knowledge is gained not just by reading books but by observing and spending quality time with those who embody spiritual wisdom in their daily lives. It is through these relationships and interactions that she has learned some of the most profound lessons of her life - lessons that she now passes on to others.

WALKING THE TALK

What truly sets Dr. Namita apart is her unwavering commitment to practicing what she preaches. Her teachings are not mere theoretical concepts but are deeply rooted in her own lived experience. She is a living example of the wisdom she imparts, and this authenticity is what makes her teachings so powerful.

Her behavior is a reflection of her teachings, and those who interact with her often describe her as a 'walking and talking embodiment of wisdom.' There is no gap between what she teaches and how she lives, and this integrity is what makes her a true teacher and guide. Her wisdom is not something that can be found in textbooks or on the internet; it is something that has been cultivated through years of dedicated practice and discipline.

EMBRACING THE 'ART OF BIOFIELD ALCHEMY'

At the core of Dr. Namita's life, is the practice of 'Biofield Alchemy' - the art of transforming and harmonizing one's energy field to align with the universal flow of life force energy. This practice is not just a theoretical concept but a living, breathing reality that Dr. Namita embodies every day. Her life is a model of how one can cultivate and enhance their biofield through disciplined spiritual practice, conscious living, and unwavering devotion to the path of dharma.

CONCLUSION

Dr. Namita Aggarwal's journey is a shining example of how a life rooted in ancient wisdom and spiritual discipline can lead to profound transformation and inner peace. Through her dedication to the principles of 'Biofield Alchemy', she has created a life that is not only fulfilling on a personal level but also serves as an inspiration to others seeking to harmonize their energy with the universe. Dr. Namita's life is a testament to the power of living in alignment with one's highest spiritual aspirations - a path that she continues to walk with grace, humility, and unwavering commitment.

FEW NAMES OF ALTERNATIVE HEALING MODALITIES

FEW COMMON NAMES OF ALTERNATIVE HEALING MODALITIES

1) NEUROLINGUISTICS PROGRAMMING (NLP)

Unlocks the subconscious code for biofield mastery, reprogramming thought patterns and behaviors to harmonize energy, enabling transformational shifts in perception, emotion, and vitality.

2) SILVA METHOD

Harnesses mental clarity to align the biofield with higher frequencies, empowering focus, intuition, and healing through deep meditation and visualization techniques that access the mind's latent potential.

3) JYOTISHA (VEDIC ASTROLOGY)

Reveals cosmic influences on the biofield, offering guidance through planetary energies that shape karmic pathways, spiritual evolution, and personal empowerment aligned with universal rhythms.

4) VAASTU SHASTRA

Transforms living spaces into biofield enhancers by aligning architectural elements with natural energies, fostering harmony, balance, and the flow of positive forces for holistic well-being.

5) NATUROPATHY

Restores biofield equilibrium through nature's remedies, supporting the body's inherent energy healing systems by integrating herbal medicine, diet, and lifestyle changes for optimal vitality.

6) FENG SHUI

Aligns spatial energy flows with the biofield, using environmental balance to invite prosperity, health, and serenity through strategic placement of objects and elements.

7) MARTIAL ARTS

Integrates physical movement with biofield strength, balancing inner energy (chi) through disciplined action, fostering physical, mental, and spiritual resilience.

8) ASHTANGA YOGA

Synchronizes breath and movement to clear blockages within the biofield, fostering physical strength, mental clarity, and deep spiritual alignment through disciplined practice.

9) HOLOGRAPHIC HEALING

Accesses multidimensional layers of the biofield, using quantum energy techniques to repair and realign energetic imprints, offering profound healing at the cellular and soul levels.

10) CRYSTAL HEALING

Amplifies and stabilizes the biofield through the vibrational frequencies of crystals, facilitating balance, protection, and healing across emotional, mental, and spiritual planes.

11) RAINBOW REIKI

Channels vibrant, multicolored energy streams into the biofield, harmonizing chakras and healing deep emotional wounds, offering advanced spiritual growth and energetic cleansing.

12) MELCHIZEDEK METHOD

Activates the light body within the biofield, accelerating spiritual evolution and facilitating ascension through powerful ancient wisdom combined with cutting-edge quantum healing.

13) HYPNOTHERAPY

Unlocks subconscious blockages in the biofield, guiding the mind into a deep state of relaxation where healing and transformation occur on emotional and energetic levels.

14) PAST LIFE REGRESSION THERAPY

Reveals karmic imprints on the biofield, helping resolve past-life traumas and emotional wounds, allowing for deep healing and liberation in the present incarnation.

15) SHAMANISM

Connects with earth and spirit energies, clearing and balancing the biofield through ancient rituals, drumming, and spirit journeys for healing and spiritual alignment.

16) AYURVEDIC MEDICINES

Balances the biofield through dosha-specific herbs, diet, and lifestyle, aligning body and mind with nature's rhythms for optimal health and energetic harmony.

17) HOMEOPATHY

Stimulates the biofield's natural healing capacity by introducing energetic remedies that resonate with the body's vibrational blueprint, restoring balance and vitality.

18) COSMETOLOGY

Enhances the biofield's outer expression, using aesthetic treatments that reflect internal energy balance, fostering beauty, confidence, and overall well-being.

19) YANTRA SCIENCE

Utilizes sacred geometry to realign the biofield, invoking divine energies through symbols and shapes that resonate with universal frequencies for spiritual growth.

20) THETA HEALING

Reprograms the biofield by accessing theta brainwaves, clearing limiting beliefs and emotional blockages, facilitating rapid healing and manifestation.

21) PRANIC HEALING

Cleanses and revitalizes the biofield by channeling prana, or life force energy, clearing energetic congestion and restoring harmony to the body's vital systems.

22) VIPASSANA

Purifies the biofield through mindful observation of the self, fostering deep inner peace and awareness by dissolving mental and emotional blockages.

23) TAROT CARDS

Accesses archetypal energies affecting the biofield, offering insight and guidance through symbolic imagery that reveals hidden influences and future potentials.

24) I - CHING

Balances the biofield with ancient wisdom, providing insights into life's transitions by interpreting the changing energies of time and space for decision-making.

25) HEARTMATH METHODS

Synchronizes the heart and brain, aligning the biofield with coherent, positive emotional states that enhance well-being and performance.

26) PYRAMID SCIENCE

Harnesses the geometric energy of pyramids to amplify and stabilize the biofield, fostering spiritual growth and enhanced energetic healing capabilities.

27) FACE READING

Interprets facial features as mirrors of the biofield, revealing emotional patterns, personality traits, and health conditions through energetic imprints.

28) BODY LANGUAGE

Unveils biofield dynamics through physical expressions, providing insight into emotional and mental states that affect interpersonal energy exchanges.

29) ACUPRESSURE

Activates meridians within the biofield by applying pressure to key points, promoting energetic flow and relieving blockages to restore balance and health.

30) FIVE ELEMENT HEALING

Restores balance in the biofield by aligning the five elements (earth, water, fire, air, ether) to harmonize body, mind, and spirit for optimal well-being.

31) HEALING RELATIONSHIP

Harmonizes the biofield through conscious energy exchange, fostering emotional healing, and strengthening bonds by resolving energetic imbalances in personal relationships.

32) VEDIC RITUALS

Channel sacred energies to cleanse and protect the biofield, aligning personal energies with cosmic forces through traditional offerings, chants, and fire ceremonies.

33) MANDALA THERAPY

Uses intricate patterns to heal and recalibrate the biofield, fostering emotional balance and spiritual alignment through creative engagement with sacred geometry.

34) HOLISTIC DIET & NUTRITION THERAPY

Nourishes the biofield by aligning dietary choices with natural rhythms, supporting energy flow, and optimizing physical and mental health.

35) COLOR THERAPY

Influences the biofield through vibrational frequencies of color, balancing emotions, enhancing mood, and restoring energetic harmony in the body.

36) MANTRA SCIENCE

Harmonizes the biofield by activating sacred sounds and vibrations, using repetitive chanting to clear negative energies and enhance spiritual resonance.

37) AROMATHERAPY

Realigns the biofield using plant essences, stimulating emotional healing, and mental clarity through the vibrational properties of aromatic oils.

38) MAGNIFIED HEALING

Accelerates spiritual growth by intensifying biofield healing, using higher-dimensional energies to restore balance, cleanse emotional blockages, and uplift consciousness.

39) HYDROTHERAPY

Uses water's healing properties to purify and balance the biofield, promoting physical detoxification and emotional release through immersion and flow.

40) SOLAR HEALING

Utilizes the sun's powerful energy to recharge the biofield, enhancing vitality, clarity, and emotional balance by absorbing natural sunlight.

41) BUILDING BIOFIELD

Cultivates a strong, resilient biofield through conscious energy practices, protecting against negative influences and enhancing overall vitality.

42) MENTAL HEALTH THERAPY

Heals the biofield by addressing psychological imbalances, nurturing emotional well-being, and fostering a healthy mind-body connection.

43) EMOTIONAL FREEDOM TECHNIQUE (EFT)

Releases trapped emotions from the biofield by tapping acupressure points, freeing energy blockages, and restoring emotional equilibrium.

44) SOUND HEALING

Realigns the biofield with sound vibrations, using tonal frequencies to dissolve energetic blockages, promote relaxation, and uplift spiritual awareness.

45) SACRED GEOMETRY

Balances the biofield through the energy of geometric patterns, harnessing the universe's natural order to foster alignment and spiritual transformation.

46) LAMA FERA

Clears the biofield of deep-seated negative energies using ancient Buddhist healing techniques, promoting spiritual evolution and energetic renewal.

47) PSYCHOTHERAPY

Heals the biofield by addressing emotional wounds and mental patterns, fostering emotional clarity and psychological well-being for overall energetic harmony.

48) REBIRTHING

Cleanses the biofield by revisiting and healing birth-related traumas through conscious breathwork, releasing deep emotional blockages.

49) MINDFULNESS MEDITATIONS

Centers and strengthens the biofield by cultivating present-moment awareness, dissolving mental clutter, and promoting inner peace.

50) LIVING ON LIGHT

Elevates the biofield by attuning to higher spiritual frequencies, sustaining life through cosmic energy rather than physical nourishment.

51) BACH FLOWER REMEDIES

Balances emotional vibrations within the biofield through flower essences, harmonizing moods, and supporting emotional healing.

52) TENSION RELEASE EXERCISES (TRE)

Discharges deep-seated tension and trauma from the biofield through controlled physical movements, freeing emotional and energetic blockages.

53) PALMISTRY

Decodes the biofield's energetic imprints by interpreting palm lines, revealing personal traits, life path, and karmic lessons through intuitive insights.

54) SWARA YOGA

Balances the biofield through breath regulation, using the power of prana to harmonize body, mind, and spirit for optimal health and awareness.

55) REFLEXOLOGY

Stimulates specific points on the feet or hands to clear energy pathways in the biofield, promoting relaxation and restoring balance.

56) KINESIOLOGY

Uncovers energetic imbalances in the biofield by testing muscle response, guiding healing interventions to restore vitality and harmony.

57) MAGNET THERAPY

Uses magnetic fields to realign the biofield, promoting healing by restoring energetic flow and balance within the body's systems.

58) WHITE LIGHT HEALING

Channels pure, high-frequency light into the biofield, clearing dense energies and uplifting the soul to higher states of consciousness.

59) QI GONG HEALING

Cultivates and directs life force energy (Qi) to heal the biofield, promoting physical vitality and spiritual harmony through slow, intentional movements.

60) ART THERAPY

Expresses and heals emotional energy through creative engagement, allowing the biofield to release blockages and cultivate balance through visual art.

61) MUSIC THERAPY

Uses musical vibrations to attune and heal the biofield, creating harmony, emotional release, and spiritual elevation through sound.

62) DANCE THERAPY

Incorporates movement to unlock and heal emotional and energetic blockages in the biofield, enhancing freedom of expression and inner joy.

63) DRAMA THERAPY

Engages the biofield in creative role-play, facilitating emotional healing and personal growth by bringing subconscious patterns to the surface.

64) PLAY THERAPY

Utilizes spontaneous play to explore and heal the biofield, helping release pent-up emotions and promote self-expression.

65) INNER CHILD HEALING

Reintegrates childhood memories into the biofield, healing past wounds, and restoring emotional harmony through love, understanding, and acceptance.

66) HIGHER - SELF CONNECTION

Aligns the biofield with the soul's highest frequencies, fostering intuitive clarity, spiritual wisdom, and deeper connection to universal consciousness.

67) PSYCHIC SURGERY

Removes energetic intrusions from the biofield through non-invasive spiritual techniques, facilitating healing on emotional and physical levels.

68) PENDULUM DOWSING

Accesses the biofield's energy currents to reveal answers, detect blockages, and guide healing using the pendulum's subtle energetic movements.

69) EMOTIONAL INTELLIGENCE COACHING

Enhances biofield resilience by improving emotional awareness, enabling healthier relationships, and fostering balance in personal energy.

70) ENERGY MEDICINE

Balances and strengthens the biofield through hands-on techniques and energy transfers, facilitating holistic healing and physical well-being.

71) TAI CHI

Cultivates life force energy in the biofield through graceful, flowing movements that promote inner harmony, strength, and spiritual connection.

72) MUDRA SCIENCE

Activates energetic pathways within the biofield using hand gestures, promoting healing and spiritual awakening by aligning with universal forces.

73) HOME SCIENCE

Optimizes the biofield by harmonizing living spaces through energy-conscious design, promoting physical health, mental clarity, and emotional well-being in everyday environments.

74) FERTILITY THERAPY

Rebalances the biofield to enhance reproductive health, clearing energetic blockages and nurturing a supportive environment for conception and vitality.

75) HEALING ORNAMENTS

Infuse personal biofields with protective and healing energies through sacred symbols, gemstones, and materials, acting as talismans to enhance well-being.

76) QUANTUM MATRIX HEALING

Engages the quantum field to realign the biofield, enabling profound transformation by dissolving energetic patterns and restoring coherence at the subatomic level.

77) WHITE MAGIC

Channels positive spiritual energies to heal and protect the biofield, manifesting well-being and balance by aligning with natural and divine forces.

78) GAIA CONNECTION HEALING

Aligns the biofield with Earth's nurturing energies, fostering healing by reconnecting with the planet's vibrations for grounding, balance, and renewal.

79) MERKABA ACTIVATION

Activates the biofield's light body by awakening sacred geometries, enabling multidimensional healing and spiritual ascension.

80) MARMA THERAPY

Stimulates vital energy points to cleanse the biofield, harmonizing physical and emotional health through ancient Ayurvedic healing techniques.

81) PANCHAKARMA

Detoxifies and revitalizes the biofield through Ayurvedic cleansing rituals, restoring energetic balance and promoting long-term health.

82) CHAKRA HEALING

Balances and energizes the biofield by clearing, aligning, and activating the body's chakra system, restoring physical and emotional harmony.

83) TRATAKA (GAZING)

Focuses the mind's energy to cleanse and purify the biofield, promoting mental clarity and spiritual vision through meditative gazing.

84) KRIYA YOGA

Elevates the biofield by harmonizing mind, body, and spirit through breath control and energy circulation, fostering spiritual awakening.

85) YAJNA (SACRED RITUAL)

Purifies the biofield through fire rituals and sacred offerings, channeling cosmic energies for protection, prosperity, and spiritual growth.

86) SUBCONSCIOUS REPROGRAMMING

Rewrites limiting beliefs imprinted in the biofield, facilitating deep healing by aligning thoughts and emotions with desired outcomes.

87) DIVINE DNA ACTIVATION

Awakens dormant spiritual potential in the biofield, unlocking higher consciousness and personal transformation at a cellular level.

88) ANCESTRAL HEALING

Cleanses inherited energetic imprints within the biofield, resolving ancestral patterns to promote healing and freedom for future generations.

89) AKASHIC RECORD READING

Accesses the soul's energetic blueprint within the biofield, offering insights into past, present, and future to guide healing and growth.

90) TRANSCENDENTAL MEDITATION

Expands and purifies the biofield by transcending thought, tapping into deeper consciousness to enhance mental clarity and inner peace.

91) ZEN MEDITATION

Cleanses the biofield through deep stillness and mindfulness, fostering a peaceful mind, heightened awareness, and a balanced energy field.

92) DIVINATION METHOD

Taps into the biofield's intuitive energies to provide insights and guidance, aligning the mind and spirit with divine wisdom.

93) SOUL RETRIEVAL THERAPY

Restores the biofield by recovering fragmented soul parts, healing trauma, and reintegrating lost energies to complete personal wholeness.

94) RUNES DIVINATION

Uses ancient symbols to read and align the biofield's energy, offering guidance and clarity by tapping into universal energies.

95) GENETIC PATTERN HEALING

Rewrites limiting genetic blueprints embedded in the biofield, promoting healing by clearing inherited emotional and energetic patterns.

96) LIGHT THERAPY

Uses the vibrational energy of light to restore the biofield's natural rhythm, promoting healing, vitality, and emotional well-being.

97) CORE HEALING

Dives into the biofield's deepest layers to release trauma and restore energetic harmony, healing from the core outward for lasting transformation.

98) LUNAR HEALING RITUALS

Synchronizes the biofield with the moon's cyclical energy, using lunar phases to cleanse, recharge, and empower the body and spirit.

99) TWIN SOUL HEALING

Heals the biofield by harmonizing twin flame energies, dissolving emotional blockages, and fostering a deep spiritual connection with one's soulmate.

100) METAL MAGIC

Utilizes the vibrational frequencies of metals to protect and heal the biofield, aligning energies with nature's elemental forces for spiritual and physical well-being.

101) GEM ELIXIRS

Imbues the biofield with healing energies from gemstones, promoting energetic balance and spiritual growth through the vibrational power of crystals.

102) KUNDALINI ACTIVATION

Awakens dormant energy in the biofield through spiritual practices, unleashing transformative power and accelerating spiritual evolution.

103) BIOFIELD TUNING

Balances the biofield by using tuning forks to detect and harmonize energy imbalances, restoring vitality and emotional clarity.

104) HEALING PREGNANCY

Nurtures the biofield of both mother and child, creating a supportive, balanced energetic environment for healthy development and emotional well-being.

105) WOMB HEALING

Clears deep emotional and energetic imprints from the biofield's reproductive energy, promoting healing and reconnection with feminine power.

106) DREAMWORK

Accesses the subconscious through dreamscapes, revealing hidden messages within the biofield to guide emotional and spiritual healing.

107) PSYCHIC PROTECTION

Shields the biofield from negative external energies, creating a strong protective barrier to safeguard emotional and spiritual integrity.

108) DIVINE BLUEPRINT HEALING

Restores the biofield's original divine design by clearing distortions, aligning personal energy with the soul's highest potential.

109) HOME ENERGIZING

Purifies the living space's energy field, harmonizing the biofield by transforming negative vibrations into a supportive, high-frequency environment.

110) METAPHYSICAL HEALING

Engages higher-dimensional energies to clear the biofield of spiritual blockages, promoting healing on physical, emotional, and soul levels.

111) SACRED EARTH HEALING

Aligns the biofield with the Earth's healing energies, grounding and nurturing the spirit through deep connection to nature.

112) PSYCHOSOMATIC HEALING

Reveals the body-mind connection within the biofield, healing emotional and mental patterns that manifest as physical ailments.

113) HOLISTIC QUANTUM HEALING

Restores balance to the biofield by accessing the quantum field, promoting healing on all levels by shifting deep energetic patterns.

114) TIME LINE THERAPY

Heals the biofield by revisiting past traumas and releasing emotional blockages, allowing for personal growth and emotional freedom.

115) HEALING GARMENTS

Infuses the biofield with protective and healing energies through specially designed clothing, promoting energetic balance and spiritual alignment.

116) LIGHT BODY ACTIVATION

Awakens the biofield's highest vibrational state, facilitating spiritual ascension by activating the body's subtle energy layers.

117) ENERGY SHIELDS

Creates a protective energy barrier around the biofield, safeguarding against negative influences and maintaining energetic integrity.

118) ACUPUNCTURE

Balances the biofield by stimulating energy meridians, promoting health and healing through precise application of fine needles.

119) KALARIPAYATTU

Strengthens the biofield through disciplined movement, blending martial arts and spiritual practice to enhance vitality and energy flow.

120) ZERO POINT ENERGY HEALING

Taps into the universal energy field to restore the biofield's balance, promoting healing and transformation by accessing infinite potential.

UPCOMING BOOK

BIOFIELD

&

THE ALCHEMY

OF

RELATIONSHIPS

LOVE - LIFE - LIGHT

NAMITA AGGARWAL

UPCOMING BOOK

BIOFIELD CURRENCY

**ALCHEMY OF THE MOST POTENT
CURRENCY OF THE UNIVERSE**

NAMITA AGGARWAL

www.ingramcontent.com/pod-product-compliance
Lightning Source LLC
LaVergne TN
LVHW061538070526
838199LV00077B/6831